French Lessons

Leçons françaises

French Lessons

Leçons françaises

Justin North

hardie grant books

MELBOURNE · LONDON

First published in 2007 by Hardie Grant Books
This edition published in 2013 by Hardie Grant Books

Hardie Grant Books (Australia)
Ground Floor, Building 1
658 Church Street
Richmond, Victoria 3121, Australia
www.hardiegrant.com.au

Hardie Grant Books (UK)
Dudley House, North Suite
34–35 Southampton Street
London WC2E 7HF
www.hardiegrant.co.uk

Cataloguing-in-Publication data is available from the National Library of Australia.

ISBN 978 1 74270 484 5

Edited and indexed by Lucy Malouf
Art direction, styling and design by Greendot Design
Photography by Steve Brown
Printed and bound in China by 1010 Printing International Limited

10 9 8 7 6 5 4 3 2 1

The publisher would like to thank the following for their generosity in supplying
props for the book: Bison Homewares, Chef's Warehouse, All Hand Made Gallery,
Food Service International, Succulent Designs, Quince Homewares, Dandi,
Villa Homewares, The Bay Tree, Prop Stop, Major + Tom and Lucienne Linen.

This book is dedicated to the loving memory of my wonderful father, the hardest-working man I have ever met, a gentleman, a lover of fine food, and a supportive and proud dad.

And to my three beautiful girls – my darling mother Hazel, my loving and supportive wife Georgia and my gorgeous daughter Sophia.

the contents
Les contents

Introduction

When I look back, it seems to me that I sort of fell into French cookery. I wasn't born in France, nor do I have French heritage, but by some happy accident, many of my formative cooking years were spent working in great French restaurants in Australia and around Europe.

I've been lucky enough to have worked with some of the greatest French chefs of our time – and I've made it a point to eat in the restaurants of many more!

To be honest, when I began my journey I didn't have the same passion for food that I do today. In fact, I don't really believe passion is something you're born with. In my experience, it's something that grows over time along with drive and determination to succeed. And it needs to be nurtured. With me, it's been something that grew as I grew, that evolved and strengthened with each year and with each chef I was lucky enough to work with.

If a passion for good food is developed over a long time, a passion for French food can take even longer because it is such a vast and comprehensive cuisine to get to know and it is so steeped in tradition. But there is no doubt that in the West, at least, la cuisine classique is the model for most cooking schools and an understanding of the techniques and methods is well worth mastering even for the home cook.

The primary goal of this book is to provide an insight into the world of French cookery in a way that is accessible and feasible for home cooks of all abilities. It's not intended to be a *Larousse Gastronomique* or to duplicate a professional Cordon Bleu cookery course, but rather, to bring a wide range of useful techniques within reach of even the most timid cook.

In my view, the somewhat rigid traditional approach to French cooking, with its reliance on heavy ingredients like butter, flour and cream, is fast disappearing in restaurant kitchens the world over. The modern choice is for lighter, more delicate and intensely flavoured foods. This shift is certainly reflected in my own approach to cooking and in the pages that follow.

Another of my goals in *French Lessons* is to encourage you, the reader and home cook, to develop a similar approach to food and to cooking to what you find in France. That is, to focus far more on quality and freshness than on convenience when it comes to selecting your produce. In many French towns, people shop for food on a daily basis, and fresh produce markets rather than giant supermarkets are still the preferred option, wherever possible. While I understand that not many people have the time or opportunity to shop daily, I do really encourage you to spend more time shopping at markets and greengrocers, to support your local butchers and fishmongers, to spend the extra dollar on organic and free-range, rather than mass-produced foodstuffs. Not only will your dinner taste better, but you will also be doing your part to keep alive the dream of the small, local and passionate producers who so greatly need your support.

It's important, too, to realise that good food takes a level of care. We all tend to rush about frantically, crying that we are 'time-poor'. Well, cooking is a great way to make yourself slow down. Try to think of cooking as something to be savoured and enjoyed, not rushed through as a means to an end. A considered approach to cooking is quite different from grabbing ingredients and tossing them together as quickly as you can. But I believe the rewards are far greater. If you take the time to understand the techniques employed when cooking, it will be reflected in the finished dish. It is certainly possible to make good stocks and sauces at home, using top-notch ingredients and with minimal fuss.

In a nutshell, one might like to say that in this book you'll find lessons that respect the traditions of the past, but with a definite nod to present trends and to the future. I hope you enjoy cooking the recipes as much as I enjoyed researching, practising and compiling them.

the essentials
Les bases

Getting started

Each chapter in *French Lessons* is based on a particular technique or a small group of related techniques. Most of the recipes are straightforward and fairly simple, and they have been chosen to demonstrate each specific technique or method.

As with all recipe books, I do suggest that before you start cooking you read the recipe through a couple of times from start to finish. This is an important step as it not only gives you a good overall idea of the extent and scope of the dish, but it also helps you develop a mental image of the finished dish; something to work towards. I also do recommend that you read the introductory part of the chapter – the lesson – so that you gain a good understanding of the 'hows' and 'whys' of the techniques employed.

You'll see that each recipe is also accompanied by a suggested accompaniment – a sauce, starch or vegetable garnish, as appropriate. Putting different flavours and textures together to create a balanced meal is one of my passions … but don't feel constrained by my suggestions. I'd love to feel that you take some of the ideas and run with them, that you develop the confidence to explore and develop your own ideas about matching different components in a dish or meal.

Choosing ingredients

It was the legendary Raymond Blanc who first instilled in me the importance of choosing good produce and not accepting second best. He used to say, 'If you start with rubbish, you end up with rubbish!' I firmly believe that you can't cook good French food with mediocre produce, especially in this modern age, when taste and flavour are so critical. These days we are more and more focused on using less cream, butter and flour, which makes the cuisine lighter, more intensely flavoured – more honest.

When I was writing my first book, *Bécasse*, I learnt some valuable lessons. I discovered that there are wonderful growers, farmers and producers all around us, if only we'd take the time to find out where they are. I firmly believe that it is worth travelling the extra distance or paying the extra dollar to get the best produce. After all, we invest so much money in the latest recipe books and the flashest new kitchen equipment, why would we not want to invest in the best food?

In my view, supermarkets are fine for washing powder and nappies (diapers), but when it comes to fresh, quality produce choose the small retailer, specialty store or local market instead. It's also well worth copying what professional chefs and restaurant kitchens do in building a relationship with their suppliers. I strongly urge you to make friends with your local butcher, fishmonger or greengrocer. Believe me, these are people who know what they're talking about; they'll welcome your interest in their produce and should be happy to assist you, offer advice and source hard-to-find ingredients for you.

Farming methods

Wherever possible I try to use produce that is farmed using free-range, organic or biodynamic methods rather than traditional mass-farming methods. Most producers who choose these approaches are passionate about their produce. They have the health of the animal or plant at the forefront of their mind, and are deeply focused on the quality and flavour of the end product, rather than their profit margin.

Meat

This is a particular passion of mine – especially when it comes to ageing. Mind you, this is a subject that only becomes relevant if you are prepared to pay what it costs to buy your meat from a good-quality butcher. Ageing meat is typically only done with export-quality carcasses. But the difference between this and the hum-drum, flabby meat that predominates in the Australian food industry is vast.

Given a choice I always tend to choose meat that's been dry-aged. This means that the carcass has been hung, uncovered in a refrigerator where the air can circulate freely. It should be aged at a steady temperature of 3–4°C (37–40°F) and 60–70% humidity. If the temperature is too cold the meat tends to tighten and age on the outside only. Above this temperature, and the meat is liable to spoil.

As the meat ages, over time it starts to dehydrate, which concentrates its flavour. Enzymes begin to breakdown within the meat and have a tenderising effect, so that you end up with a flavoursome meat that is wonderfully tender. Generally, the optimum ageing time is from 4–6 weeks, up to a maximum of 8 weeks. Any longer and you start to enter dangerous territory with the meat beginning to break down and spoil.

Perhaps more readily available (and less pricey) is wet-aged meat. This is meat that has been boned out and vacuum-sealed using cryovac technology. It is then aged in the refrigerator at a temperature of 0–2°C (32–36°F). Soft-textured cuts such as the fillet (tenderloin) are aged for around 2 weeks. More robust cuts, such as rump (top sirloin) or strip loin (short loin), will be aged from 6–8 weeks.

Meat that is wet-aged retains its moisture content and doesn't require such specialised conditions. The downside is that there is inevitably some seepage of blood out of the meat, which can impart an odour and liver-ish flavour to it. If you buy vacuum-sealed meat check to see that there is an absorbent pad in the bag which will minimise these negatives.

Another important decision to make at the premium end of the beef market is whether to choose grass or grain fed beef. Good-quality grass fed beef tends to have an earthy, beefier flavour, but it can be tougher in texture. Nearly all cattle are fed on grass initially, but many are then moved on to a grain diet as it allows for a more consistent product. (The quality of grass is of course susceptible to all sorts of other external factors.) A grain diet has the effect of increasing the marbling within the meat, making it more tender and juicier. Most of the meat sold in Australian supermarkets has been grain fed for up to 70 days, whereas specialty stores and quality butchers will buy meat that's been grain fed for up to 150 days. This meat will be evenly marbled and have an even texture. At the very high end of the market is export-quality Wagyu beef that is grain fed for up to 600 days. But this is not readily available. Save your pennies and enjoy it at a top-notch restaurant.

Eggs, cheese and dairy

The golden rule is to always check the 'packed' date and 'use by' date to ensure you are buying a product at its optimum freshness.

With eggs, always try to buy organic, or at least free-range eggs, as these will have a much better flavour, colour and shelf-life. It's a good idea to buy regularly and in small quantities so you always have the freshest products to hand. Store them in the fridge – but remember that their porous shells mean they risk absorbing flavours from other unwrapped ingredients. And use eggs as soon as you can: the fresher they are the firmer and plumper is the white; over time, this breaks down and becomes watery.

With cream, the flavour of an organic or biodynamically produced product is far richer and lusher than that from a large dairy. Remember, too, that the fresher it is, the better the flavour and the less likely it is to split.

Cheeses that are oozingly ripe, with a full, rich flavour, will be more appreciated by your guests than a cheese that is immature and somewhat chalky. It's often a good idea to let the cheese seller guide you as to which cheeses are at their peak, rather than have a preconceived idea about what you think you want. Cheese should be wrapped in waxed paper (this will allow the cheese to breathe) and stored in airtight containers to avoid mingling aromas. Serving cheese at the correct temperature is imperative in order to release its full flavour and appreciate its true characteristics and depth of flavour.

Chef's notes

Choosing quality applies as much with general ingredients for your larder or fridge as it does with fresh fruit, vegetables, meat, poultry and seafood. There are a few specific choices that I make for the recipes that follow, and they are:

- Salt is specified as fine table salt, or sea salt – preferably Maldon, fleur de sel or pink salt.
- Pepper is freshly ground white pepper, unless black is specified.
- Sugar is caster (superfine) sugar, unless otherwise specified.
- Chocolate is the best quality dark chocolate you can afford.
- Oil is non-scented, either good-quality vegetable or canola, grapeseed or rice bran. These have no aroma and a clean, non-greasy flavour. I generally only use olive oil or other strong flavoured oils for dressings or to finish a dish.
- Butter is always unsalted, as it allows better control over the quantity of salt you use in each dish.
- Milk is always fresh, full-fat (whole).
- Cream is 35% butterfat content (whipping cream), unless thick (double/heavy) cream (45% butterfat) is specified.
- Eggs are free-range and weigh about 60 g (2 oz).

Batterie de cuisine

Essential items which are the foundation of every good kitchen.

For the hands

Knives – boning, carving, paring, chef's
    knife, serrated knife, filleting knife
Carving fork
Sharpening stone and steel
Vegetable peeler
Kitchen scissors
Tweezers
Whisks, wooden spoons, slices and
    spatulas, slotted spoons, grater
Zester, rolling pin, pastry brush, juicer
Mandoline
Mortar and pestle
Salad spinner, sieve, colander

For the benchtop

Chopping boards
Food processor
Electric mixer
Blender
Hand blender
Ice-cream machine

For the stove top

Stockpot
Saucepans
Frying pans
Omelette pan
Roasting tray
Steamer basket or pot
Griddle plate

Measuring

Weighing scales
Cups and spoons
Thermometer
Timer

For the oven

Baking sheets
Roasting pans
Casserole
Cake and patty (muffin) tins
Silicone baking sheets

conversion tables

Oven temperatures

C°	F°
125	240
140	275
150	300
160	320
170	340
180	350
190	375
200	400
210	410
220	430

teaspoons, tablespoons and cups

1 teaspoon	5 ml
1 tablespoon	20 ml
¼ cup	60 ml
⅓ cup	80 ml
½ cup	125 ml
1 cup	250 ml

Weight

METRIC	IMPERIAL
10 g	½ oz
20 g	¾ oz
30 g	1 oz
50 g	2 oz
80 g	3 oz
125 g	4 ½ oz
150 g	5 ½ oz
175 g	6 oz
200 g	7 oz
225 g	8 oz
250 g	9 oz
275 g	10 oz
300 g	10 ½ oz
350 g	12 oz
400 g	14 oz
450 g	1 lb
500 g	1 lb 2 oz
600 g	1 lb 5 oz
650 g	1 lb 7 oz
750 g	1 lb 10 oz
900 g	2 lb
1 kg	2 lb 3 oz

Volume

METRIC	IMPERIAL
10 ml	¼ fl oz
15 ml	½ fl oz
30 ml	1 fl oz
40 ml	1 ¼ fl oz
60 ml	2 fl oz
75 ml	2 ½ fl oz
100 ml	3 ½ fl oz
150 ml	5 fl oz
300 ml	10 fl oz
500 ml	17 fl oz
750 ml	25 fl oz
1 litre	34 fl oz

the lessons

Les leçons

Flavourings

As far as I'm concerned, when it comes to cooking (and eating!) this is where it all begins. It's no mistake that the very first lesson drummed home to all apprentice chefs the world over is, 'Taste what you're cooking!'

Taste it again and again and again! And while all the senses play their part at the dinner table, when we think about food and eating, above all else it's the flavour that interests us.

Yet this thing that we call flavour is complex and difficult to define. The broad-brush grouping of sweet, salty, sour and bitter is really only part of a much more complex story.

Intuitively, we think of flavour as being the way something tastes. In fact, two senses work together to help us determine the flavour of a foodstuff. Yes, people are often surprised to hear that our sense of smell plays almost as large a part in detecting flavour as our tongue. We are only able to detect the flavour of something as the result of a complex physiological reaction in our brain between these two senses.

But enough of the scientific stuff ... now let's talk philosophy! My whole approach to cooking is about maximising the natural flavours of the foods that we eat. It's about purity and integrity, and not masking these natural flavours by dulling our tastebuds with too much fat or starch or confusing our palate by complicating things too much.

While some ingredients taste most intense and pure in their natural raw state, often some sort of action is needed to bring out the inherent flavour. It can be as simple as changing the temperature (by cooking) or by adding other ingredients – such as salt, herbs, spices, acids or alcohol.

Herbs

Herbs play a huge part in French cookery, and of course in all cuisines.

They are the edible leaves and stalks of aromatic plants and each has its own unique flavour.

Herbs can be used on their own or in combination, as in a bouquet garni, to add a magical depth of flavour to a dish.

They can be divided into two groups: hard and robust or soft and delicate. Hard herbs tend to have woody stalks and tougher leaves; think of rosemary, thyme or bay leaves. They can withstand excessive heat and prolonged cooking, and are often added early on in the cooking so that their flavours meld and infuse over time. Soft herbs, such as basil and mint or chives and chervil, are more fragile and tend to be added at the very end of the cooking time or used raw, as heat destroys their delicate flavour.

When choosing herbs, try to select ones that look fresh and vibrant – not limp and tired. They should smell fragrant and the colour should be vivid. Grow your own if you can – or buy living herbs that you can snip as required. Otherwise, buy them in small quantities, wrap them in a damp (not wet) cloth and store them in an airtight container in the refrigerator. Soft herbs will keep well for up to 5 days and hard herbs will keep for up to 7 days if stored correctly.

Before preparing herbs it's a good idea to give them a quick wash. Submerge them gently in a bowl or sink of water and swirl them around gently. Remove straight away and dry them on paper towels or in a salad spinner. Never wash herbs under running water as the pressure is enough to bruise and damage them.

Different herbs require different preparation, but generally the aromatic leaves need to be picked from the stalks, which are then discarded. Use your fingers or scissors to pick small sprigs, or for woody herbs, such as rosemary, strip the leaves off quickly by pulling against the direction of growth.

To chop herbs, gather together the leaves in a tight bundle and roll them up tightly. Use a very sharp knife to slice across the bundle – the resulting shreds are known as a chiffonnade, which is often used as a garnish. To chop more finely, gather the shreds together and chop across the pile in a rocking motion. With some of the more delicate herbs, such as chervil and basil, you need to be careful not to overchop as you run the risk of bruising them and losing their aroma.

I'm not a big fan of dried herbs – fresh ones are so readily available that frankly I just don't see the point of using dried ones. At all costs avoid the little jars and packets that sit for months on supermarket shelves. If you want to dry your own, then tie them into small bunches and hang them in an airy spot for a few days until they are completely dry. Store in an airtight container and use within a few months while they are still fragrant. Use more sparingly than fresh herbs as the flavour tends to be more intense.

Herbes de Provence

This is a classic French combination of robust, savoury herbs, which is great to use in marinades for meats and grills. Herbes de Provence can also be added to stocks, braises and even kneaded into bread dough before baking.

This is hardly a recipe as such, but more an assembly of various herbs. Traditionally the mixture includes thyme, rosemary, bay leaf, basil and savoury (if savoury is not available it can simply be omitted), combined according to your own taste. Tie the herbs together to form a bundle, or strip the leaves and chop them together roughly.

Fines herbes

Another classic French mixture, this time of delicate, fragile herbs. Fines herbes are generally added at the end of the cooking time, or used as a garnish for sauces, soups, sautés and seafood dishes.

Again, the choice of herbs depends largely on personal taste and on the particular dish, but the mix may include parsley, chives, chervil and tarragon. Take care not to overdo the tarragon, however, as it can be a little overpowering. I prefer French tarragon as it has a milder flavour.

Bouquet garni

This selection is my preferred combination, but vary the quantities according to your own taste.

makes 1 bouquet garni (enough for 2 litres/68 fl oz of stock)

PREP TIME 5 MINUTES

3 sprigs parsley

2 sprigs thyme

1 bay leaf

1 stick celery

1 piece leek

Tie the herbs and vegetables together with a piece of string, or to wrap the piece of leek around the stalks and tie the string around it. Sometimes I even place a piece of streaky bacon on top of the leek and tie it all up together. Alternatively, tie everything up in a small muslin (cheesecloth) bag.

Use immediately, or store in the refrigerator for up to 3 days.

A bundle of aromatic herbs and vegetables used for flavouring stocks, soups and braises. The classic combination is bay leaf, thyme and parsley, although it can include other herbs, and sometimes spices or vegetables.

Spices

Spices are often dry-roasted, which brings out their flavour even more. You can either roast them in the oven or in a dry frying pan.

Although spices don't play such a starring role in French cookery as they do in some other cuisines (such as Asian or Middle Eastern, for instance), they do play an important part in marinades, brines and salt-cures, charcuterie, soups, sauces and pastries.

Whereas herbs are the leafy green parts of edible plants, spices are the other bits; generally speaking that means the intensely aromatic buds, berries, bark, roots, seeds and fruit. And while herbs are familiar, friendly kinds of plants that grow in most people's back gardens, spices tend to come from far more exotic and far-flung lands.

Spices are used in the same way as herbs, to heighten and enliven the flavour of a dish. But you do need to be a bit careful not to overuse them – you don't want to overpower the underlying ingredients, but rather to complement and enhance them. As a general principle I advise you to err on the side of caution – add less rather than more to start off with, after all you can always add more later on.

For maximum freshness, always purchase spices from a specialty food shop or spice retailer. To maintain flavour and aroma, store spices in an airtight container in a cool dry place. And only buy spices in small quantities; they will lose their aroma and flavour if they sit in your cupboard for years on end!

Spices can be used whole or ground, depending on the dish. Add a whole cinnamon stick or a few whole cloves to a stock syrup for instance – these can be fished out after cooking, whereas ground cinnamon or cloves would ruin the clarity of the syrup. But if you want to use spices in marinades, rubs, casseroles or in cakes or biscuits (cookies) they need to be ground to a fine powder so they mix in readily with the other ingredients.

To grind spices, use a mortar and pestle or an electric spice or coffee grinder. With the latter though, be careful not to overgrind the spices, which will burn the essential oils and alter the flavour.

Spices are often dry-roasted, which brings out their flavour even more. You can either roast them in the oven or in a dry frying pan. Spread them out in an even layer and roast for a few minutes until they start to colour and become intensely fragrant. You'll need to keep the pan moving so they don't burn.

The recipes that follow use spices in two different ways. In the aromatic spice mix the spices are roughly crushed with salt and then toasted to release and intensify their flavour. In the sweet spice mix, the spices are infused in a warm solution of alcohol, which is used as a marinade.

Quatre épices

This is a classic French spice mixture of 4 spices – allspice, cinnamon, nutmeg and cloves – is used in baking cakes, biscuits (cookies) and desserts. Usually the ratio is 7 parts allspice to 1 part each of the other spices. The allspice, cinnamon and cloves are roughly pounded in a mortar, and the nutmeg grated. I then whiz everything to a powder in a spice or coffee grinder.

16

Aromatic spice mix

This is one of my favourite spice mixes; I find the fennel and star anise are particularly good with crustaceans, such as marron, yabby, crayfish, lobster and scampi (langoustine), and one of my all-time favourite dishes, roasted Lobster Tails (see page 205).

makes enough for 2 x 600 g (1 lb 5 oz) lobster tails

✎ PREP TIME 5 MINUTES

20 g (¾ oz) sea salt

1 cinnamon stick

4 garlic cloves

4 sprigs thyme

2 star anise

6 coriander seeds

8 fennel seeds

Mix all the ingredients in a mortar and gently crush with the pestle until just broken but not too crushed.

Heat a heavy-based frying pan over a medium heat. Add the spices and toast for 3–5 minutes without colouring, until the flavours are released. Use immediately.

Sweet spice mix for cherries

makes enough to bottle 1 kg (2 lb 3 oz) of cherries (1 large Kilner/preserve jar)

✎ PREP TIME 20 MINUTES   🍲 COOK TIME 60 MINUTES

1 kg (2 lb 3 oz) fresh cherries, pitted

2 litres (68 fl oz) red wine

1 litre (34 fl oz) ruby port

1 cinnamon stick

3 star anise

6 cloves

Place all ingredients in a heavy-based saucepan and bring to the boil over a moderately high heat. Lower the heat and simmer for 45 minutes, until the liquid has reduced enough to just cover the cherries. It should have an intensely spiced aroma.

Allow to cool before tipping into a large sterilised Kilner jar. The bottled cherries will keep in the fridge for 1 month.

Salt

Salt is as fundamental to French cooking as it is to all cuisines. It is not only an essential mineral that the human body requires (although not to excess), but it acts as an important trigger to the production of saliva in our mouth and the gastric juices in our stomach. It is, if you like, the ultimate flavour enhancer.

As well as being used as a seasoning to heighten the flavour of other foods, the other main use of salt is as a food preserver. Traditionally salt has been used to dry- or wet-cure, or to pickle perishable foodstuffs in a brine solution. Since the advent of freezing and refrigeration, however, the necessity for this method of preserving has all but disappeared.

Whereas herbs and spices introduce new and different flavours to a dish, salt, when used properly, should be neutral. Poor quality mass-produced salts may have chemicals added to keep them free-flowing, but these will definitely impact on the flavour of your final dish. Wherever possible, try to use unrefined salts with no added chemicals.

I use two different kinds of salt in my kitchen: fine cooking salt that I use to cook with, and salt flakes or crystals that I use to season at the end of cooking and as a condiment on the dinner table. Good-quality salts such as Maldon sea salt and fleur de sel (wet salt) from Brittany are both readily available. All salts should be stored in an airtight container in a cool dry place.

Finally, if you are using ingredients such as olives, anchovies, capers or botaga roe, don't forget that these are naturally salty (and extra salt is used in their production) so you will not need to add much – if any – more salt to the dish.

Asian spiced salt mix for pork

Makes 150 g (5½ oz) (enough for 1 large pork belly)

PREP TIME 20 MINUTES

100 g (3½ oz) wet salt

20 g (¾ oz) brown sugar

1 lime

2 stalks fresh coriander (cilantro)

½ cinnamon stick

2 garlic cloves

4 sprigs thyme

15 g (½ oz) fresh ginger

2 star anise

6 coriander seeds

4 cloves

Place the salt and sugar in a mortar. Grate the lime onto the salt and sugar, making sure you capture all the spray and oils released by the fruit. Squeeze the lime and add the juice to the mix.

Add the remaining ingredients and pound with the pestle until crushed and aromatic.

This salt will keep in an airtight container in the refrigerator for up to 2 weeks.

Wet citrus salt

makes 150 g (5½ oz)

PREP TIME 20 MINUTES

100 g (3½ oz) wet salt

30 g (1 oz) sugar

1 lime

1 orange

1 lemon

4 coriander seeds

2 peppercorns

Place the salt and sugar in a mortar, and grate the citrus fruits over. Add the coriander seeds and peppercorns and pound with the pestle until crushed and aromatic. This salt will keep in an airtight container in the refrigerator for up to 2 weeks.

Aromatic confit salt

makes around 150 g (5½ oz)

PREP TIME 20 MINUTES

100 g (3½ oz) wet salt

½ cinnamon stick

2 garlic cloves

4 sprigs thyme

1 sprig rosemary

½ bay leaf

1 star anise

2 peppercorns

4 coriander seeds

Place all the ingredients in a mortar, pound well until well crushed and aromatic. This salt will keep in an airtight container in the refrigerator for up to 2 weeks.

Alcohol and vinegar solutions

Wine is splashed around with great abandon in the French kitchen, and spirits and liqueurs are often used at the end of cooking to add a final flavour and lift to a sauce, soup or stew.

Similarly, I like to use vinegar – especially wine-based vinegars – to add a sharp, acid note to all kinds of dressings, sauces and casseroles.

There are a few things to keep in mind, though. Firstly, there are obviously many differences between red and white wines – so use the appropriate wine for each dish, as directed in the recipe. Secondly, alcohol shouldn't be used 'raw' in a dish as it is far too overpowering – and this is especially true if you're using wines that are less than top-notch! Usually the alcohol will be evaporated off as you cook it, leaving the wine flavour behind. But the more you cook it, the more concentrated and acidic the flavours will become; always exercise caution and taste continuously. Often, a few minutes' vigorous simmering will be sufficient to burn off the alcohol and still maintain the freshness of flavour.

When it comes to distilled spirits or liqueurs, though, it's a different story and they should only be used raw – or very briefly boiled or flamed – as the flavours are far more volatile and delicate. The impact they make can be stunning. Think about adding a splash of Armagnac or rum to a sweet custard or pastry cream or a drop of cognac to a velvety seafood bisque.

Similarly, sweet and fortified wines such as a sauterne, port, Madeira or sherry should only really be added towards the end of the cooking time – or only given the briefest simmer – so as not to destroy their wonderful sweet intensity of flavour.

When it comes to vinegar, I use the whole gamut, from pricy 'boutique' vinegars made from cabernet sauvignon, chardonnay or champagne to more generic white or red wine vinegars, sherry vinegar or balsamic vinegar. Remember that vinegar also becomes much more intense and acidic when it's simmered and reduced. So once again, be guided by the way it's being used in the dish.

White wine vinegar reduction

This reduction is the base for the famous hollandaise sauce and all its various derivatives. I tend to make it in a reasonable amount as it keeps for many months and is always useful.

makes 150 ml (5 fl oz)

PREP TIME 10 MINUTES   COOK TIME 10 MINUTES

200 ml (7 fl oz) white wine

100 ml (3 ½ fl oz) white wine vinegar

1 shallot, finely sliced

1 garlic clove, finely sliced

1 sprig thyme

½ bay leaf

3 peppercorns

Place all ingredients in a saucepan and bring to the boil. Lower the heat and simmer until reduced by half. Transfer to a container with a tight-fitting lid and refrigerate. The reduction will keep in a sealed container in the refrigerator for many months.

Red wine vinegar reduction

I splash this around into salads and whisk it into vinaigrettes; I add it to sauces, as a finishing touch and I even like to drizzle it straight onto platters of cured meats to liven them up a bit.

makes 200 ml (7 fl oz)

PREP TIME 5 MINUTES   COOK TIME 30 MINUTES

500 ml (17 fl oz) cabernet sauvignon vinegar

250 ml (8 ½ fl oz) red wine

250 ml (8 ½ fl oz) ruby port

Place all the ingredients in a heavy-based saucepan over a high heat. Bring to the boil, then simmer until reduced to 200 ml (7 fl oz), or until thick and syrupy. Pour into a screwtop jar and keep refrigerated for up to 2 weeks.

Port and red wine reduction

makes 200 ml (7 fl oz)

PREP TIME 5 MINUTES   COOK TIME 30 MINUTES

700 ml (23 fl oz) red wine

300 ml (10 fl oz) ruby port

2 sprigs thyme

1 crushed clove garlic

Place all the ingredients in a heavy-based saucepan over a high heat. Bring to the boil, then simmer until reduced to 200 ml (7 fl oz), or until thick and syrupy.

Pour into a screwtop jar and keep refrigerated for up to 2 weeks. Remove the thyme and garlic before use.

Vanilla and apple cider reduction

This reduction is especially good with pork dishes – either splashed onto roasts or added to their accompanying sauces.

makes 200 ml (7 fl oz)

✎ PREP TIME 5 MINUTES ☞ COOK TIME 30 MINUTES

700 ml (23 fl oz) dry cider

300 ml (10 fl oz) clear apple juice

1 vanilla pod, seeds scraped

Place the ingredients in a heavy-based saucepan over a high heat. Simmer until reduced to 200 ml (7 fl oz) or until thick and syrupy. Pour into a screwtop jar and keep refrigerated for up to 2 weeks. Remove the vanilla pod before use.

Solution for poaching or pickling red beetroot

Home-pickled beetroot (beet) is *so* much better than shop-bought. I love them in salads and sandwiches, at barbecues and picnics, and even with the Sunday roast!

makes enough for 1 kg (2 lb 3 oz) beetroot (2 medium Kilner/ preserve jars)

✎ PREP TIME 20 MINUTES ☞ COOK TIME 2 HOURS FOR LARGE BEETROOT OR 1 HOUR FOR BABY BEETROOT

1 kg (2 lb 3 oz) large or baby red beetroot (beets)

100 ml (3½ fl oz) cabernet sauvignon vinegar

2 litres (68 fl oz) water

50 g (2 oz) sugar

200 ml (7 fl oz) red wine

1 teaspoon salt

100 ml (3½ fl oz) ruby port

Wash the beetroot well to remove all grit and sand and place them in a large saucepan. Combine the remaining ingredients in a large pitcher and stir until the sugar and salt have dissolved. Pour onto the beetroot, making sure they are completely covered.

Heat gently until nearly simmering. Poach gently, uncovered, for about 2 hours or until tender when tested with a sharp skewer. Allow to cool slightly and peel away the skin while still warm. Cut into small pieces.

Pour the poaching liquor through a piece of muslin (cheesecloth) and then tip back into to the saucepan. Return the pan to the heat and bring to the boil. Simmer until reduced by a third. You are looking for a good depth of flavour and a balance of sweetness and acidity.

Spoon the beetroot pieces into 2 sterilised Kilner jars and pour in enough liquor to cover them completely. Store in the refrigerator for up to 3 weeks.

Elderflower champagne

This is a lovely refreshing, lightly floral sparkling drink, perfect for those hot summer months. I also love to use it to make jellies (gelatin desserts) and refreshing sorbets (sherbets). The recipe comes from my head chef James; he remembers making this as a child, with his grandmother, when growing up in England.

Makes 2 x 750 ml (25 fl oz) bottles

PREP TIME 20 MINUTES · INFUSING TIME 24 HOURS
FERMENTING TIME 2 WEEKS

2.5 litres (85 fl oz) water

1 large head or bunch elderflower

1 whole lemon

250 g (9 oz) sugar

1 teaspoon white wine vinegar

Place the water and elderflower in a clean container. Cut the lemon in half, squeeze the juice into the water mix and add the lemon halves. Mix in the sugar and vinegar.

Cover tightly with plastic wrap and leave to stand and infuse at room temperature for 24 hours.

Strain through a piece of muslin or fine cheesecloth and pour into sterilised bottles. Secure tightly with tie-down or screwtop lids – this is important, as the build up of pressure can make the lids burst off if they are not well secured. Leave in a cool dry place for 2 weeks to ferment.

Transfer the bottles to a cool dark cupboard. Once opened, the cordial will keep for a couple of weeks in the refrigerator. Otherwise, store unopened in a cool dark place for up to 6 months.

Sweet flavourings

In French cooking, sweet flavourings tend to be used mainly in desserts and the most common sweet additions are sugar, natural fruit sugars and honey, and spices with sweet undertones, such as vanilla, cloves, nutmeg and cinnamon.

I love to use sugar as a medium to carry other flavours (in the same way as I use salt in savoury dishes). So, for instance, I'll infuse a jar of sugar with a vanilla pod or a few strips of orange, lemon or lime peel, or I'll add a splash of sherry vinegar or a grating of lime zest to a caramel.

Sugar can also be used as a flavour enhancer – that is to bring out the natural sweet flavours of other ingredients. People often add a teaspoon of sugar to a home-made tomato sauce, for example, or a pinch of sugar to baby peas or carrots.

Vanilla sugar

This is a good way of extending the use of those expensive vanilla pods, once they've been scraped of their seeds. Place them in your sugar canister, so they're completely covered in sugar. The vanilla will infuse the sugar with a delicate sweet scent. The resulting vanilla sugar is perfect for sprinkling over shortbread biscuits (cookies) before you bake them or for using when you make custards and sweet sauces. It will keep for several months in a cool dry place.

Vanilla gastrique

This amazing caramel is finished with lime juice. It adds a wonderful sour-sweet finish to all sorts of sauces.

makes 200 ml (7 fl oz)

✐ PREP TIME 5 MINUTES ☕ COOK TIME 20 MINUTES

200 g (7 oz) sugar

200 ml (7 fl oz) water

juice of 1 lime

1 vanilla pod, seeds scraped

Place the sugar and 100 ml (3½ fl oz) of water in a heavy-based saucepan. Cook over a moderate heat to dissolve the sugar. When completely clear, add the vanilla pod and seeds and bring to the boil. Simmer gently for 5–6 minutes, to form a light caramel.

Remove from the heat and add the lime juice and remaining water. Allow to cool and refrigerate until required for up to 4 weeks. Remove the vanilla pod before you serve. The gastrique may set quite thick once refrigerated; if this is the case, simply warm slightly before using.

tea

Although tea has been around for centuries as a hot refreshing drink, using it in other culinary applications has only started to become fashionable in French cooking fairly recently.

I'm delighted that tea is being used more widely because I love the light delicate flavours that different varieties of tea add to different types of food. The use of herbal infusions is fairly obvious, of course, but think of the elegant, citrus notes of Earl Grey tea, for instance, which perfectly complement a delicate Tomato Essence (page 49). Or imagine the way a more robust Marco Polo tea will enhance an earthy, lemongrass-infused dressing.

There are a few recipes in the following chapters that use tea as an unexpected additional flavour; they include Date Purée (page 245), Lemon Verbena Tea Granita (page 263) and Date and Earl Grey Parfait (page 273).

Although you might be unfamiliar with the idea of using tea as a 'flavour', I do encourage you to try it in these recipes. As is always the case with cooking, you need to think about the aroma and flavour and try to imagine how it will interact with other component parts of the dish. Why not have a bit of fun in the kitchen?

As is the case with spices, always purchase your tea from a reputable specialty tea shop to ensure a tea with integrity and freshness. Store tea leaves in airtight jars in a cool dry place.

Stocks

The French word for stock is 'fond', foundation, which to me says everything about their importance in French cooking. Stocks are indeed the foundation upon which all kinds of dishes are built. Without good stocks there would be few soups, sauces, ragoûts or braises.

It's probably true to say that without good stocks, French cuisine would not exist in the form that it does today.

The interesting thing about stocks is that they are never made simply as an end in their own right. They are always used as the basis to create some other dish or sauce. Perhaps this is one reason why making stocks at home has fallen out of fashion somewhat – this and the fact that, while not difficult to make, they are time consuming. Somehow, in this fast-paced world, it all seems just a bit too hard.

But to be honest, learning to make decent stocks is an absolutely essential part of learning to cook French dishes. In this chapter I hope to convince you that simple stock making is just that: simple. All that you really need is a few basic ingredients and patience.

The first thing to understand is that it's just plain silly to start a recipe by making a stock. It makes much better sense to cook stocks in large batches and freeze them in convenient amounts – say 500 ml (17 fl oz) or 1 litre (34 fl oz) – so that they're always on hand for immediate use. I also recommend having at least one white stock and one brown stock in your freezer.

So what's the difference? French cuisine generally divides stocks into brown (fond brun) and white (fond blanc). Both are made in the same way, using raw bones, with vegetables and herbs added for additional flavour. For brown stocks, though, the bones and vegetables are thoroughly browned (usually by roasting in the oven) before adding water. Brown stocks are richer, fuller-flavoured and more concentrated than white stocks.

For all stocks, it's important to use good-quality ingredients and the method is, essentially, the same. Once the water has been added to the bones (roasted or raw), vegetables and other flavourings, the stock is slowly brought to the boil over a low heat. When it boils, the stock is then skimmed and left to simmer gently, virtually unattended. The stock shouldn't be allowed to boil, as it will turn cloudy and can develop an unpleasant taste. It's a good idea to skim off any impurities from time to time, as they rise to the top – this also helps to ensure a clear and richly flavoured stock.

At the end of the cooking time all the flavour will have been extracted from the bones and vegetables. As well as gaining flavour and colour, a good stock also attains body from the bones' marrow, and will set to a gorgeous jelly when chilled.

One final point: it is possible to buy good-quality stocks these days, and I strongly encourage you to choose the best you can afford. It's generally preferable to buy the home-made variety from specialty food stores or delis – many local butchers make or sell good-quality stocks as well. If possible, avoid buying stock from supermarket chains. Their products tend to be price-driven, and the quality nearly always suffers as a result.

WHITE STOCKS

White stocks are made from unroasted bones and are generally lighter in flavour than brown stocks. They can be made from chicken or game carcasses, veal bones, fish bones or vegetables. They are used with delicate white meats and seafood and for making pale sauces, and can also be used instead of water as a base for making brown stocks when a greater depth of flavour is required.

White chicken stock

Use the same general method for other white-fleshed game birds, such as quail, guinea fowl, pheasant or even squab.

makes 2 litres (68 fl oz)

/ PREP TIME 5 MINUTES ⌒ COOK TIME 2 HOURS

3 kg (6 lb 9 oz) raw chicken carcasses, skin and fat removed

1 bulb garlic, cut in half

8 sprigs thyme

Roughly chop the bones into small, even-sized pieces. Put them in a stockpot or large saucepan and pour on just enough water to cover.

Bring to the boil slowly. Use a ladle to skim away the scum and impurities as they rise to the surface, to prevent them cooking back into the stock, making it cloudy and bitter. When the stock boils, reduce the heat. Add the garlic and thyme and simmer gently, uncovered, for 2 hours, skimming frequently.

Leave to cool slightly then strain through a fine sieve into a pitcher or bowl. Allow to cool completely then skim again and refrigerate overnight. When the stock is cold most of the fat will have solidified into a layer on the surface. This can be easily scraped away.

If not using immediately, divide into 500 ml (17 fl oz) batches and freeze. If using from frozen, leave to thaw in the refrigerator overnight, or defrost quickly in the microwave. This minimises the risk of harmful bacteria forming.

The stock will keep in sealed containers in the fridge for 2 days or up to 3 months in the freezer.

White veal stock

Use the same general method for white lamb and pork stocks. Ask your butcher to cut the bones on the band saw to the size of a small fist. Choose bones that have a good covering of meat on them, as this will ensure a good depth of flavour to your stock.

makes 2 litres (68 fl oz)

PREP TIME 5 MINUTES COOK TIME 3 HOURS

3 kg (6 lb 9 oz) raw veal neck bones

1 garlic bulb, cut in half

8 sprigs thyme

1 bay leaf

5 white peppercorns

Roughly chop the bones into small, even-sized pieces, or ask your butcher to do it for you. Put them in a stockpot or large saucepan and pour on just enough water to cover.

Bring to the boil slowly. Use a ladle to skim away the scum and impurities as they rise to the surface, to prevent them cooking back into the stock, making it cloudy and bitter. When the stock boils, reduce the heat. Add the garlic, thyme, bay leaf and peppercorns and simmer gently, uncovered, for 3 hours, skimming frequently.

Leave to cool slightly then strain through a fine sieve into a pitcher or bowl. Allow to cool then skim again and refrigerate overnight. When the stock is cold most of the fat will have solidified into a layer on the surface. This can be easily scraped away.

If not using immediately, divide into 500 ml (17 fl oz) batches and freeze. If using from frozen, leave to thaw in the refrigerator overnight, or defrost quickly in the microwave. This minimises the risk of harmful bacteria forming.

The stock will keep in sealed containers in the fridge for 3 days or up to 3 months in the freezer.

Fish stock

Fish stock is best made from white fish, such as snapper or John Dory. It is quick and easy to make.

makes 2 litres (68 fl oz)

⁄ PREP TIME 5 MINUTES ⌒ COOK TIME 20 MINUTES

1 kg (2 lb 3 oz) raw fish bones

2.5 litres (85 fl oz) water

1 onion, finely sliced

2 garlic cloves, roughly crushed

2 celery stalks, roughly chopped

1 fennel bulb, roughly chopped

1 bay leaf

10 coriander seeds

2 star anise

Chop the fish bones into large pieces and rinse them under cold running water for a few minutes. Put the fish bones in a stockpot or large saucepan and pour on the water.

Bring to the boil slowly. As soon as the stock boils, reduce the heat. Add the remaining ingredients and simmer gently, uncovered, for 20 minutes, skimming frequently.

Drain the stock through a colander, then pass through a fine sieve into a pitcher or bowl. Allow to cool then skim and refrigerate overnight.

If not using immediately, divide into 500 ml (17 fl oz) batches and freeze. If using from frozen, leave to thaw in the refrigerator overnight, or defrost quickly in the microwave. This minimises the risk of harmful bacteria forming.

The stock will keep in sealed containers in the fridge for 2 days or up to 3 months in the freezer.

Vegetable stock

makes 2 litres (68 fl oz)

PREP TIME 15 MINUTES   COOK TIME 20 MINUTES   INFUSING TIME 30 MINUTES

1 onion, finely sliced

2 carrots, finely sliced

½ leek, finely sliced

2 celery stalks, finely sliced

1 fennel bulb, finely sliced

4 garlic cloves

4 white peppercorns

6 coriander seeds, crushed

3 star anise

3 sprigs thyme

2.5 litres (85 fl oz) water

4 sprigs tarragon

6 sprigs chervil

2 sprigs coriander (cilantro)

Put the sliced vegetables, garlic, peppercorns, coriander seeds, star anise and thyme in a stockpot or large saucepan and pour on the water.

Bring to the boil over a high heat. As soon as the stock boils, reduce the heat and simmer gently, uncovered, for 10 minutes. Remove the pan from the heat, add the herbs, cover with a tight-fitting lid and leave to infuse for 30 minutes.

Strain through a fine sieve into a pitcher or bowl and refrigerate overnight. If not using immediately, divide into 500 ml (17 fl oz) batches and freeze. If using from frozen, leave to thaw out in the refrigerator overnight, or defrost quickly in the microwave. This minimises the risk of harmful bacteria forming.

The stock will keep in sealed containers in the fridge for 2 days or up to 3 months in the freezer.

BROWN STOCKS

Brown stocks can be made from chicken or game bird carcasses, veal or lamb bones. Roasting the bones and vegetables gives the stock a deeper colour and a more intense flavour. Once roasted, the pan is déglacé (deglazed), by adding water to the pan and stirring around the caramelised deposits to colour and flavour the liquid.

Brown chicken or game stock

Although this stock can be made with water, I like to use a white stock as the base liquid, which results in a richer, deeper flavour. Use white chicken stock for your base if making brown chicken stock, white game stock as the base for brown game stock. For an even more intense flavour use a base of half white stock and half Brown Veal Stock (opposite). To ensure the final stock is clear, use chilled white stock, straight from the refrigerator. As it warms through, any impurities will rise to the surface. Use a ladle to skim these away immediately.

makes 2 litres (68 fl oz)

/ PREP TIME 10 MINUTES ☐ COOK TIME 45 MINUTES

50 ml (2 fl oz) vegetable oil

2 kg (4 lb 6 oz) meaty chicken wings and carcasses (or game bones, as appropriate)

150 g (5½ oz) cold butter, diced

300 g (10½ oz) shallots, finely sliced

300 g (10½ oz) button mushrooms, finely sliced

½ garlic bulb

6 sprigs thyme

3 litres (102 fl oz) white stock (chicken or game, as appropriate)

salt and pepper

Preheat the oven to 190°C (375°F). Put the oil in a roasting pan and heat in the oven. Roughly chop the bones into small, even-sized pieces. Add them to the roasting pan and roast for 10–15 minutes, stirring occasionally to prevent them sticking and burning.

Once the wings are golden brown, scatter on the butter and return to the oven until it foams. Add the vegetables, garlic and thyme and return to the oven for a further 10 minutes, until everything is a deep golden brown.

Remove the roasting pan from the oven. Tip the contents into a colander to drain, then transfer them to a stockpot or large saucepan. Tip out all the fat from the roasting pan and place it over a medium heat. Add a few splashes of water and stir to scrape up any caramelised residue; this is called deglazing. Pour the deglazing liquid over the roasted bones and vegetables, then pour on the cold stock.

Bring to the boil slowly. Use a ladle to skim away the scum and impurities as they rise to the surface. When the stock boils, reduce the heat and simmer gently, uncovered, for 30 minutes, skimming frequently.

Leave to cool slightly then strain through a fine sieve into a pitcher or bowl. Allow to cool completely, then skim again and refrigerate overnight. When the stock is cold most of the fat will have solidified into a layer on the surface. This can be easily scraped away.

If not using immediately, divide into 500 ml (17 fl oz) batches and freeze. If using from frozen, leave to thaw out in the refrigerator overnight, or defrost quickly in the microwave. This minimises the risk of harmful bacteria forming.

The stock will keep in sealed containers in the fridge for 3 days or up to 3 months in the freezer.

Brown veal stock

Veal bones and calf or pig's feet are all available from the butcher. I prefer to use veal neck bones to make brown veal stock as they have a superior flavour and their meatiness assists in the caramelisation. Ask your butcher to cut the bones on the band saw to the size of a small fist. The calf's foot is not added for flavour, but for the wonderful gelatine it releases. It gives the finished stock body, ensuring it sets to a good firm jelly with a bright, sparkling sheen.

makes 2 litres (68 fl oz)

PREP TIME 20 MINUTES COOK TIME 6 HOURS

100 ml (3 ½ fl oz) vegetable oil	100 g (3 ½ oz) tomato paste (concentrated purée)
6 kg (13 lb 2 oz) veal neck bones	150 ml (5 fl oz) red wine
1 garlic bulb, cut in half	1 split calf or pig's foot
1 onion, quartered	1 bay leaf
2 carrots, halved lengthwise	6 white peppercorns
4 celery stalks, quartered	6 sprigs thyme
1 leek, halved lengthwise	

Preheat your oven to 220°C (430°F). Divide the oil between 2 roasting pans and heat them in the oven. Add the veal bones to the roasting pans, spreading them out evenly, and roast for 45 minutes, stirring occasionally to prevent them sticking and burning. Even the slightest burn will taint the flavour of the whole stock. Once the bones are a lovely golden brown tip them into a colander to drain, then set aside.

Add the onions to one roasting tray and the carrots to the other and return the trays to the oven. After about 10 minutes add some celery and leek to both trays and roast until everything is caramelised a deep golden brown. Stir half the tomato paste into each pan and roast for a further 10–15 minutes. Remove both pans from the oven and deglaze each with the red wine.

Place half the reserved bones in a stockpot or large saucepan. Place the split calf's foot on top, followed by all the roasted vegetables, and then the remaining bones. It is important that the calf's foot and vegetables be submerged in the middle of the pan, for maximum flavour release. Pour on enough water to cover the bones and bring to the boil slowly.

Use a ladle to skim away the scum and impurities as they rise to the surface. When the stock boils, reduce the heat and simmer gently, uncovered for 6 hours, skimming from time to time.

Leave to cool slightly then strain through a fine sieve into a pitcher or bowl. Allow to cool, then skim again and refrigerate overnight. When the stock is cold most of the fat will have solidified into a layer on the surface of the stock. This can be easily scraped away.

If not using immediately, divide into 500 ml (17 fl oz) batches and freeze. If using from frozen, leave to thaw out in the refrigerator overnight, or defrost quickly in the microwave. This minimises the risk of harmful bacteria forming.

The stock will keep in sealed containers in the fridge for 3 days or up to 3 months in the freezer.

VEAL GLACE

Veal glace is simply a reduction of brown veal stock. Heat in a heavy-based saucepan over a high heat until reduced by half. Skim continuously to ensure the glace is clear and the flavour is intense. I like to divide the veal glace into 200 ml (7 fl oz) batches and store it in the freezer. That way you'll always be ready to make a superbly flavoured sauce with minimal fuss.

Brown lamb or pork stock

makes 2 litres (68 fl oz)

⟋ PREP TIME 10 MINUTES ⌇ COOK TIME 3 HOURS

50 ml (2 fl oz) vegetable oil

4 kg (8 lb 8 oz) meaty lamb or pork bones, chopped small

1 onion, chopped to a large mirepoix (see page 208)

1 carrot, chopped to a large mirepoix

2 celery stalks, chopped to a large mirepoix

½ garlic bulb

200 ml (7 fl oz) white wine

4 litres (136 fl oz) cold white stock (lamb or pork, as appropriate)

4 sprigs thyme

2 sprigs rosemary (for lamb stock only)

Preheat the oven to 220°C (430°F). Put the oil in a roasting pan and heat in the oven. Roughly chop the bones into small, even-sized pieces. Add them to the roasting pan and roast for 30 minutes, stirring occasionally to prevent them sticking and burning.

Once the bones are a lovely golden brown, add the vegetables and garlic and return to the oven for a further 20 minutes, until everything is a deep golden brown.

Remove the roasting pan from the oven and tip the contents into a colander to drain. Return the contents to the roasting pan over a medium heat and deglaze with the white wine.

Tip everything into a stockpot or large saucepan then pour on the cold stock. Bring to the boil slowly. Use a ladle to skim away the scum and impurities as they rise to the surface. When the stock boils, reduce the heat, add the herbs and simmer gently, uncovered, for 2 hours, skimming frequently.

Leave to cool slightly then strain through a fine sieve into a pitcher or bowl. Allow to cool, then skim again and refrigerate overnight. When the stock is cold most of the fat will have solidified into a layer on the surface of the stock. This can be easily scraped away.

If not using immediately, divide into 500 ml (17 fl oz) batches and freeze. If using from frozen, leave to thaw in the refrigerator overnight, or defrost quickly in the microwave. This minimises the risk of harmful bacteria forming.

The stock will keep in sealed containers in the fridge for 3 days or up to 3 months in the freezer.

Soups

According to Beethoven, 'Only the pure in heart can make good soup.' I'm not entirely sure what the great composer knew about soup making, but this comment certainly rings true with me.

I think there is a danger of thinking about soups as a bit of an exercise in recycling leftovers. But good soup is not something that you can cheat with! It really is something that comes from the heart and the soul, and requires a certain sort of culinary honesty. By this I mean you need to begin with good ingredients and take the proper time – without shortcuts – to achieve the magic that transforms the mundane into something intensely flavoursome and satisfying.

Apparently simple, in French cooking soups are incredibly varied and can range from humble and hearty to subtle and sophisticated. The substantial soupes and potages of provincial cooking are popular family fare, and will often be the mainstay of an evening meal, followed perhaps by just a small salad or fruit. At the other end of the spectrum, elegant consommés, complex bisques and silky-smooth veloutés take their place proudly at the start of an elaborate dinner party or restaurant meal.

The simplest and most sophisticated soups all require the same approach to achieve the desired purity and depth of flavour. It's not about chucking a whole lot of ingredients into the pot and hoping for the best. Some of the best soups, such as Potato Velouté (page 52) or intensely flavoured Tomato Essence (page 49), are made from only one or two ingredients. It's far more important to use top-quality fresh ingredients, and to season appropriately.

In my view, the soup course is a good example of the way in which classical French cooking is evolving. Thankfully, cooks are moving away from the heavy, roux-based varieties of soups that tended to mask the flavour of the ingredients and dull the palate with their reliance on cream, butter and flour. These days, home cooks and restaurant chefs have access to excellent produce and we have a better understanding of how to extract the freshness and flavour from these ingredients for a lighter and more intensely flavoured result.

In my restaurant we tend to divide soups into two broad styles: clear – of which the consommé is the ultimate expression – and thick. Thickening is not achieved the old-fashioned way with flour, but by puréeing the ingredients or by adding a little cream to smooth and enrich.

clear soups

Oxtail broth

Oxtail broth is wonderful served with Roasted Baby Carrots (page 224) and slivers of gelatinous bone marrow, which you can get from your butcher. At the restaurant we serve the soup with freshly grated horseradish and a generous sprinkle of chopped parsley.

makes 2 litres (68 fl oz), enough for 4 serves

PREP TIME 20 MINUTES   MARINATING TIME 12 HOURS   COOK TIME 4 HOURS

1 carrot	500 ml (17 fl oz) red wine
1 onion	500 ml (17 fl oz) ruby port
1 celery stalk	1 kg (2 lb 3 oz) oxtail, jointed
1½ garlic bulbs	2 litres (68 fl oz) Brown Veal Stock (page 35)
3 sprigs thyme	salt and pepper
1 bay leaf	30 ml (1 fl oz) vegetable oil

Cut the vegetables into large pieces and put them in a large saucepan with the garlic, herbs, wine and port. Bring to the boil over a high heat and cook for 5 minutes. Remove from the heat and allow to cool slightly. Put the oxtails in a large bowl and pour the hot marinade over the oxtails. Once cool, cover in plastic wrap and refrigerate for at least 12 hours.

Tip into a colander, reserving the marinade. Reserve the vegetables and pat the oxtails dry using paper towels. Bring the marinade to the boil over a high heat and simmer until reduced by a third. Skim off any impurities that rise to the surface. Once the marinade has reduced, add the veal stock to the pan and set aside.

Preheat the oven to 110°C (230°F). Season the oxtails with salt and pepper. Heat a heavy-based braising pan over a moderate heat and add the oil, then oxtails. Cook until brown and caramelised all over, then remove from the pan and set aside.

Now add the reserved vegetables to the braising pan and cook until deep brown. Return the oxtails to the pan and pour on the marinade-stock mixture. Cut a circle of baking paper to the size of the pan to make a cartouche and place on the surface. Place in the oven and cook for 3 hours until the meat is soft and gelatinous and falls away from the bones easily. You'll probably need to turn the meat every 30 minutes or so to ensure it cooks evenly.

Strain the cooking stock through a colander and then through a fine sieve. Transfer this clear, flavoursome broth to a saucepan and keep warm. Pick the meat from the bones and add to the broth. Taste and season to your liking. Serve immediately or transfer to a container with a tight-fitting lid and refrigerate.

The soup will keep in a sealed container in the refrigerator for 4 days or up to 3 months in the freezer.

Potage quat' saisons

This is a very light vegetarian broth using the freshest and best seasonal ingredients. You'll need to be guided by the time of year – hence the name, Four Seasons Soup – as each season favours a different selection of vegetables. Use common sense to vary the cooking times, depending on the texture of each vegetable.

makes 2 litres (68 fl oz), enough for 4 serves

PREP TIME 30 MINUTES   COOK TIME 10 MINUTES

1 carrot

½ celeriac

1 leek, tough outer leaves discarded, cut into neat squares

100 g (3 ½ oz) green beans, diced into small rounds

1 baby zucchini (courgette), sliced

30 ml (1 fl oz) vegetable oil

salt and pepper

1 litre (34 fl oz) Vegetable Stock (page 32)

½ tablespoon cream

1 cup watercress sprigs

2 tomatoes, blanched, deseeded and diced

few drops lemon juice

2 tablespoons Fines Herbes (page 15)

½ cup sorrel, finely shredded

Peel the carrot and celeriac and cut them to a macédoine (page 208). Prepare all the remaining vegetables.

Heat the oil in a heavy-based saucepan and sweat the carrot and celeriac for 5 minutes. Season well then add the leek, beans and zucchini and sweat for a further minute.

Pour on the stock and bring to the boil. Simmer for 5 minutes, skimming occasionally. Stir in the cream and remove the pan from the heat. Add the watercress and tomatoes, season again and add the lemon juice.

Serve the soup straight away, garnished with the herbs and shredded sorrel. This is a soup that should be made and served immediately – it should not be prepared ahead of time.

Smoked ham broth

makes 2 litres (68 fl oz), enough for 4 serves

PREP TIME 20 MINUTES COOK TIME 4 HOURS

2 onions

1 carrot

2 celery stalks

1 leek, white only

2 smoked ham hocks

200 g (7 oz) piece pancetta

1 garlic bulb

6 sprigs thyme

1 bay leaf

2 litres (68 fl oz) White Chicken Stock (page 29)

salt and pepper

I serve this broth with a tasty Persillade (page 70) and Braised Borlotti Beans (page 221).

Chop all the vegetables to a rough mirepoix (page 208) and put in a stockpot or large saucepan with the ham hocks, pancetta, garlic and herbs. Pour on the chicken stock and bring to the boil over a high heat. Skim well, then lower the heat and simmer very gently for 3–4 hours until the meat is very soft and tender.

Remove the ham hocks and pancetta and use your fingers to break the meat into flakes. Discard the bones. Strain the cooking liquor through a fine sieve, reserving the vegetables. Return the broth to a clean saucepan. Add the meat and vegetables, taste and season to your liking. Serve immediately or transfer to a container with a tight-fitting lid and refrigerate.

The soup will keep in a sealed container in the refrigerator for 3–4 days or up to 2 months in the freezer.

Consommés

The art of making good consommés comes from good technique and following a few simple steps. It is possible to transform any intensely flavoured double stock or rustic broth into a refined, restaurant-quality consommé by clarifying it with a 'raft'.

This is a thick paste made from minced (ground) meat, vegetables and egg whites. As the consommé heats, the egg whites coagulate and the raft rises to the surface, trapping any impurities on the way. Once the raft sets on the surface, make a little hole in it to allow the steam to escape and let the consommé simmer gently for around 20 minutes. It is important not to let it boil or the raft will break up and the consommé will become cloudy.

Remember to make a raft that is appropriate to the consommé – use minced fish or seafood for a seafood consommé, minced game trimmings for a game consommé, and so on.

Game consommé (page 48)

Game consommé

makes 2 litres (68 fl oz), enough for 4 serves

/ PREP TIME 30 MINUTES ☞ COOK TIME 20 MINUTES

150 g (5 ½ oz) game meat trimmings from breast or legs, trimmed of fat and sinew
½ carrot
1 shallot
½ celery stalk
1 garlic clove
2 sprigs thyme
5 egg whites
2.5 litres (85 fl oz) Game Stock (page 34), at room temperature
salt and pepper
30 ml (1 fl oz) Madeira
20 ml (¾ fl oz) Armagnac

This consommé is absolutely gorgeous served with gooey Foie Gras and Thyme Dumplings (page 226).

To make the raft, put the meat into a food processor and whiz until smooth. Tip into a mixing bowl. Put the vegetables, garlic and thyme into the processor and whiz to a coarse purée. Add the vegetables to the meat and stir in the egg whites until well combined.

Put the stock in a large saucepan and whisk in the raft thoroughly. Heat very gently, whisking from time to time to stop the solids from sticking and burning. As the stock comes to a simmer the raft will begin to coagulate and rise to the surface. Once it has set on the surface, make a little hole in it to allow the steam to escape. Simmer very gently for 20 minutes then remove from the heat.

When cool, carefully ladle the consommé through a sieve double-lined with muslin (cheesecloth). Taste and adjust the seasoning then add the Madeira and Armagnac. Serve immediately or transfer to a container with a tight-fitting lid and refrigerate. The consommé will keep in a sealed container in the refrigerator for 3–4 days or up to 3 months in the freezer.

LOBSTER CONSOMMÉ

This consommé is made in exactly the same way as Game Consommé (above), except we replace the game trimmings with trimmings from white fish, lobster or scallops. Use Lobster Bisque (page 58) instead of game stock and omit the Madeira.

It will keep in a sealed container in the refrigerator for 2 days or up to 2 months in the freezer.

Tomato essence

This exquisite soup is not a true consommé of course, but it certainly looks the part as it is crystal clear and intensely flavoured. Think of it as a sort of cheat's consommé – and it's incredibly simple to make. For a variation of flavour, add 100 ml (3 ½ fl oz) of strong-brewed Earl Grey tea, leaves and all, as it infuses.

makes 2 litres (68 fl oz), enough for 4 serves

⟋ PREP TIME 20 MINUTES ⬕ MARINATING TIME 4–6 HOURS

Serve with a brightly coloured Pistou of Vegetables (page 226) garnish, or a scattering of baby basil leaves.

2 kg (4 lb 6 oz) ripe tomatoes	100 ml (3 ½ fl oz) white wine
6 shallots, finely sliced	50 ml (2 fl oz) chardonnay vinegar
1 garlic clove	1 tablespoon sea salt
1 cup basil leaves	pinch sugar
½ cup tarragon leaves	

Roughly chop the tomatoes and place them in a large bowl with all remaining ingredients. Mix together well, then pulse briefly in batches in a food processor – just enough to release all the liquid from the tomatoes. Cover with plastic wrap and refrigerate for at least 4 hours to infuse.

Ladle into a double-layered muslin (cheesecloth) bag and suspend for 1–2 hours over a large bowl. Press gently from time to time to extract the last of the juice. Pour the juice through a coffee filter paper, taking great care not to disturb any sediment. Season and adjust to your liking. Serve immediately or transfer to a container with a tight-fitting lid and refrigerate. The consommé will keep in a sealed container in the refrigerator for 2 days or up to 2 months in the freezer.

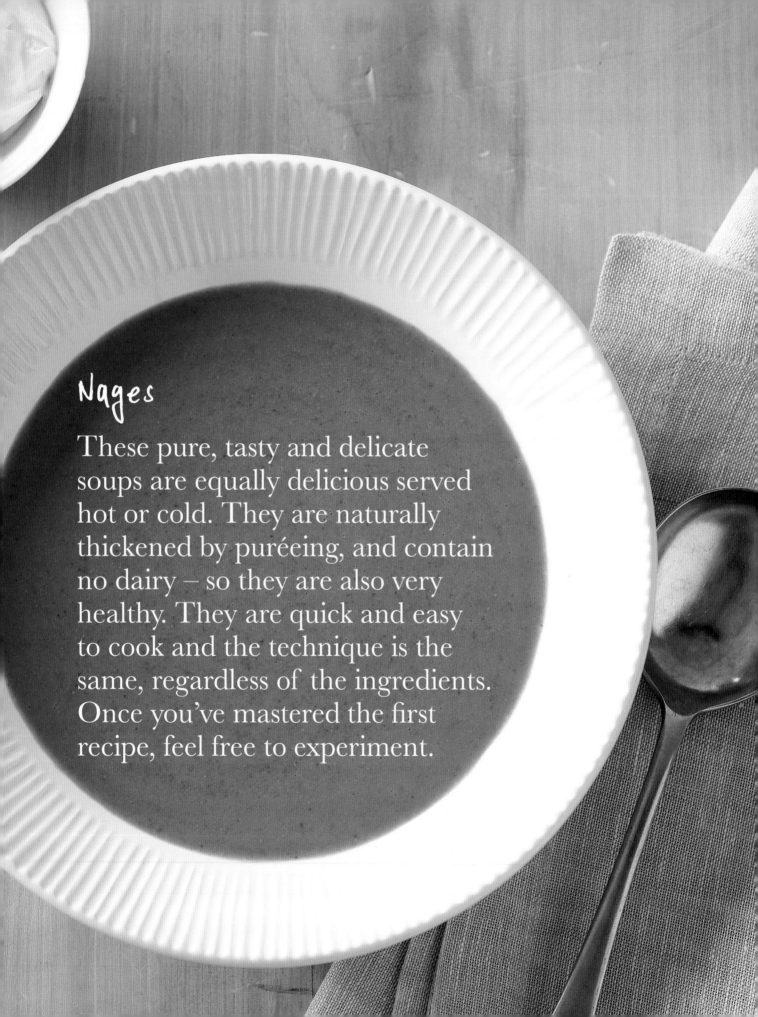

Nages

These pure, tasty and delicate soups are equally delicious served hot or cold. They are naturally thickened by puréeing, and contain no dairy – so they are also very healthy. They are quick and easy to cook and the technique is the same, regardless of the ingredients. Once you've mastered the first recipe, feel free to experiment.

Spring pea nage

makes 2 litres (68 fl oz), enough for 4 serves

PREP TIME 15 MINUTES   COOK TIME 20 MINUTES

80 ml (3 fl oz) vegetable oil

½ bay leaf

1½ onions, finely sliced

salt and pepper

3 garlic cloves, finely sliced

600 g (1 lb 5 oz) fresh peas

2 sprigs thyme

2 litres (68 fl oz) White Chicken or
    Vegetable Stock (page 29 or 32)

Serve topped with grilled (broiled) scallops or a dollop of Smoked Bacon Chantilly (page 79).

Heat the oil in a heavy-based saucepan. Add the onions, garlic, thyme and bay leaf and season well. Sweat over a low heat until onion is soft and translucent, about 10 minutes.

Add the peas and stock to the pan and bring to the boil. Season again then lower the heat and simmer gently for 10 minutes until the peas are soft. Ladle into a blender in batches and whiz to a very smooth purée. Push the soup through a fine sieve, taste and adjust the seasoning to your liking. Serve immediately or transfer to a container with a tight-fitting lid and refrigerate. The nage will keep in a sealed container in the refrigerator for 2 days or up to 2 months in the freezer.

ASPARAGUS NAGE

This soup is made in exactly the same way as the Spring pea nage. Just replace the peas with the same weight of finely sliced asparagus spears and 2–3 very thin slices of potato, and follow the same method. This nage will keep in a sealed container in the refrigerator for 2 days or up to 2 months in the freezer.

Watercress nage

makes 2 litres (68 fl oz), enough for 4 serves

PREP TIME 15 MINUTES   COOK TIME 20 MINUTES

80 ml (3 fl oz) cooking oil

1½ onions, finely sliced

3 garlic cloves, finely sliced

2 sprigs thyme

½ bay leaf

salt and pepper

50 g (2 oz) potato, peeled and finely sliced

2 litres (68 fl oz) White Chicken or
    Vegetable Stock (page 29 or 32)

4 cups watercress leaves

I like to serve this nage with a drizzle of crème fraîche.

Heat the oil in a heavy-based saucepan. Add the onions, garlic, thyme and bay leaf and season well. Sweat over a low heat until onion is soft and translucent, about 10 minutes.

Add the potato and stock to the pan and bring to the boil. Season again then lower the heat and simmer gently for 10 minutes until the potato is soft. Stir in the watercress leaves then ladle into a blender in batches and whiz to a very smooth purée. Push the soup through a fine sieve, taste and adjust the seasoning to your liking. Serve immediately or transfer to a container with a tight-fitting lid and refrigerate. The nage will keep in a sealed container in the refrigerator for 2 days or up to 2 months in the freezer.

Cauliflower vichyssoise

Based on a classic vichyssoise, this version uses cauliflower and is incredibly light. It is traditionally served chilled, but is also good served warm or hot.

makes 2 litres (68 fl oz), enough for 4 serves

PREP TIME 15 MINUTES COOK TIME 30 MINUTES

60 ml (2 fl oz) vegetable oil

1 onion, finely sliced

1 leek, white part only, finely sliced

2 garlic cloves, finely sliced

½ cauliflower, broken into small florets

3 sprigs thyme

salt and pepper

2 litres (68 fl oz) White Chicken Stock (page 29)

few drops lemon juice

Heat the oil in a heavy-based saucepan. Add the vegetables and thyme and season well. Sweat over a low heat until onion is soft and translucent, about 10 minutes.

Add the stock to the pan and bring to the boil. Season again then lower the heat and simmer gently for 20 minutes. Ladle into a blender in batches and whiz to a very smooth purée. Push the soup through a fine sieve, taste and adjust the seasoning to your liking. Chill and serve cold.

The vichyssoise will keep in a sealed container in the refrigerator for 2 days, but is not suitable for freezing.

Potato velouté

This soup is wonderful served with a sprinkling of dried cep (porcini) mushroom powder, which can be purchased from most good food stores.

makes 2 litres (68 fl oz), enough for 4 serves

PREP TIME 10 MINUTES COOK TIME 30 MINUTES

60 g (2 oz) butter

2 onions, finely sliced

4 garlic cloves, finely sliced

2 sprigs thyme

1 bay leaf

salt and pepper

300 g (10½ oz) potato, peeled and finely sliced

2 litres (68 fl oz) White Chicken Stock (page 29)

100 ml (3½ fl oz) cream

few drops lemon juice

Melt the butter in a heavy-based saucepan. Add the onions, garlic and thyme and season well. Sweat over a low heat until onion is soft and translucent, about 6–8 minutes. Add the potatoes to the pan and sweat for a further 2 minutes.

Add the stock to the pan and bring to the boil. Season again then lower the heat and simmer gently for 20 minutes, until the potato is very soft. Add the cream and bring the soup back to a simmer. Ladle into a blender in batches and whiz to a very smooth purée. Push the soup through a fine sieve, taste and adjust the seasoning to your liking. This soup is best served immediately and piping hot – it should not be made ahead of time.

Veloutés

A velouté is all about texture – it should be light and smooth as silk, thanks to the addition of cream and a little butter. Use the Potato Velouté as a base recipe, then work your way through the other delicious variations!

Smoked haddock and whisky velouté

This is an absolutely brilliant winter soup, one of my all-time favourites. I strongly urge you to try it at least once, even if you're not mad about whisky; it is really just a subtle background flavour.

makes 2 litres (68 fl oz), enough for 4 serves

PREP TIME 30 MINUTES ☐ COOK TIME 1 HOUR

This soup is even better served with a Slow-cooked Egg (page 110) and Lemon Sabayon (page 92) – and if you want to be really extravagant, a dollop of iodine-rich salty caviar.

500 g (1 lb 2 oz) smoked haddock

80 g (3 oz) butter

1 onion, finely sliced

½ leek, white part only, finely sliced

2 garlic cloves, finely sliced

salt and pepper

pinch curry powder

pinch saffron

100 ml (3 ½ fl oz) Scotch whisky

600 ml (20 ½ fl oz) Fish Stock (page 31)

600 ml (20 ½ fl oz) milk

400 ml (13 fl oz) cream

Remove the skin and bones from the haddock and chop it roughly.

Melt the butter in a heavy-based saucepan until it froths. Add the onion, leek and garlic and season well. Sweat over a low heat for a few minutes, then add the haddock, curry powder and saffron and sweat for a further 5 minutes.

Add the whisky (reserving a few drops to finish at the end) and bring to the boil. Add the stock, milk and cream, bring to the boil and simmer gently for 30 minutes. Ladle into a blender in batches and whiz to a very smooth purée. Push the soup through a fine sieve, taste and adjust the seasoning to your liking. Serve immediately, or transfer to a container with a tight-fitting lid and refrigerate.

This velouté will keep in a sealed container in the refrigerator for 2 days. Because of the high fat content it does not freeze well.

Sweetcorn and basil velouté

This velouté is based on a lovely earthy stock made from sweetcorn cobs.

makes 2 litres (68 fl oz), enough for 4 serves

/ PREP TIME 20 MINUTES ☞ COOK TIME 90 MINUTES

6 sweetcorn cobs, outer husks and fibres removed	**Sweetcorn sorbet/sherbet (optional)**
3 litres (102 fl oz) water	150 ml (5 fl oz) sweetcorn velouté (without the basil)
1 garlic bulb	1 tablespoon liquid glucose
8 sprigs thyme	
80 g (3 oz) unsalted butter	
1 onion, finely sliced	
salt and pepper	
100 ml (3½ fl oz) cream	
½ bunch basil, leaves and stalks	

Top it with a spoonful of Basil Chantilly (page 79) or serve it chilled with a scoop of sweetcorn sorbet (sherbet).

Cut the cobs in half and use a sharp knife to slice the kernels away. Reserve the kernels for the soup. Cut the cobs in half again and place in a stockpot or large saucepan with the water, half the cloves from the garlic bulb and 4 sprigs of thyme. Bring to the boil, skimming well. Lower the heat and simmer gently for 20 minutes, skimming frequently. Remove from the heat and strain through a fine sieve. Reserve the corn stock.

Melt the butter in a heavy-based saucepan until it froths. Finely slice the remaining garlic cloves and add them to the pan with the onion. Season well and sweat over a low heat for about 5 minutes until onion is soft and translucent. Add the reserved corn kernels and sweat for a few more minutes.

Add the reserved corn stock to the pan and bring to the boil. Add the remaining thyme, season again then lower the heat and simmer gently for 25 minutes, skimming regularly. Add the cream and bring the soup back to a simmer. Ladle into a blender in batches and whiz to a very smooth purée. If making the sorbet, reserve 150 ml (5 fl oz) of the puréed velouté. Use the back of a heavy knife to bruise the basil and add it to the soup. Allow to infuse for around 30 minutes.

Push the soup through a fine sieve, taste and adjust the seasoning to your liking. Serve immediately or transfer to a container with a tight-fitting lid and refrigerate.

This velouté will keep in a sealed container in the refrigerator for 3 days. Because of the high fat content it does not freeze well.

To make the sweetcorn sorbet, simply reserve 150 ml (5 fl oz) of the velouté before you add the basil, mix well with the glucose and churn it in an ice-cream machine.

Bisques

Light and intensely aromatic, bisques are traditionally made from seafood. They are flavoured with wine and Cognac and lightly thickened with cream.

Bouillabaisse (page 60)

Lobster bisque

You can make this bisque using the shells from lobster heads, which are available from fish markets and some fishmongers, or use the same recipe to make a prawn (shrimp) bisque. Buy fresh whole prawns and use the shells and heads for the soup base, then reserve the prawn meat to serve as a garnish, grilled or sautéed with a little butter.

makes 2 litres (68 fl oz), enough for 4 serves

PREP TIME 20 MINUTES ☞ COOK TIME 40 MINUTES

2 kg (4 lb 6 oz) lobster heads or large whole prawns (shrimp)	100 ml (3 ½ fl oz) white wine
	50 ml (2 fl oz) Cognac, Armagnac or cooking brandy
50 ml (2 fl oz) vegetable oil	4 sprigs thyme
150 g (5 ½ oz) butter	3 litres (102 fl oz) water
2 carrots, 1 onion and 2 celery stalks, chopped to a large mirepoix (see page 208)	80 ml (3 fl oz) cream
	salt and pepper
4 garlic cloves	squeeze of fresh orange juice
2 tablespoons tomato paste (concentrated purée)	

Serve with Armagnac and Orange Crème (page 80), or to make it really special with Lobster Tail Roasted on Aromatics (page 205).

Rinse the lobster heads well. Use kitchen scissors to cut them into small pieces and bash them roughly with a meat mallet to loosen as much meat as you can. This adds flavour to the soup.

Heat the oil in a heavy-based roasting pan. Add the crushed lobster pieces and sauté until bright pink and lightly caramelised. Add 100 g (3½ oz) of the butter, the vegetable mirepoix and garlic. Sauté for another 10 minutes, until everything is aromatic and coloured. Add the tomato paste, stir well and cook for 2 minutes. Pour in the white wine and deglaze the pan, stirring well. Add the Cognac (reserving a splash to finish the soup) and the thyme.

Add the water and bring to the boil, then lower the heat and simmer gently for 40 minutes, stirring from time to time to prevent the shells sticking and burning.

Strain the soup through a sieve, pushing forcefully with the back of the ladle to extract as much of the juice and pulp as you can. Pass through a finer sieve and return to a clean saucepan over a medium heat. Use a whisk or hand blender to whisk in the remaining butter and the cream. Taste and adjust seasoning to your liking. Serve immediately with an extra splash of Cognac and fresh orange juice, or transfer to a container with a tight-fitting lid and refrigerate. The butter, cream, Cognac and orange juice should be added just before serving.

This bisque will keep in a sealed container in the refrigerator for 2 days or up to 2 months in the freezer.

Freshwater bisque

The more earthy quality of freshwater shellfish gives this bisque an earthier, sweeter dimension. The method is the same, substituting yabby, crayfish or marrons for the lobster or prawns (shrimp). You'll probably struggle to find yabby shells, so buy whole live yabbies or crayfish and reserve the tail meat to serve as a garnish, grilled (broiled) or sautéed with a little butter.

makes 2 litres (68 fl oz), enough for 4 serves

/ PREP TIME 25 MINUTES ☐ COOK TIME 45 MINUTES

2 kg (4 lb 6 oz) live yabbies or crayfish	50 ml (2 fl oz) Cognac, Armagnac or cooking brandy
50 ml (2 fl oz) vegetable oil	4 sprigs thyme
150 g (5½ oz) butter	3 litres (102 fl oz) water
2 carrots, 1 onion and 2 celery stalks, chopped to a large mirepoix (page 208)	80 ml (3 fl oz) cream
	salt and pepper
4 garlic cloves	additional 30 ml (1 fl oz) vegetable oil
2 tablespoons tomato paste (concentrated purée)	additional 50 g (2 oz) butter
100 ml (3½ fl oz) white wine	few drops fresh lemon juice

Place the yabbies in the freezer for 10 minutes or so to put them to sleep (no longer, or they'll freeze). Twist off their heads, and pull out the intestinal tract by twisting and pulling the middle part of their tail base. Bring a large pan of salted water to the boil and blanch the yabby tails, still in the shell, for 30 seconds. This is just enough to 'set' the meat so the shell can be easily removed. Refresh the tails in iced water to stop the cooking process. Drain well and gently peel off the shells, being careful not to damage the meat. Refrigerate until ready to use.

Follow the method for the Lobster Bisque, substituting the yabby shells and heads for the lobster heads. Just before serving, heat the oil in a heavy-based frying pan over a moderate heat. Season the yabby tails and add to the pan. Sauté gently for 1–2 minutes. Raise the heat and add the additional 50 g (2 oz) butter to the pan, allowing it to foam, but not colour. Turn the yabby tails around in the foaming butter so they are just coloured, but still translucent in the middle. Add the lemon juice and divide the yabby tails between 4 serving bowls. Pour on the hot bisque and serve straight away.

Bouillabaisse

A specialty from the south of France, bouillabaisse is more of a meal than a mere soup. It is really all about the seafood, which is served whole, suspended in an intense saffron-flavoured broth. Don't be daunted by the long list of ingredients: the trick is being organised. All the trimmings and fish bones are used to make the stock. Shortly before serving, the fish fillets and seafood are quickly poached in the stock for maximum flavour.

serves 4

PREP TIME 1 HOUR ▪ MARINATING TIME 2 HOURS ▪ COOK TIME 40 MINUTES

1 kg (2 lb 3 oz) fish bones	10 coriander seeds
3 x 300 g (10½ oz) red mullet or red snapper	good pinch saffron threads
1 whole snapper, about 1 kg (2 lb 3 oz)	1 small piece of orange rind
12 large mussels, scrubbed and beards removed	100 ml (3½ fl oz) white wine
12 large prawns (shrimp), peeled and deveined	80 ml (3 fl oz) Pernod
12 large scallops	80 ml (3 fl oz) brandy
1 fennel bulb	50 ml (2 fl oz) extra-virgin olive oil
1 carrot	1 tablespoon tomato purée
½ celery stalk	2 stalks basil
1 onion	80 ml (3 fl oz) cooking oil
2 garlic cloves	80 g (3 oz) butter
4 vine-ripened tomatoes	3 litres (102 fl oz) water
2 star anise	salt and pepper

If you are not confident about preparing the fish yourself, ask your fishmonger to fillet it for you. Just make sure you ask him to give you the trimmings and bones back for your stock, plus extra if needed to make up the 1 kg (2 lb 3 oz). The red mullet should give 6 fillets and the snapper 2 fillets. Cut each snapper fillet in half to give 4 portions. Prepare all the remaining seafood and refrigerate until ready to use.

Chop the fish carcasses into small pieces and place in a large bowl with the prawn shells.

Chop all the vegetables to a rough mirepoix (page 208) and add them to the bowl with all the remaining ingredients, except for the fish and seafood, salt and pepper, oil, butter and water. Mix well to combine, cover with plastic wrap and refrigerate for a few hours to marinate.

Tip into a colander to drain, and keep the liquid separate from the solids. Heat the oil in a large roasting pan or heavy-based casserole pan over a high heat. Add the marinated bones and vegetables and toss over the heat for a few moments. Add the butter and allow it to foam and caramelise. Sauté for 10–15 minutes until everything has coloured a deep golden red.

Add the reserved marinade to the pan and deglaze. Pour on the water and bring to the boil. Lower the heat and simmer gently for 40 minutes, stirring occasionally to prevent things sticking and burning.

Strain the soup through a sieve, pushing forcefully with the back of the ladle to extract as much of the juice and pulp as you can. Pass through a finer sieve and return to a clean saucepan over a medium heat. Add the snapper fillets and mussels to the pan and poach for 2 minutes. Add the red mullet and prawns and poach for a further minute. Just before you serve, add the scallops, which will cook in the heat by the time the bowl reaches the table. Season to taste. Serve piping hot.

Serve the bouillabaisse in a large serving bowl so everyone can help themselves. I serve it with Rouille (page 72) and a big bowl of Crushed Potatoes (page 218) to soak up the extra broth.

Savoury sauces

If stocks are the foundation stones of French cooking then sauces are the essential finishing touch that brings the whole dish together in a unified coherence.

Just as an undecorated house feels bare and unfinished, so, too, does an unsauced dish. A sauce complements the basic architecture of a particular dish, and the vast range and variety of sauces in the French chef's repertoire means that almost every conceivable taste preference can be accommodated.

At this point, you might be asking, what is the point of a sauce? Well, the ideal sauce is a lightly thickened, flavoursome liquid that adds moisture, mouth-feel and an extra dimension of flavour to a dish. Sauces may be hot or cold, savoury or sweet (see pages 229–45 for sweet sauces). In classical French cuisine, the range of sauces encompasses those made from stocks, which may be given extra body with a flour-and-fat roux, or emulsified with egg yolks or butter; it includes purées made from fresh herbs or vegetables, and vinaigrettes and mayonnaise-style dressings for salads. I also include compound (flavoured) butters in this chapter, as they are a simple and effective way of adding instant sauce to a plate!

Sauces are treated with great reverence by the French and they are generally considered to be the crowning glory of its cuisine. But as is the case with stocks, they are often thought of as being mainly the domain of the professional kitchen. Many home cooks seem to be frightened of sauces – even of knocking up the simplest pan gravy (or jus gras, as it is known technically). Perhaps it's a deep-seated fear of lumps, or the misconception that sauces are too rich and heavy and will drown the other ingredients on the plate.

Well, there may have been some truth to this in the 'bad old days'. But modern French cooking is all about embracing purity of flavour. These days there is less interest in making the traditional roux-based sauces or a thick, overly concentrated demi-glace (or sauce espagnole, as it used to be called). Instead the focus is on lighter sauces that are less rich, less complex and easier to prepare. I revel in these wonderful emulsions, vegetable-based sauces and delicate stock reductions, which typify sauce making in the twenty-first century.

Whichever sauce you make, remember that its function is to enhance and complement the ingredients it is accompanying. Once you've familiarised yourself with the various techniques in this chapter you will know the fundamental principles of good sauce-making. In the end, your own taste buds will determine the final flavour of your sauce, through careful and frequent tasting and seasoning. With time you'll learn how to develop a sort of mental 'palette' of flavours. And you'll learn how to achieve what you want through constant tasting, skimming, reducing and seasoning. Creating a well-balanced, good-textured and beautiful sauce is something of an art. But it is a simple art that is well worth learning; the results will repay your effort ten-fold.

COLD SAUCES

The most obvious cold sauces are vinaigrettes, dressings and mayonnaises that are used with cold dishes such as salads.

But the range also extends to dipping sauces, to condiments, to flavoured oils, creams and butters – some of which are also used to provide a delicious temperature contrast with hot dishes.

In my view, many of the cold sauces are sublime examples of the new flavour-based approach to French cooking. They are about extracting maximum taste from fresh-tasting ingredients – be they vegetables, herbs or other flavourings. Unlike most hot sauces, cold sauces can usually be made in just a few minutes and with minimal fuss. They are a wonderful way of using up any extra vegetables or herbs that you have in the refrigerator, instead of leaving them to rot!

Vinaigrettes

These simple, tasty sauces are most often used for salads, to bring out the flavour of delicate leaves and herbs. All vinaigrettes use the same basic ingredients, good-quality vinegar and oil, which are whisked together with seasonings to form an emulsion.

But the vinaigrette is endlessly versatile; you can alter the flavour and acidity by using different vinegars or citrus juices, and the oil can also be varied, from a full-flavoured fruity extra-virgin olive oil to more delicate nut oils. When you throw mustards, herbs and spices into the equation, you'll start to use this type of dressing for all kinds of dishes, hot and cold.

Lemon vinaigrette

makes 200 ml (7 fl oz)

PREP TIME 5 MINUTES

50 ml (2 fl oz) freshly squeezed lemon juice

pinch salt and pepper

75 ml (2½ fl oz) olive oil

75 ml (2½ fl oz) grapeseed oil

Put the lemon juice in a mixing bowl and whisk in the salt and pepper to dissolve. Slowly add the oils, whisking constantly. Taste and adjust the seasoning to your liking. Use immediately, or transfer to a small container with a tight-fitting lid and refrigerate until ready to use. The vinaigrette will keep in a sealed container in the refrigerator for 3 days.

Herb vinaigrette

makes 200 ml (7 fl oz)

PREP TIME 10 MINUTES   MARINATING TIME OVERNIGHT

50 ml (2 fl oz) chardonnay vinegar

pinch salt and pepper

2 garlic cloves, roughly crushed

½ cup Herbes de Provence (page 14), left whole, not chopped

75 ml (2½ fl oz) olive oil

75 ml (2½ fl oz) grapeseed oil

Put the chardonnay vinegar in a mixing bowl and whisk in the salt and pepper to dissolve. Whisk in the garlic and herbs then slowly add the oils, whisking constantly. Transfer to a small container with a tight-fitting lid and refrigerate overnight for the flavours to infuse.

An hour before use, bring the vinaigrette to room temperature. Strain through a fine sieve, taste and adjust the seasoning to your liking. The vinaigrette will keep in a sealed container in the refrigerator for 3 days.

Walnut vinaigrette

makes 200 ml (7 fl oz)

PREP TIME 15 MINUTES

2 teaspoons Dijon mustard

30 ml (1 fl oz) sherry vinegar

2 tablespoons roasted walnuts

pinch salt and pepper

70 ml (2¼ fl oz) walnut oil

60 ml (2 fl oz) grapeseed oil

Put the mustard, vinegar, nuts and seasonings in a mortar and pound to a coarse paste (or use a food processor). Slowly add the oils, whisking constantly. Taste and adjust the seasoning to your liking. Use immediately, or transfer to a small container with a tight-fitting lid and refrigerate until ready to use. The vinaigrette will keep in a sealed container in the refrigerator for 3 days.

HAZELNUT VINAIGRETTE

Make in the same way as the walnut vinaigrette, substituting roasted hazelnuts and hazelnut oil for the walnuts and walnut oil.

Verbena tea vinaigrette

makes 300 ml (10 fl oz)

PREP TIME 15 MINUTES   MARINATING TIME 2 HOURS

½ cup lemon verbena

1 stick lemongrass, roughly chopped

3 sprigs lemon thyme

zest and juice of 1 lemon

1 teaspoon finely chopped fresh ginger

pinch salt and pepper

70 ml (2¼ fl oz) strong-brewed Marco Polo
  tea, warm

30 ml (1 fl oz) chardonnay vinegar

100 ml (3½ fl oz) olive oil

100 ml (3½ fl oz) grapeseed oil

Place the lemon verbena, lemongrass, lemon thyme, lemon zest and juice, ginger and salt and pepper in a mortar and pound to a coarse paste (or use a food processor). Transfer to a bowl, add the tea and vinegar, cover and leave in a warm place for 2 hours to infuse.

Press through a fine sieve into a mixing bowl. Slowly add the oils, whisking constantly. Taste and adjust the seasoning to your liking. Use immediately, or transfer to a small container with a tight-fitting lid and refrigerate until ready to use. The vinaigrette will keep in a sealed container in the refrigerator for 3 days.

Dressings

These vegetable and herb-based
sauces are a superb accompaniment
to all sorts of fish, meat or poultry.

Caponata dressing

makes 200 ml (7 fl oz), enough for 4 serves
PREP TIME 20 MINUTES COOK TIME 5 MINUTES

50 ml (2 fl oz) olive oil

2 long, thin eggplants (aubergines), finely diced

1 small red (Spanish) onion, finely diced

1 small yellow zucchini (courgette), finely diced

1 small green zucchini (courgette), finely diced

1 Roasted Sweet and Sour Capsicum (page 225), finely diced

2 Tomatoes Concasse (page 219)

2 tablespoons finely chopped black olives

1 tablespoon finely chopped capers

2 tablespoons finely chopped anchovies

2 tablespoons Fines Herbes (page 15)

100 ml (3½ fl oz) Herb Vinaigrette (page 66)

pepper

Heat a heavy-based frying pan over a medium heat. Add the oil, then the diced vegetables. Fry for 2 minutes, until soft and lightly coloured. Tip into a large mixing bowl and add all the remaining ingredients.

Mix well to combine, then taste and adjust the seasonings to your liking. The olives, capers and anchovies are all quite salty, so it's unlikely you'll need to add more salt. Use immediately, or transfer to a small container with a tight-fitting lid and refrigerate until ready to use. The dressing will keep in a sealed container in the refrigerator for 3 days.

Salsa verde

makes 200 ml (7 fl oz)
PREP TIME 20 MINUTES

½ cup finely chopped parsley

½ cup finely chopped basil

6 leaves mint, finely chopped

1 garlic clove, finely chopped

1 teaspoon finely chopped capers

1 teaspoon chopped anchovies

1 teaspoon Dijon mustard

1 tablespoon red wine vinegar

100 ml (3½ fl oz) olive oil

salt and pepper

few drops lemon juice

Place all the ingredients in a large mixing bowl and whisk well to combine. Taste and adjust the seasoning to your liking. Use immediately, or transfer to a small container with a tight-fitting lid and refrigerate until ready to use. The dressing will keep in a sealed container in the refrigerator for 2 days.

Gremolata

makes 200 ml (7 fl oz)
PREP TIME 5 MINUTES

80 ml (3 fl oz) olive oil

6 cloves Slow-roasted Garlic (page 219), finely
chopped

½ cup finely chopped parsley

zest and juice of 1 lemon

salt and pepper

Place all the ingredients in a large mixing bowl
and whisk well to combine. Taste and adjust the
seasoning to your liking. Use immediately, or transfer
to a small container with a tight-fitting lid and
refrigerate until ready to use. The dressing will keep
in a sealed container in the refrigerator for 2 days.

Persillade

makes 200 ml (7 fl oz)
PREP TIME 5 MINUTES

¼ cup chopped parsley leaves

4 tablespoons Slow-roasted Garlic (page 219),
crushed to a paste

salt and pepper

2 tablespoons olive oil

Place all the ingredients in a large mixing bowl
and whisk well to combine. Taste and adjust the
seasoning to your liking. Use immediately, or transfer
to a small container with a tight-fitting lid and
refrigerate until ready to use. The dressing will keep
in a sealed container in the refrigerator for 1–2 days.

Cherry tomato coulis

makes 200 ml (7 fl oz)
PREP TIME 20 MINUTES

1 punnet vine-ripened cherry tomatoes
(about 1 ½ cups)

pinch salt and pepper

few drops lemon juice

½ tablespoon olive oil

Cut the tomatoes in half and squeeze out the seeds
and juice. Push the juice and seeds through a fine
sieve, discard the seeds and reserve the juice. Transfer
the tomatoes to a blender and whiz to a fine purée.
Push through a fine sieve and thin with the reserved
tomato juice until the consistency of thin cream.

Whisk in the remaining ingredients, taste and adjust
the seasonings to your liking. Use immediately, or
transfer to a small container with a tight-fitting lid and
refrigerate until ready to use. The dressing will keep
in a sealed container in the refrigerator for 2 days.

cold emulsions

Emulsified sauces can be hot (page 80) or cold, but all depend upon the magical ability of egg yolks to absorb fats such as oil or butter, and to hold them in a thick, smooth, glossy suspension. People are often scared about making emulsified sauces because of their reputation for 'splitting' – separating and curdling. The secret is to make sure all the ingredients are at room temperature, and to add the fat very slowly.

Mayonnaise

This is possibly the most popular cold sauce, and forms the base of endless variations. I like to use a neutral-flavoured oil, such as grapeseed, sunflower or canola, as olive oil is rather overwhelming. It's well worth learning how to make mayonnaise – you'll never buy shop-bought again.

makes 200 ml (7 fl oz)

PREP TIME 20 MINUTES

1 egg yolk
150 ml (5 fl oz) grapeseed oil
few drops lemon juice
1 teaspoon Dijon mustard (optional)
salt and pepper

Make sure all the ingredients, especially the egg and oil, are at room temperature before you begin. It is harder for them to emulsify to the desired lightness and smoothness if they are cold.

Place the egg yolk in a bowl and set it on a dampened tea (dish) towel on your work surface (this holds the bowl steady as you whisk). Slowly trickle in the oil, drop by drop to begin with, whisking all the time. As the sauce begins to thicken, add the oil in a slow, steady stream, whisking continuously. When it has all been incorporated, add the lemon juice and mustard (if using) and adjust the seasoning to your liking.

If you add the oil too quickly, you run the risk of the mayonnaise curdling and separating. To rescue, place a tablespoon of hot water into another clean bowl and slowly trickle in the split sauce, whisking continuously. This will bring it back together to a smooth, glossy sauce.

Use immediately, or transfer to a small container with a tight-fitting lid and refrigerate until ready to use. The dressing will keep in a sealed container in the refrigerator for 1 month.

AIOLI

To the base Mayonnaise recipe, add 8 cloves of Slow-roasted Garlic (page 219) that have been pounded to a paste. Use immediately, or transfer to a small container with a tight-fitting lid and refrigerate until ready to use. The aioli will keep in a sealed container in the refrigerator for up to 2 weeks.

ROUILLE

In French, this means 'rust', which is exactly the orange-red colour of the finished sauce. To 100 ml (3½ fl oz) of the Mayonnaise base recipe add 50 g (2 oz) warm Potato Purée (page 212), a pinch of saffron threads and 4 cloves Slow-roasted Garlic (page 219) that have been pounded to a paste. For a little kick, you can also add a few drops of Tabasco or harissa paste. Use immediately, or transfer to a small container with a tight-fitting lid and refrigerate until ready to use. The rouille will keep in a sealed container in the refrigerator for up to 1 week.

Sauce gribiche

makes 200 ml (7 fl oz)

PREP TIME 20 MINUTES

2 tablespoons finely chopped cornichons
  (baby gherkins)

2 tablespoons finely chopped pickled onions

1 tablespoon finely chopped capers

2 tablespoons Fines Herbes (page 15)

1 hard-boiled egg, finely chopped

100 ml (3½ fl oz) Mayonnaise (opposite)

salt and pepper

few drops lemon juice

Place all the ingredients in a large mixing bowl and whisk gently to combine. Taste and adjust seasonings to your liking. Use immediately, or transfer to a small container with a tight-fitting lid and refrigerate until ready to use. The sauce will keep in a sealed container in the refrigerator for up to 2 weeks.

Hazelnut emulsion

makes 200 ml (7 fl oz)

PREP TIME 15 MINUTES

1 teaspoon Dijon mustard

1 tablespoon sherry vinegar

2 tablespoons Roasted Hazelnuts (page 162)

2 tablespoons hot water

70 ml (2¼ fl oz) hazelnut oil

60 ml (2 fl oz) grapeseed oil

salt and pepper

Put the mustard, vinegar, hazelnuts and water in a blender and whiz to a smooth purée. With the motor running, slowly trickle in the oils until emulsified, in the same way as making a mayonnaise. Taste and adjust seasoning to your liking. Use immediately at room temperature or transfer to a small container with a tight-fitting lid and refrigerate until ready to use. The emulsion will keep in a sealed container in the refrigerator for up to 1 week.

Parsley and fennel coulis

Use just parsley, or a combination of parsley and fennel. The fennel fronds are difficult to emulsify when used on their own, but the parsley helps add body. Basil or chives can also be added or substituted.

makes 200 ml (7 fl oz)

PREP TIME 20 MINUTES

2 cups parsley leaves

2 cups fennel fronds

80 ml (3 fl oz) grapeseed oil

1 tablespoon hot water

salt and pepper

Bring a large saucepan of salted water to the boil, and prepare a bowl of iced water. Blanch the parsley for 1 minute and refresh in the iced water. Blanch the fennel for 2 minutes and refresh in the iced water. When cold, squeeze out the excess water, but leave them damp.

Chop the parsley and fennel roughly and tip into a blender. Add half the oil and whiz to a fine purée. Add the hot water and then slowly trickle in remaining oil until emulsified, in the same way as making a mayonnaise. Taste and adjust seasoning to your liking. The sauce should be silky-smooth and vibrant green. Use immediately at room temperature or transfer to a small container with a tight-fitting lid and refrigerate until ready to use. The emulsion will keep in a sealed container in the refrigerator for up to 3 days.

Sweet and sour capsicum emulsion

makes 200 ml (7 fl oz)

PREP TIME 15 MINUTES

2 Roasted Sweet and Sour Capsicums and reserved juices (page 225)

1 tablespoon red wine vinegar

60 ml (2 fl oz) olive oil

sugar, salt and pepper

Peel the roasted capsicums (peppers) and remove all the seeds. Chop them roughly and tip into a blender. Add the vinegar and whiz to a fine purée. Slowly trickle in the oil until emulsified, in the same way as making a mayonnaise. Taste and adjust seasoning to your liking. Pass through a fine sieve. The sauce should be silky-smooth and vibrant orange-red. Use immediately at room temperature or transfer to a small container with a tight-fitting lid and refrigerate until ready to use. The emulsion will keep in a sealed container in the refrigerator for up to 3 days.

Flavoured oils

These are simple oils infused with flavourings such as citrus, herbs and spices. I have started with a basic lemon oil; to this we can add lemon thyme, basil, lime and so on.

Lemon oil

Vary this base recipe with lemon thyme, lime or basil.

makes 200 ml (7 fl oz)

PREP TIME 10 MINUTES ☼ INFUSING TIME 24 HOURS

100 ml (3½ fl oz) grapeseed oil

100 ml (3½ fl oz) olive oil

zest of 2 lemons

Mix the oils together in a saucepan. Grate the lemons over the pan to capture the spray and oils that are released. Heat oil gently until warm then remove the pan from the heat. Cover and leave to infuse for at least 24 hours before use. The oil will keep in a sealed container in the refrigerator for up to 1 month.

Home-made truffle oil

makes 200 ml (7 fl oz)

PREP TIME 5 MINUTES ☼ INFUSING TIME 5 DAYS

200 ml (7 fl oz) grapeseed oil

50 g (2 oz) fresh black truffle

Put the oil in a saucepan and shave in the truffle. Heat gently until warm then remove the pan from the heat. Cover and leave to infuse for 5 days before use. The oil will keep in a sealed container in the refrigerator for up to 1 month.

Herb oil

Vary this base recipe with watercress, basil or chives according to your fancy. Use single herbs, or in any combination that you like.

makes 200 ml (7 fl oz)

PREP TIME 20 MINUTES ☼ INFUSING TIME 15 MINUTES

2 cups Fines Herbes (page 15), leaves unchopped

150 ml (5 fl oz) grapeseed oil

salt

Bring a large saucepan of salted water to the boil, and prepare a bowl of iced water. Blanch the herbs for 1 minute and refresh in the iced water. When cold, squeeze out the excess water, but leave them damp.

Chop the herbs roughly and tip into a blender with the oil. Whiz to a fine purée and season with the salt. Tip into a pitcher or bowl and leave to infuse for 15 minutes. The chlorophyll will leach out of the leaves, turning the oil a deep, vibrant green.

Tip into a piece of muslin (cheesecloth) and suspend it over a bowl for 2–3 hours to catch the oil. Discard the contents of the bag and transfer the infused oil to a sealed container. It will keep in the refrigerator for up to 3 days.

compound butters

These are simple to make with all sorts of flavourings. Add your choice of flavourings to the butter, roll tightly to a log shape and wrap in baking paper. Keep a selection in the freezer or refrigerator and simply slice off a portion as needed. They make a delicious 'instant sauce' when popped on top of grilled meats, poultry, fish or baked potatoes.

Foie gras butter

makes 200 g (7 oz)

/ PREP TIME 20 MINUTES

100 g (3½ oz) unsalted butter, diced

100 g (3½ oz) cooked foie gras, diced

splash Armagnac

salt and pepper

Put the butter and foie gras in a bowl, cover with plastic wrap and leave in a warm place to soften (do not allow to melt).

Push through a fine sieve into a bowl. Add the remaining ingredients. Use a wooden spoon and mix well to combine.

Roll the butter in baking paper to a sausage shape, twist the ends securely and chill until required. The butter will keep in a sealed container in the refrigerator for 2 weeks or up to 3 months in the freezer.

Garlic and rosemary butter

makes 200 g (7 oz)

/ PREP TIME 20 MINUTES

150 g (5½ oz) unsalted butter, diced

½ cup finely chopped rosemary

10 cloves Slow-roasted Garlic (page 219), pounded to a paste

few drops lemon juice

salt and pepper

Put the butter in a bowl, cover with plastic wrap and leave in a warm place to soften (do not allow to melt).

Add the remaining ingredients. Use a wooden spoon and mix well to combine.

Roll the butter in baking paper to a sausage shape, twist the ends securely and chill until required. The butter will keep in a sealed container in the refrigerator for 2 weeks or up to 3 months in the freezer.

Lemon and parsley butter

makes 200 g (7 oz)

PREP TIME 20 MINUTES

150 g (5 ½ oz) unsalted butter, diced

2 lemons

½ cup finely chopped parsley

splash of brandy

salt and pepper

Put the butter in a bowl, cover with plastic wrap and leave in a warm place to soften (do not allow to melt).

Grate both lemons over the butter to capture the spray and oils. Add the juice of 1 lemon to the butter with the parsley, brandy and seasoning. Use a wooden spoon and mix well to combine.

Roll the butter in baking paper to a sausage shape, twist the ends securely and chill until required. The butter will keep in a sealed container in the refrigerator for 2 weeks or up to 3 months in the freezer.

Truffle butter

makes 200 g (7 oz)

PREP TIME 20 MINUTES

150 g (5 ½ oz) unsalted butter, diced

50 g (2 oz) fresh black truffle, finely chopped

salt and pepper

Put the butter in a bowl, cover with plastic wrap and leave in a warm place to soften (do not allow to melt). Add the remaining ingredients. Use a wooden spoon and mix well to combine. Roll the butter in baking paper to a sausage shape, twist the ends securely and chill until required. The butter will keep in a sealed container in the refrigerator for 2 weeks or up to 3 months in the freezer.

Café de Paris butter

This French brasserie classic is zesty and full of strong flavours. Feel free to taste and adjust the balance according to your preference.

makes 250 g (9 oz)

PREP TIME 20 MINUTES

200 g (7 oz) unsalted butter, softened

2 tablespoons finely chopped shallots

1 tablespoon finely chopped garlic

2 tablespoons finely chopped parsley

1 tablespoon finely chopped tarragon

4 anchovy fillets, very finely diced

2 tablespoons brandy

1 tablespoon Worcestershire sauce

1 lemon

few drops Tabasco, to taste

½ teaspoon salt

pinch of freshly ground black pepper

Put all the ingredients in a large mixing bowl. Using a wooden spoon, mix well to combine.

Roll the butter in baking paper to a sausage shape, twist the ends securely and chill until required. The butter will keep in a sealed container in the refrigerator for 2 weeks or up to 3 months in the freezer.

Savoury chantilly creams

Chantilly creams may be savoury or sweet (page 233). Savoury creams give a perfect, luxurious finishing touch to cream-based soups and veloutés. I also like to add a dollop to ragoûts or risottos at the last minute.

Chervil chantilly

Substitute herbs of your choice, such as basil, tarragon, lemon verbena or thyme.

makes 200 ml (7 fl oz)

/ PREP TIME 5 MINUTES

100 ml (3 ½ fl oz) chilled cream

3 tablespoons chopped chervil

few drops lemon juice

salt and pepper

Make sure the cream is very cold. Use a balloon whisk to whip the cream until it thickens to the ribbon stage; i.e. if you lift the whisk above the cream it will fall onto the surface and hold a ribbon shape (see page 233). You can whip the cream in an electric mixer, but it is harder to gauge the correct consistency.

Fold in the remaining ingredients and continue to whip the cream to soft peaks (page 233). It should be soft and fluffy, but fairly firm. Chill until ready to use and use within 24 hours.

Smoked bacon chantilly

makes 200 ml (7 fl oz)

/ PREP TIME 10 MINUTES

50 g (2 oz) smoked bacon or pancetta

100 ml (3 ½ fl oz) chilled cream

few drops lemon juice

salt and pepper

Finely mince (grind) the bacon and fry in a hot pan for 1 minute. Drain on paper towels and allow to cool.

Use a balloon whisk to whip the cream until it thickens to the ribbon stage; i.e. if you lift the whisk above the cream it will fall onto the surface and hold a ribbon shape (see page 233). You can whip the cream in an electric mixer, but it is harder to gauge the correct consistency.

Fold in the remaining ingredients and continue to whip the cream to soft peaks (page 233). It should be soft and fluffy, but fairly firm. Chill until ready to use and use within 24 hours.

Armagnac and orange crème

makes 200 ml (7 fl oz)

PREP TIME 5 MINUTES

100 ml (3 ½ fl oz) chilled cream

1 orange

few drops Armagnac

salt and pepper

Use a balloon whisk to whip the cream until it thickens to the ribbon stage; i.e. if you lift the whisk above the cream it will fall onto the surface and hold a ribbon shape (see page 233). You can whip the cream in an electric mixer, but it is harder to gauge the correct consistency.

Grate the orange over the bowl to capture the spray and oils. Add a squeeze of orange juice and the remaining ingredients. Continue to whip the cream to soft peaks (page 233). It should be soft and fluffy, but fairly firm. Chill until ready to use and use within 24 hours.

HOT SAUCES

In classical French cooking, hot sauces are based on the sauces mères – mother sauces – and are either white or brown. Old-fashioned white sauces are based on a basic béchamel, which is made from milk that is thickened with a white roux. In contemporary kitchens though, white sauces are increasingly based on a velouté, which is made from a chicken, veal or fish stock and is then lightly enriched and thickened with cream.

Brown sauces are all based on good-quality brown stock, which acquires its dark colour and richer flavour by roasting the bones (page 33). The original brown sauce – the espagnole – was always considered the cornerstone of the classic French repertoire of sauces. In its simplest form, it was made with a rich brown stock, thickened with a brown roux (where oil replaces butter), enriched with additional flavourings and simmered slowly for 2–3 days.

But contemporary cooking has again parted company with tradition. The espagnole is time-consuming and too rich and heavy for modern palates. Today, most brown sauces tend to be either rustic pan sauces or more refined jus-based sauces.

Pan sauces are simplicity itself, made from the caramelised sediment in a roasting pan and a generous splash of stock. More refined sauces will be skimmed of much of the fat and given body and a lovely sheen from the addition of jus – a lovely reduced veal glace (page 36).

The modern-day trend away from roux-thickened sauces is further exemplified in emulsified sauces, which instead rely on butter or egg yolks for body and texture. The stars of this type of sauce are the hollandaise and béarnaise, and the simpler beurre blanc.

White sauces

I have a bit of a horror of that kitchen basic, the béchamel, as I find the flour, however well cooked out it is, always dulls the flavour of the other ingredients. My cooking is all about maintaining and intensifying the purity of flavour, so all my white sauces are stock-based, and only lightly thickened with a little cream.

Chicken velouté

makes 500 ml (17 fl oz)

PREP TIME 20 MINUTES   COOK TIME 40 MINUTES

30 g (1 oz) butter	80 ml (3 fl oz) white wine
4 shallots, finely sliced	300 ml (10 fl oz) White Chicken Stock (page 29)
8 button mushrooms, finely sliced	500 ml (17 fl oz) cream
1 garlic clove, finely sliced	salt and pepper
2 sprigs thyme	few drops lemon juice
500 g (1 lb 2 oz) chicken wings, cut into small pieces	

Heat the butter in a heavy-based saucepan until it foams. Add the vegetables and thyme and stir well. Sweat for 5 minutes until the onion is translucent. Add the chicken wings and sweat for a further 3 minutes. Pour on the white wine and simmer vigorously until it has almost reduced, then add the chicken stock and simmer until reduced by a third.

Add the cream to the pan and simmer for 10 minutes. Taste and season to your liking then add the lemon juice. Strain through a fine sieve and serve straight away. Otherwise, transfer to a container with a tight-fitting lid and refrigerate. The sauce will keep in a sealed container in the refrigerator for 3 days.

Albufera sauce

A classic velouté-based sauce which is often made from gently sautéed capsicums (peppers) or, as in this case, with foie gras.

500 ml (17 fl oz) Chicken Velouté (page 81)

50 g (2 oz) Foie Gras Butter (page 76)

½ tablespoon Madeira

1 tablespoon Armagnac

Gently warm the velouté. Add the foie gras butter, Madeira and Armagnac and use a hand blender to whiz to a smooth, shiny sauce.

Fish velouté

makes 500 ml (17 fl oz)

PREP TIME 20 MINUTES   COOK TIME 40 MINUTES

30 g (1 oz) butter

4 shallots, finely sliced

8 button mushrooms, finely sliced

1 garlic clove, finely sliced

2 sprigs thyme

150 g (5½ oz) white fish trimmings, such as snapper or John Dory

80 ml (3 fl oz) white wine

300 ml (10 fl oz) Fish Stock (page 31)

500 ml (17 fl oz) cream

salt and pepper

few drops lemon juice

Heat the butter in a heavy-based saucepan until it foams. Add the vegetables and thyme and stir well. Sweat for 5 minutes until onion is translucent. Add the fish trimmings and sweat for a further 3 minutes. Pour on the white wine and simmer vigorously until it has almost reduced, then add the fish stock and simmer until reduced by a third.

Add the cream to the pan and simmer for 10 minutes. Taste and season to your liking then add the lemon juice. Strain through a fine sieve and serve straight away. Otherwise, transfer to a container with a tight-fitting lid and refrigerate. The sauce will keep in a sealed container in the refrigerator for 2 days.

RIESLING VELOUTÉ

Make the Fish Velouté as described above and finish with a good splash of your favourite riesling.

NOILLY PRAT AND CHERVIL VELOUTÉ

To 250 ml (8½ fl oz) of Fish Velouté add 2 tablespoons chopped chervil and Noilly Prat to taste.

Lemon-scented clam jus

makes 500 ml (17 fl oz)

PREP TIME 20 MINUTES   COOK TIME 30 MINUTES

30 ml (1 fl oz) vegetable oil

4 shallots, very finely sliced

1 garlic clove, very finely sliced

3 cm (1 ¼ in) piece fresh ginger, very finely sliced

1 lemongrass stalk, very finely sliced

200 ml (7 fl oz) white wine

500 g (1 lb 2 oz) clams

500 ml (17 fl oz) water or Fish Stock (page 31)

salt and pepper

few drops lemon juice

Heat the oil in a heavy-based saucepan. Add the shallots, garlic, ginger and lemongrass and sweat gently for 5 minutes or so until onion is soft and translucent. Add the white wine and simmer until reduced by two-thirds.

Meanwhile, place the clams in a double-lined plastic bag and smash with a rolling pin until completely crushed. Be careful not to let any juices escape. Add them to the saucepan and cover with the water or stock. Bring to the boil and simmer gently for 5 minutes.

Remove from the heat, taste and season with salt and pepper. Add the lemon juice and cover the pan with a tight-fitting lid. Leave to infuse for 15 minutes before straining through a fine sieve. Then pour the strained liquid through a sieve lined with a double layer of muslin (cheesecloth). The jus will keep in a sealed container in the refrigerator for 2 days.

Bread sauce

makes 500 ml (17 fl oz)

PREP TIME 20 MINUTES   COOK TIME 10 MINUTES
INFUSING TIME 30 MINUTES

½ onion

½ bay leaf

3 cloves

20 ml (¾ fl oz) vegetable oil

200 ml (7 fl oz) milk

6 slices thick white bread cut into large squares

100 ml (3 ½ fl oz) cream

pinch of nutmeg

salt and pepper

Divide the onion in half and dice one piece to a fine brunoise (page 208). Fix the bay leaf to the other piece of onion with the 3 cloves and set it to one side.

Heat the oil in a small saucepan and sweat the onion brunoise until soft and translucent. Add the milk to the pan with the onion and bring to the boil. Remove the pan from the heat, cover and leave to infuse for 30 minutes.

Add the remaining ingredients to the infused milk and stir well. Heat gently to a simmer and keep warm until ready to serve. Remove half onion, with bay leaf and cloves, before serving. This sauce will only keep for 1–2 hours.

Brown sauces

Brown sauces are based on brown stocks; they can be made from poultry, game, veal, lamb or pork. They are characterised by a richness and intensity of flavour and their dark brown colour. I tend to divide them into simple pan-based sauces and more refined, elegant jus-based sauces.

Pan sauce (jus gras)

Also known as jus gras – fatty gravy – at their simplest, pan sauces are simple, home-style sauces made in the roasting pan from meat juices, rendered fat and caramelised sediment from the bottom of the pan. Sometimes, though, especially if you roast your meat or poultry on a rack, there won't be much sediment left. This is a useful recipe to have if you want to knock some up relatively quickly; it uses the same principle and yields a lovely tasty sauce.

makes 500 ml (17 fl oz)

/ PREP TIME 10 MINUTES ☗ COOK TIME 30 MINUTES

30 ml (1 fl oz) vegetable oil	3 garlic cloves, finely sliced
500 g (1 lb 2 oz) chicken wings, chopped into small pieces	200 ml (7 fl oz) white wine
200 g (7 oz) butter	300 ml (10 fl oz) Brown Chicken Stock (page 34)
5 shallots, finely sliced	3 sprigs thyme
10 button mushrooms, finely sliced	salt and pepper

Heat the oil in a heavy-based saucepan. Add the chicken wings and sauté for 5 minutes or so until brown and caramelised. Add the butter and leave to foam. Add the vegetables and garlic to the pan and continue to sauté for a further 5 minutes or so, until everything is a deep golden brown.

Add the white wine and deglaze the pan, then add the chicken stock and thyme and simmer gently for 20 minutes until reduced to a sauce consistency. Strain through a fine sieve and serve straight away. Otherwise, transfer to a container with a tight-fitting lid and refrigerate. The sauce will keep in a sealed container in the refrigerator for 5 days.

Red wine sauce

makes 500 ml (17 fl oz)

⟋ PREP TIME 10 MINUTES ⬜ COOK TIME 25 MINUTES

500 ml (17 fl oz) red wine

100 ml (3½ fl oz) ruby port

3 sprigs thyme

2 garlic cloves, roughly crushed

¼ bay leaf

2 peppercorns

400 ml (13 fl oz) Veal Glace (page 36)

Put all the ingredients except for the veal glace in a medium-sized, heavy-based saucepan and bring to the boil over a high heat. Boil vigorously to reduce the alcohol to about one-sixth of its original volume.

Add the veal glace, lower the heat and simmer gently for 8 minutes, skimming from time to time. Pour through a fine sieve, taking care not to allow any sediment to pass into the sauce. Serve straight away, or transfer to a container with a tight-fitting lid and refrigerate. The sauce will keep in a sealed container in the refrigerator for 5 days or 3 months in the freezer.

BORDELAISE SAUCE

For every 100 ml (3½ fl oz) of Red Wine Sauce add 1 tablespoon finely diced shallots, 1 tablespoon finely chopped parsley and 2 tablespoons diced rinsed bone marrow. Whisk together well and serve piping hot.

jus-based sauces

These are more complex, intensely flavoured sauces that are given body and sheen by adding Veal Glace (page 36).

Lamb jus

makes 500 ml (17 fl oz)

PREP TIME 10 MINUTES   COOK TIME 30 MINUTES

30 ml (1 fl oz) vegetable oil	1 tomato, roughly chopped
300 g (10½ oz) lamb meat trimmings, cut small	3 sprigs thyme
4 shallots, finely sliced	1 sprig rosemary
2 garlic cloves, finely sliced	1 litre (34 fl oz) Brown Lamb Stock (page 37)
250 ml (8½ fl oz) white wine	

Heat the oil in a large heavy-based saucepan. Add the lamb pieces and sauté until caramelised a deep golden brown. Add the shallots and garlic to the pan and continue to sauté for a further 5 minutes or so, until everything is a deep golden brown.

Tip everything into a colander to drain off the fat. Return the meat and vegetables to the pan and deglaze with the white wine. Add the tomato, herbs and stock and simmer gently for 20 minutes, skimming from time to time. Strain through a fine sieve and serve straight away or transfer to a container with a tight-fitting lid and refrigerate. The sauce will keep in a sealed container in the refrigerator for 5 days or up to 3 months in the freezer.

PIPERADE SAUCE

For every 100 ml (3½ fl oz) of hot lamb jus add the following, just before serving;

1 teaspoon finely diced shallots
1 tablespoon diced Roasted Capsicums (page 225)
1 tablespoon chopped green olives
1 teaspoon chopped capers
1 teaspoon chopped anchovies
1 teaspoon chopped parsley

Caramelised veal jus

This sauce is one of my absolute favourites, full of flavour and vitality. It is based on a simple principle: caramelised meat juices. Remember, though, that for a great sauce you need to begin with a great stock.

makes 500 ml (17 fl oz)

/ PREP TIME 15 MINUTES ☞ COOK TIME 45 MINUTES

50 ml (2 fl oz) vegetable oil

300 g (10½ oz) veal meat trimmings, cut small

50 g (2 oz) cold butter, diced

5 shallots, finely sliced

10 button mushrooms, finely sliced

3 garlic cloves, finely sliced

150 ml (5 fl oz) white wine

1 litre (34 fl oz) Brown Veal Stock (page 35)

Heat the oil in a large heavy-based saucepan. Add the veal pieces in a single layer and sear on a high heat to colour. If necessary, sear in batches as you don't want them to stew. Add the butter and allow to foam. Lower the heat and sauté the veal in the butter until the sugars caramelise and the veal browns. Sauté for 5–10 minutes, stirring all the time to scrape the sticky sediment up from the bottom of the pan.

Add the vegetables and garlic to the pan and continue to sauté for a further 5 minutes or so, until everything is a deep golden brown. Tip everything into a colander to drain off the fat. Return the meat and vegetables to the pan and deglaze with the white wine. Simmer until the wine has reduced to a syrupy consistency. Add the stock and simmer gently for 30 minutes, skimming from time to time. Strain through a fine sieve and serve straight away. Otherwise, transfer to a container with a tight-fitting lid and refrigerate. The sauce will keep in a sealed container in the refrigerator for 3 days or up to 3 months in the freezer.

LIME JUS

To 250 ml (8½ fl oz) Caramelised Veal Jus add the juice and chopped flesh (membranes removed) of 1 lime.

PÉRIGUEUX SAUCE

To 250 ml (8½ fl oz) Caramelised Veal Jus add 30 ml (1 fl oz) Madeira and 1 tablespoon chopped fresh black truffle.

Roast pork jus

makes 500 ml (17 fl oz)

PREP TIME 10 MINUTES COOK TIME 45 MINUTES

30 ml (1 fl oz) vegetable oil	1 Granny Smith apple, roughly chopped
300 g (10½ oz) pork meat trimmings, cut small	2 sprigs thyme
50 g (2 oz) butter	100 ml (3½ fl oz) white wine
5 shallots, finely sliced	1 litre (34 fl oz) Brown Pork Stock (page 37)
2 garlic cloves, finely sliced	salt and pepper

Heat the oil in a large heavy-based saucepan. Add the pork pieces and sear on a high heat to colour. Add the butter and allow to foam. Lower the heat and sauté the pork in the butter until the sugars caramelise and the meat browns. Add shallots, garlic and apple to the pan and continue to sauté for a further 5 minutes or so, until everything is a deep golden brown.

Tip everything into a colander to drain off the fat. Return everything to the pan, add the thyme and deglaze with the white wine. Simmer until the wine has reduced to a syrupy consistency. Add the stock and simmer gently for 30 minutes, skimming from time to time. Strain through a fine sieve, season and serve straight away. Otherwise, transfer to a container with a tight-fitting lid and refrigerate. The sauce will keep in a sealed container in the refrigerator for 5 days or up to 3 months in the freezer.

SMOKED BACON AND GRAIN MUSTARD JUS

For every 100 ml (3½ fl oz) of hot Roast Pork Jus
add 2 tablespoons finely diced pancetta and
1 tablespoon wholegrain mustard just before serving.

Roasted poultry or game jus

makes 500 ml (17 fl oz)

PREP TIME 10 MINUTES ☐ COOK TIME 30 MINUTES

30 ml (1 fl oz) cooking oil	100 ml (3 ½ fl oz) Madeira
500 g (1 lb 2 oz) poultry or game carcasses, chopped small	1 litre (34 fl oz) Brown Chicken or Game Stock (page 34)
50 g (2 oz) butter	2 sprigs thyme
8 shallots, finely sliced	½ bay leaf
10 button mushrooms, finely sliced	few drops Armagnac
2 garlic cloves, finely sliced	

Heat the oil in a large heavy-based saucepan. Add the chopped carcasses and sear on a high heat to colour. Add the butter and allow to foam, then add the vegetables and garlic to the pan and continue to sauté for a further 5 minutes or so, until everything is a deep golden brown.

Tip everything into colander to drain off the fat. Return everything to the pan and deglaze with the Madeira. Simmer until reduced to a syrupy consistency. Add the stock and herbs and simmer gently for 20 minutes, skimming from time to time. Strain through a fine sieve and finish with the Armagnac. Serve straight away or transfer to a container with a tight-fitting lid and refrigerate. The sauce will keep in a sealed container in the refrigerator for 5 days or up to 3 months in the freezer.

SPICED CHERRY JUS

For every 100 ml (3½ fl oz) of hot Game Jus add 50 g (2 oz) Spiced Cherries (page 17) blitzed to a purée with a hand blender. This makes a wonderful sauce to serve with roast duck and game birds, such as the Butterflied Quail (page 187) with Choucroute (page 220).

Vegetable and herb jus

These make intensely flavoured, light sauces, with a wonderful sweet finish. I love to serve them with roasted meats, poultry or lobster – or even add a splash to my favourite salad.

Thyme jus

makes 500 ml (17 fl oz)

PREP TIME 5 MINUTES COOK TIME 15 MINUTES
INFUSING TIME 15 MINUTES

20 ml (¾ fl oz) vegetable oil

½ onion, finely diced

1 garlic clove, finely sliced

½ bunch thyme

500 ml (17 fl oz) milk

salt and pepper

few drops lemon juice

Heat the oil in a large heavy-based saucepan. Add the onion and garlic and sweat for about 5 minutes until translucent. Add the thyme and milk and bring to the boil. Lower the heat and simmer for 5 minutes. Remove from the heat, cover with a tight-fitting lid and leave in a warm place to infuse for 15 minutes.

Pass through a fine sieve then taste and season to your liking, finishing with a few drops of lemon juice. This sauce is best served as fresh as possible, although it will keep for a few hours.

Carrot jus

makes 200 ml (7 fl oz)

PREP TIME 10 MINUTES COOK TIME 35 MINUTES

3 large carrots

4 sprigs thyme

1 star anise

500 ml (17 fl oz) water

10 ml (¼ fl oz) vegetable oil

salt and pepper

pinch sugar (optional)

Peel the carrots and slice them finely. Place the peelings in a saucepan with one of the carrots, 2 sprigs of the thyme, the star anise and water. Bring to the boil, then lower the heat and simmer for 15 minutes. Strain the carrot stock through a fine sieve and reserve.

Heat the oil in a large heavy-based saucepan. Add the rest of the carrots and sweat for a few minutes until they soften. Add the rest of the thyme and the reserved carrot stock and simmer for 10 minutes. Taste and season to your liking, adding a little sugar if need be.

Tip into a colander and drain, transferring the liquor to a blender with 2 tablespoons of the pulpy cooked carrots. Whiz to a smooth purée and pass though a fine sieve. This sauce is best served as fresh as possible, although it will keep for a few hours.

White asparagus jus

You can use the asparagus tips for the main part of your dish and reserve the stalks for this sauce.

makes 500 ml (17 fl oz)

PREP TIME 5 MINUTES ☞ COOK TIME 15 MINUTES
INFUSING TIME 15 MINUTES

1 tablespoon vegetable oil

½ onion, finely diced

1 garlic clove, finely sliced

8 white asparagus spears, finely sliced

2 sprigs thyme

100 ml (3 ½ fl oz) white wine

150 ml (5 fl oz) Vegetable Stock (page 32)

150 ml (5 fl oz) milk

salt and pepper

few drops lemon juice

Heat the oil in a large heavy-based saucepan. Add the onion and garlic and sweat for about 5 minutes until onion is translucent. Add the asparagus and thyme and sweat for a few more minutes. Add the wine and deglaze the pan. Simmer until reduced by a third. Add the stock and milk and bring to the boil. Lower the heat and simmer for 5 minutes.

Tip into a blender and whiz to a light, smooth purée. Pass through a fine sieve then taste and season to your liking, finishing with a few drops of lemon juice. This sauce is best served as fresh as possible, although it will keep for a few hours.

Hot emulsions

As is the case with cold emulsions, hot emulsions depend primarily upon the magical binding properties of egg yolks.

The best known is the hollandaise, a smooth, light-as-a-feather sauce that is also addictively rich. It's a bit like a hot, looser mayonnaise, and like mayonnaise is the perfect accompaniment to poached fish and vegetables. Hollandaise sauce can be flavoured with all sorts of other ingredients, most famously perhaps with tarragon to create béarnaise sauce – the classic French accompaniment to grilled (broiled) steak.

Hollandaise and other emulsions can be made with melted butter, but I prefer to use clarified butter as it gives a purer, smoother flavour. Clarified butter is simply normal butter that is melted gently until the white milk solids separate and sink to the bottom of the pan. The vibrant yellow clarified liquid is then skimmed off and the solids discarded. The great virtue of clarified butter, apart from the flavour, is that it can be heated to higher temperatures than regular butter without burning.

Hollandaise sauce

makes 200 ml (7 fl oz)

PREP TIME 5 MINUTES   COOK TIME 10 MINUTES

3 tablespoons White Wine Vinegar Reduction (page 21)

2 egg yolks

150 ml (5 fl oz) clarified butter (see page 91)

salt and pepper

few drops lemon juice

Put the vinegar reduction in a stainless-steel bowl and set it over a pan of simmering water; the base of the bowl should not come into contact with the water. Add the egg yolks and whisk together until the mixture is thick, pale and creamy. Slowly trickle in the clarified butter, whisking continuously, until the sauce is thick and shiny. Remove from the heat, season and add the lemon juice. Serve straight away, or keep it in a warm place until ready to serve. It will keep for 1–2 hours.

BÉARNAISE SAUCE

Make in the same way as a Hollandaise Sauce and add a generous tablespoon of chopped tarragon at the end. Serve with grilled (broiled) steak and French fries.

CHORON SAUCE

Make in the same way as a Hollandaise Sauce and add a generous tablespoon of tomato purée at the end. Serve with grilled steak or fish or Poached Eggs (page 109).

PALOISE SAUCE

Make in the same way as a Hollandaise Sauce and add a generous tablespoon of chopped mint at the end. Serve with grilled lamb or boiled potatoes.

CHIVE SABAYON

Make in the same way as Hollandaise Sauce but add 50 ml (2 fl oz) of white wine at the beginning as you start to whisk – this will give you a much lighter sauce, closer to a sabayon. At the end add 2 tablespoons chopped chives. Serve with poached lobster, salmon or trout – or even with poached or coddled eggs.

LEMON SABAYON

Make in the same way as Chive Sabayon, but omit chives and add a few drops of fresh lemon juice and ½ tablespoon grated lemon zest.

Beurre blanc

makes 200 ml (7 fl oz)

PREP TIME 5 MINUTES COOK TIME 5 MINUTES

50 ml (2 fl oz) White Wine Vinegar Reduction
   (page 21)

1 tablespoon cream

200 g (7 oz) cold butter, diced

salt and pepper

few drops lemon juice

Put the vinegar reduction and cream in a small
heavy-based saucepan and bring to the boil. Lower
the heat and whisk in the butter, just a few pieces
at a time, whisking continuously until the sauce is
completely emulsified, thick and shiny. Remove from
the heat, season and add the lemon juice. Serve
straight away, or keep it in a warm place until ready
to serve. It will keep for 1–2 hours.

LEMON THYME BEURRE BLANC

Make in the same way as a Beurre Blanc and add a
generous tablespoon of chopped lemon thyme at the
end. Allow to infuse in a warm place for 5 minutes or
so. Then strain before serving with grilled (broiled)
asparagus, Petits Pois à la Française (page 219),
roasted fish or poultry.

HERB BEURRE BLANC

Make in the same way as a Beurre Blanc and add
a generous tablespoon of chopped herbs at the end.
Vary according to your preference, using parsley,
basil or chervil. Allow to infuse in a warm place for
5 minutes or so. Then strain before serving with
poached or steamed fish, sautéed shellfish, seared
scallops or even savoury tarts.

Beurre noisette – hazelnut butter

This has an intoxicating nutty aroma and
flavour and is great to use as a simple
sauce, especially for fish.

makes 200 ml (7 fl oz)

PREP TIME 5 MINUTES COOK TIME 10 MINUTES

250 g (9 oz) butter

salt and pepper

few drops lemon juice

Put the butter in a saucepan and heat gently
until melted. Increase the temperature and cook
until the butter begins to froth. Continue cooking until
it darkens to a light, then dark brown. Remove from
the heat immediately and allow to cool. It will have
a distinctive hazelnut aroma. Pour through a fine
sieve, season and add the lemon juice. Serve
straight away, hot or warm. Otherwise, transfer to
a container with a tight-fitting lid and refrigerate.

The sauce will keep in a sealed container in the
refrigerator for up to a month. It will solidify, and you
will need to gently warm it through before serving.

ROSEMARY AND TRUFFLE BEURRE NOISETTE

Make in the same way as a Beurre Noisette and add
a tablespoon of chopped rosemary and a tablespoon
of chopped fresh black truffle to the finished sauce.
Serve with grilled (broiled) or sautéed fish, steamed
green vegetables, Poached Eggs (page 109) or even
Slow-cooked Eggs (page 110).

Salads

Over the years the 'salade' has come to mean different things to different people, and no more so than in the French kitchen. Traditionally, and most usually in a French meal, salad pretty much just meant green lettuce leaves tossed in a vinaigrette dressing and it was served after the main course as a sort of digestif before cheese and dessert.

With the advent of the nouvelle cuisine movement in the 1970s, a new type of salad emerged. Served more as a starter to stimulate the mind and the palate, these various salades – folle, gourmande, nouvelle and so on – were all about visual impact and letting the imagination run wild.

While this all seems a bit passé these days, I still really love the idea of a composée salad, or salade composée. To me salads are worthy of far more than being simply relegated to 'side' status. With all the endless options available in respect of colour, texture and flavour, salads make wonderful dishes in their own right, either as a light starter or as a light main meal. And remember, whatever part they play in a meal they are always intended to be refreshing and light, rather than filling.

Given that salad ingredients are usually (but not always) eaten raw, it is imperative that you choose absolutely top-notch produce. And really, there's no excuse not to do this. We are spoilt for choice these days when it comes to the vast array of baby vegetables, salad leaves, miniature herbs, cresses and even edible flowers that are readily available.

In my view, local market gardens and growers' markets are likely to be your best bet for finding an interesting array of salad ingredients. And don't just assume that all green leaves taste the same! It's very important not to be shy, but always to ask if you can have a little taste of what's on offer. That way you'll start to learn about the different textures and flavours that are available, from the pepperiness of wild rocket (arugula) and watercress, or the sharp bite of sorrel, to bitter radicchio (Italian chicory) and endive (chicory) or sweet butter lettuce. As with herbs, every salad leaf has its own unique flavour and texture, and it's the way you put the various components together that creates a great salad. Even the simplest salad should focus on colour, texture and flavour – in ways that complement and contrast each other, and the dishes that are to follow.

When choosing ingredients for your salads, look for crisp, fresh leaves and bright vivid colours. It's a good idea to buy cresses and baby leaves in punnets (small plastic containers), wherever possible – and always buy in smallish quantities for maximum freshness.

Store salad leaves in their original packaging, or wrapped in a damp (not wet) tea (dish) towel. Keep them in the fridge but make sure there is plenty of air circulating around them – you don't want to crush and bruise delicate leaves.

With a few exceptions, all salad leaves, herbs and cresses should be prepared in the same way: trim off the stems, discard any wilted leaves and separate the inner leaves ready for washing. Most herbs should be picked into little sprigs – or pluches, if you want to be fancy.

All salad ingredients must be well washed to remove sand or grit. The best way of washing is to place the leaves in a sink or large bowl filled with cool water. Move them around gently to loosen any dirt, then leave them to sit for a few moments to allow sand or grit to fall to the bottom of your bowl. Lift the leaves out gently and shake lightly before drying in a salad spinner or on absorbent paper towels. Don't miss this step – if your leaves are not well dried the dressing will not cling and the salad will be limp and will taste watery.

There are all sorts of dressings you can use for your salads, and you should think about them in the same way you think about a sauce: a good dressing is one that brings out the flavour of the ingredients it is paired with, rather than overwhelming them. A good dressing will also be well balanced and well seasoned – but this is very much dependent on the palate of the dressing maker! In the end, you want to achieve a happy harmony of sweetness, acidity and oil. One final tip: I often rub the inside of my salad bowl with a cut clove of garlic just before I add the salad and its dressing. This adds a fresh hint of garlic, without being overpowering.

Salade simple

As the name suggests, this sort of salad is simplicity itself, and can be varied with the seasons or according to your taste. Experiment with different combinations of leaves and fresh herbs. Play around with the dressings too, although simple salads usually need nothing more than a simple dressing. I particularly like Lemon Vinaigrette (page 66), Herb Vinaigrette (page 66) and Walnut Vinaigrette (page 67).

serves 4

PREP TIME 10 MINUTES

3 cups mixed salad leaves (any combination of cos/romaine lettuce, butter lettuce, wild rocket/arugula, watercress, sorrel, radicchio/ Italian chicory, witlof/chicory/Belgian endive or curly endive)

1 cup fresh herbs (parsley, chives, basil, mint, chervil or fennel fronds)

60 ml (2 fl oz) Lemon Vinaigrette (page 66)

salt and pepper

Tear the larger leaves into smaller pieces and place in a mixing bowl with the herbs. Pour in just enough vinaigrette to moisten the leaves — you don't want to drown them. Season and use your fingers to tumble everything together gently. You need to ensure that all the leaves are evenly and lightly coated, but above all you don't want to bruise the delicate leaves.

Pissaladière with baby leaves and soused tuna

This makes a wonderful supper dish – it's sort of half salad and half pizza! It is my favourite kind of meal, because it's all about contrasts: there's the hot crunch of the pizza base and cold smooth slices of tuna; there's the rich creaminess of the onions and the saltiness of the olives and anchovies; and then there's the sharp pepperiness of the cress leaves and the lemony tartness of the vinaigrette. What more could you want?

serves 4

PREP TIME 20 MINUTES

1 x Pissaladière (page 340)

400 g (14 oz) tuna loin or belly fillet, very finely sliced

salt and pepper

100 ml (3½ fl oz) Lemon Vinaigrette (page 66)

1 cup baby watercress

1 cup baby mustard cress

1 cup baby radish cress

extra-virgin olive oil

Preheat your oven to 180°C (350°F). Warm the pissaladière in the oven for 5–10 minutes while you prepare the other ingredients.

Place the tuna slices in a shallow bowl, season with salt and pepper and pour on the lemon vinaigrette. Place in the refrigerator for a few minutes to marinate. Toss the cresses together in a large mixing bowl.

To serve, cut the pissaladière into quarters and arrange on serving plates. Top with slices of the soused tuna and a mound of the baby cresses. Drizzle with a little extra-virgin olive oil and serve straight away.

Salade Provençale

This lovely seafood salad is full of flavours from the south of France. It is hearty enough to serve as a light meal, perhaps with some crusty bread on the side.

serves 4 as a light meal

PREP TIME 20 MINUTES   COOK TIME 2 MINUTES

400 g (14 oz) squid tubes or cuttlefish, cleaned
60 ml (2 fl oz) olive oil
12 scallops
salt and pepper
few drops lemon juice
2 cups mixed salad leaves of your choice
½ cup shredded basil
1 cup black or green olives (or a selection of both), stones removed
100 ml (3 ½ fl oz) Herb Vinaigrette (page 66)
Pistou of Vegetables (page 226)
12 cherry tomatoes

Slice the squid tubes along one side and open them out flat. Cut each tube into 12 neat rectangles and lightly score the surface with a sharp knife in a criss-cross pattern.

Heat the oil in a heavy-based frying pan. Add the squid and scallops and sauté for 2 minutes until golden brown. Season and add the lemon juice.

Put the salad leaves, basil and olives in a large mixing bowl and toss with half the vinaigrette. Arrange a mound in the centre of each plate. In the same mixing bowl, toss the pistou of vegetables with the remaining dressing. Top each salad with 3 cherry tomatoes and divide the squid and scallops evenly between the plates. Spoon on the pistou of vegetables and serve immediately.

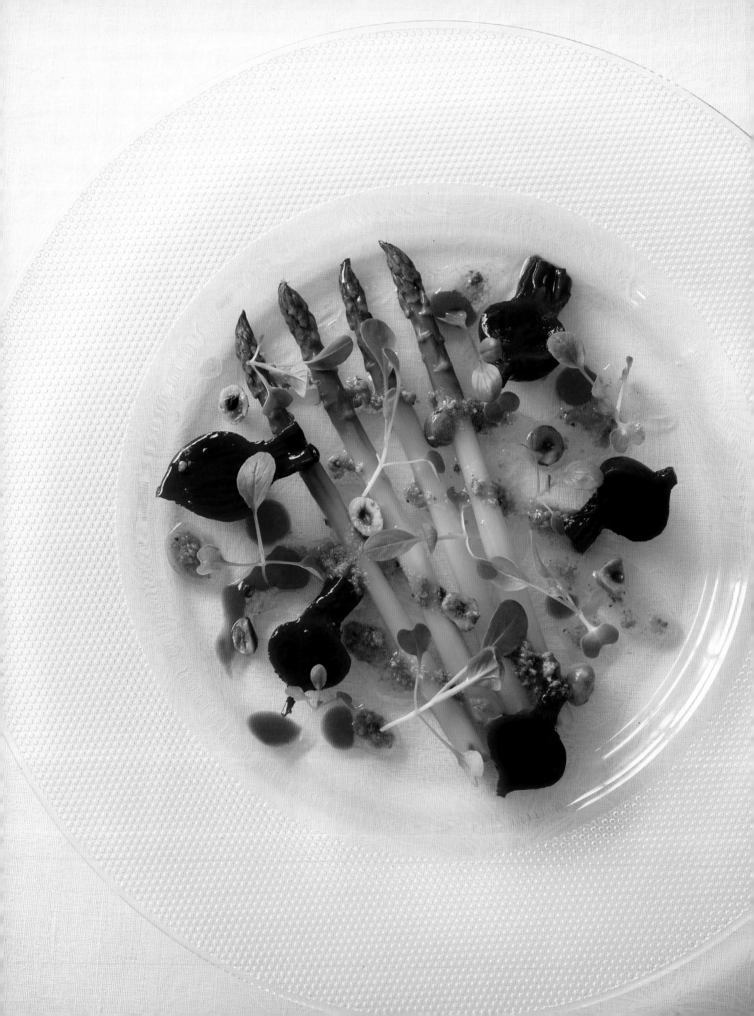

Asparagus salad with hazelnuts and tatsoi

White asparagus is very elegant, but this salad is just as delicious made with green asparagus. For a contrasting tang, scatter in a few slices of pickled beetroot (beets), which are also very pretty against the pale green of the salad. For a special occasion I like to place a few spoonfuls of frothy White Asparagus Jus (page 91) around the warm salad just before serving.

serves 4

PREP TIME 20 MINUTES

50 ml (2 fl oz) olive oil

16 white or green asparagus spears, peeled

salt and pepper

4 cups tatsoi leaves, washed and dried

250 g (9 oz) Pickled Red Beetroot (page 22) or good-quality deli beetroot (beets), sliced

200 ml (7 fl oz) Hazelnut Vinaigrette (page 67)

Heat the olive oil in a heavy-based frying pan over a moderate heat. Add the asparagus, season with salt and pepper and sauté for 3 minutes or so, until spears start to colour. They should be tender, but still firm.

Arrange 4 spears of asparagus on each serving plate. Place a mound of tatsoi leaves on top and scatter on the beetroot slices. Drizzle with the hazelnut vinaigrette and serve straight away.

Salad of golden frisée and smoked trout

I love the way the bitter frisée leaves work as a foil to the richness of the smoked trout and avocado. This salad is delicious dressed with Cherry Tomato Coulis, but works just as well with a simple Lemon Vinaigrette (page 66). Hot-smoked trout is fairly readily available from most delis and fish markets.

serves 4

PREP TIME 20 MINUTES

2 x 300 g (10 ½ oz) whole hot-smoked rainbow trout

1 head of frisée lettuce, inner golden leaves only

2 avocados, sliced

½ cup finely chopped chives

200 ml (7 fl oz) Cherry Tomato Coulis (page 70)

salt and pepper

To prepare the trout, cut off the head and tail and slide your finger under the skin to loosen it; it should peel away easily. Use a fork or your fingers to pull the flesh away from the bones and place in a large mixing bowl. Break into medium-sized flakes and set aside.

Tear the frisée leaves into smallish pieces and put into a mixing bowl with the avocado, chives and flaked trout. Pour in just enough tomato coulis to moisten the leaves – you don't want to drown them. Season and use your fingers to tumble everything together gently. Divide between 4 plates and drizzle extra tomato coulis around the plate. Serve immediately.

Lamb's lettuce with lardons

Lettuce and bacon is a classic salad combination that everyone loves. Instead of dressing it with a predictable vinaigrette, I like to use Sauce Gribiche, which adds plenty of crunch and a wonderful salty, vinegary tang. To turn it into more of a meal, add slices of sautéed Chicken Confit (page 138) or top with a soft-poached egg.

serves 4

PREP TIME 20 MINUTES

2 cups lamb's lettuce (corn salad/mâche), washed and dried

200 g (7 oz) smoked bacon, cut into thick batons (strips)

1 tablespoon olive oil

splash Home-made Truffle Oil (page 75)

few drops lemon juice

sea salt

200 ml (7 fl oz) Sauce Gribiche (page 73)

Put the lamb's lettuce in a large mixing bowl and set aside.

Heat the oil in a heavy-based frying pan and fry the bacon until golden brown. Remove from the pan and drain briefly on paper towels. Scatter the bacon into the mixing bowl, then add a generous splash of truffle oil, a squeeze of lemon and a sprinkling of sea salt. Use your fingers to tumble everything together gently.

To serve, spoon a neat mound of sauce gribiche in the centre of each serving plate. Decorate the plate with the salad and serve immediately while the bacon is still warm.

Winter salad of roasted walnuts, mushrooms and golden celery hearts

A warming salad full of earthy flavours. Serve it on its own, or garnish with Confit Duck (page 138) or thin slices of any smoked meats of your choice.

serves 4

PREP TIME 20 MINUTES

50 g (2 oz) walnut halves

drizzle of walnut oil

salt and pepper

1 bunch celery, inner golden heart and leaves only (use the outer stalks for making soups or stock)

100 g (3½ oz) shiitake mushrooms

200 ml (7 fl oz) Walnut Vinaigrette (page 67)

80 ml (3 fl oz) Port and Red Wine Reduction (page 21)

sliced Confit Duck (page 138) or smoked meat (optional)

Preheat your oven to 180°C (350°F). Heat a baking tray over a medium heat. Break the walnuts in half and scatter onto the hot tray. Drizzle with oil, season with salt and pepper and roast for 10 minutes until a deep golden brown.

Pick the leaves from the celery stalks and set aside. Finely slice the celery stalks and the shiitake mushrooms and put them in a large mixing bowl. Scatter in the celery leaves and the roasted walnuts. Pour in enough walnut vinaigrette to moisten the leaves and use your fingers to tumble everything together gently.

Divide the salad between 4 serving plates. Top with slices of confit or meat (if using) and drizzle more of the vinaigrette and a little port and red wine reduction around the plate. Serve immediately while the walnuts are still warm.

Eggs

Unquestionably one of the most versatile foods, the humble egg is put to good use in French cooking. There are literally hundreds of recipes for cooking whole eggs – from omelettes and baked eggs, to soft- and hard-boiling, scrambling, poaching or frying. And that's just the start of it.

As well as being eaten on their own, there are even more uses for eggs as an ingredient within a dish. Whole eggs are used to help bind stuffings or terrines and to add richness to cakes. When separated, egg yolks and whites are used to achieve very different results. Egg yolks are high in fat and protein, which enable them to thicken and enrich sauces (page 81) and custards (page 236) and to emulsify ingredients – such as oils and liquids – which otherwise do not combine (page 71). Egg whites increase in volume dramatically when beaten with air; this makes them indispensable in adding airy lightness and volume to cakes, soufflés, meringues and mousses.

One of the most important rules when buying eggs is to check for freshness – and really fresh eggs tend only to be reliable when bought as free-range, organic or farm eggs. Although it is rare to get a 'bad egg' these days, there is a marked difference in taste and quality with eggs that are really fresh and eggs that are a bit old. Very fresh eggs have plump, rounded yolks that sit up proudly. The whites hold their shape and cling closely to the yolk. As they age the albumen deteriorates and the whites become watery and the yolks become flabby. It makes sense to buy regularly and in small quantities so you always have the freshest possible eggs to hand.

My preference is to store eggs in the refrigerator, but remember that the shells are porous and they will absorb aromas from other unwrapped items. This is fine if you happen to have some truffles on hand, but not so good if they are sitting next to a stinky cheese. Remember, too, to take your eggs out of the refrigerator several hours in advance of using to allow them to come to room temperature.

Poached eggs and mushrooms with brioche soldiers

Poached eggs, with their lovely runny yolks, are the perfect brunch or light supper dish. Always use the freshest possible eggs; the whites are thicker and less watery, so the eggs keep their shape in the water better. The recipe that follows is my take on eggs on toast with mushrooms. For a special finishing touch, stir some Fines Herbes (page 15) into Hollandaise Sauce (page 92) and spoon it over the eggs as you serve them.

serves 4

PREP TIME 5 MINUTES   COOK TIME 4–6 MINUTES

4 free-range eggs at room temperature	30 g (1 oz) butter or duck fat
1 teaspoon white vinegar	200 ml (7 fl oz) Hollandaise Sauce (optional)
200 g (7 oz) Mushroom Duxelles (page 223)	2 tablespoons Fines Herbes (optional)
4 thick slices Brioche (page 343)	

Bring a large saucepan of water to a gentle boil and add the vinegar. Break each egg into a cup without breaking the yolk. Use a long metal spoon to stir the water in the pan, creating a mini whirlpool. Place the egg in the centre and allow the swirling water to shape it into a neatish ball. Poach for 3–5 minutes, or until the white is completely set. Remove the egg carefully and place on a clean tea towel to drain while you poach the remaining eggs. The eggs can be poached to this stage ahead of time. Reheat them in a pan of gently simmering water for 30–60 seconds just before you serve them.

Warm through the mushroom duxelles until gently simmering. Taste and adjust the seasoning to your liking.

Melt the butter in a hot frying pan. Cut the brioche slices into soldiers (fingers) and fry them on both sides until golden brown. To serve, spoon a generous mound of mushroom duxelles in the centre of each plate. Top with an egg and arrange a stack of soldiers on the side. Mix herbs with hollandaise, if using. Spoon some of the warm herb hollandaise over the eggs and serve straight away.

OEUFS À LA HOLLANDAISE

The classic accompaniment to poached eggs is Hollandaise Sauce (page 92). To ring the changes, try adding freshly chopped Fines Herbes (page 15) or any herbs of your choice.

OEUFS À LA FLORENTINE

Serve the poached eggs on a bed of Buttered Spinach (page 227) and top with a spoonful of Hollandaise Sauce (page 92).

EGGS WITH ROSEMARY AND TRUFFLE BEURRE NOISETTE

Poached eggs and truffles work brilliantly together. If you're lucky enough to have some fresh truffles in the house, knock up a lovely nutty Beurre Noisette (page 93) and flavour it with some fresh rosemary and chopped black truffles (page 93).

Slow-cooked eggs with herb and parmesan purée and crisp pancetta

This recipe demonstrates an unusual but extraordinarily effective way of cooking eggs. The very slow gentle cooking transforms the whites and yolks into a quivering, silky kind of jelly that is quite unique. It makes a very sophisticated dinner party dish. And if you can get hold of some duck eggs, you'll be bowled over by the colour and flavour. For this dish you really do need to have a thermometer as it's important that the temperature be maintained at a constant 65°C (150°F).

serves 4

PREP TIME 10 MINUTES   COOK TIME 90 MINUTES

4 free-range eggs

8 thin slices of pancetta

200 g (7 oz) Herb and Parmesan Purée (page 226)

sea salt and pepper

Heat a large saucepan of water to 65°C (150°F). Place the eggs in the water, making sure they are completely submerged. Leave for 1–1½ hours. It is important that temperature of the water does not rise above 65°C (150°F) but doesn't matter too much if it falls slightly below.

When you're nearly ready to serve, preheat the oven to 180°C (350°F). Lay the pancetta slices on a lightly oiled baking tray and place another baking tray on top to keep it flat. Bake for 8 minutes until golden and crisp, then drain on paper towels.

Gently warm through the herb and parmesan purée. Spoon a generous mound in the centre of each serving bowl. (If you really want to be fancy, serve this dish in a martini glass!) Very carefully crack the eggs on top of the purée and season lightly with salt and pepper. Finish with 2 slices of crisp pancetta and serve straight away.

Oeufs en cocotte

This is one of my favourite ways of cooking eggs: it's sort of a cross between poaching and baking. The eggs are cracked into little dishes of rendered duck fat and baked until just set. The result: a superb melting texture and flavour enriched by the duck fat. A few shavings of fresh truffle would be the perfect luxurious finishing touch.

serves 4

PREP TIME 20 MINUTES COOK TIME 10 MINUTES

300 ml (10 fl oz) rendered duck fat

4 free-range eggs

12 asparagus spears

salt and pepper

Rosemary and Truffle Beurre Noisette (page 93)

1 tablespoon chopped parsley

1 Cured Duck Ham (page 125) or pancetta, finely sliced

Preheat your oven to 180°C (350°F) then turn heat down to 90°C (195°F). Pour the rendered duck fat into 4 ramekin dishes and heat in the oven.

Meanwhile, heat an ovenproof frying pan over a moderate heat. Add the extra duck fat and sauté the asparagus for a few moments, tossing gently in the fat. Season generously and transfer to the oven to roast for 3–5 minutes, until golden but still quite firm.

Gently warm the beurre noisette in a small saucepan and add the chopped parsley.

Crack the eggs into the ramekins, and cook in the oven for about 6 minutes, until just set – or longer if you prefer your eggs firmer. To serve, divide the roasted asparagus between 4 warmed serving plates. Arrange an egg on top and scatter over a few slices of duck ham. Finally, drizzle on a little of the beurre noisette and serve immediately.

Warm egg yolk with mustard potatoes and salt cod

serves 4

/ PREP TIME 20 MINUTES 🍲 COOK TIME 90 MINUTES

4 free-range eggs, slow-cooked as on page 110

400 g (14 oz) Crushed Potatoes (page 218)

2 tablespoons wholegrain mustard

400 g (14 oz) poached Salt Cod, plus a little
    poaching liquor (page 127)

1 tablespoon horseradish cream

1 tablespoon chopped chives

½ cup chervil sprigs

Prepare the slow-cooked eggs, as described on page 110.

Gently warm through the crushed potatoes, then stir in the mustard.

Warm the salt cod in a little of its poaching liquid, then strain and use a fork to break it into medium-sized flakes.

Gently crack the slow-cooked eggs against a bowl and carefully separate the yolks from the whites. The yolks will hold their shape, like a thick hot wax, while the whites will be a warm soft jelly.

To serve, spoon a generous mound of crushed potatoes in the centre of each serving plate. Scatter the salt cod flakes around the potatoes and place an egg yolk on top.

Add the horseradish cream and the chives to the warm egg whites and whisk together briefly to form a dressing. Drizzle over the salt cod and garnish the whole dish with a sprig of chervil. Serve straight away.

Scallop mousse

This is a lovely delicate mousse that works brilliantly in Steamed Zucchini Flowers (page 151).

makes 500 g (1 lb 2 oz)

/ PREP TIME 20 MINUTES

250 g (9 oz) scallop meat

1 teaspoon salt

2 egg yolks

200 ml (7 fl oz) cream

few drops lemon juice

Place the bowl of your food processor in the freezer for 15 minutes until well chilled. Add the scallops and salt then blitz for 2 minutes to a smooth paste. Add the yolks and continue to blitz for another minute.

With the motor still running, trickle in half the cream to emulsify everything to a shiny, velvety mousse. Taste and adjust the seasoning to your liking and add the lemon juice. Pass the mousse through a fine sieve, into a bowl set onto ice. Fold in the remaining cream.

At this point I like to check on the flavour. The best way to do this is to take a teaspoon of the mix, wrap it in plastic wrap and poach it gently in simmering water for a couple of minutes. Taste the cooked mousse and adjust the balance of seasoning in the mix according to your liking.

The mousse will keep refrigerated for 2 days, but is not suitable for freezing.

Little gruyère and onion tartlets with
chive sabayon (page 116)

Lobster and parmesan omelette (page 117)

Little gruyère and onion tartlets with chive sabayon

These tartlets make wonderful canapés if you're having a party. Otherwise serve them as a starter or as a light lunch with a simple mixed salad.

serves 4

PREP TIME 20 MINUTES COOK TIME 10 MINUTES

250 g (9 oz) Shortcrust Pastry (page 322)
1 tablespoon grapeseed oil
½ onion, finely sliced
100 g (3 ½ oz) gruyère cheese, grated
2 eggs
280 ml (9 ½ fl oz) cream
salt and pepper
200 ml (7 fl oz) Hollandaise Sauce (page 92)
2 tablespoons finely chopped chives
pinch paprika
10 ml (¼ fl oz) Clarified Butter (page 91) (optional)

To prepare the tartlet shells, roll out the pastry on a lightly floured surface to a 3 mm (⅛ in) thickness. Use an 8 cm (3¼ in) pastry cutter to cut out 12 circles and use to line a 12 hole tartlet tin. Prick the bases with a fork and rest in the refrigerator for 30 minutes.

Preheat your oven to 180°C (350°F). Blind bake the pastry shells for 10 minutes, pricking the bases again if they start to puff up. When crisp and golden, remove them from the oven. Leave to firm up for a few minutes then carefully lift them out of the tin and leave to cool on a wire rack. The tartlet cases may be made ahead of time.

To make the filling, heat the oil in a heavy-based frying pan and sweat the onion for 5 minutes, until it is soft and translucent. Allow to cool. Divide the cool onion and the grated cheese between the 12 tartlets and arrange them on a baking tray.

Whisk together the eggs and 200 ml (7 fl oz) of the cream. Season with salt and pepper and pour into the tart shells, so they are not quite filled to the top. Bake in the preheated oven for 8 minutes, or until the filling is barely set. Remove from the oven and heat an overhead grill (broiler) to its highest temperature.

Whisk the rest of the cream to soft peaks and fold it into the hollandaise sauce with the chives and paprika. Spread a spoonful on top of each tartlet and place under the grill for a minute, until the topping puffs up to a golden glaze – watch carefully to make sure the tartlets don't burn. Just before serving, brush the warm tartlets with a little clarified butter and serve straight away.

116

Lobster and parmesan omelette

A simple omelette is one of life's great pleasures. This version is unashamedly luxurious, but I urge every person who reads this book to try the recipe … it is to die for! Instead of lobster, the omelette can be made with fresh crab, marron, crayfish, rock lobster or yabby tails, prawns (shrimp) or even smoked salmon.

serves 4

 PREP TIME 20 MINUTES COOK TIME 4 MINUTES

1 roasted Lobster Tail (page 205)

200 ml (7 fl oz) Hollandaise Sauce (page 92)

250 ml (8½ fl oz) Lobster Bisque (page 58), reduced to 100 ml (3½ fl oz)

80 g (3 oz) freshly grated parmesan

½ tablespoon brandy

1 teaspoon English mustard

salt and pepper

few drops lemon juice

80 ml (3 fl oz) cream

8 eggs

20 g (¾ oz) butter

Remove the roasted lobster tail from the shell, cut into large chunks and set to one side.

Combine the hollandaise, reduced bisque, parmesan, brandy and mustard in a mixing bowl. Season with salt and pepper, add a few drops lemon juice and stir to combine. Whip the cream to soft peaks (page 233) and fold it into the sauce.

Preheat your oven grill (broiler) to its highest temperature.

Break the eggs into another mixing bowl and whisk together well. Lightly butter 4 roesti pans (or an egg-poaching pan with four holes) and place over a moderate heat. Divide the eggs between the 4 pans and cook for 2 minutes – they will still be quite runny in the middle.

Divide the lobster meat evenly between the 4 omelettes and spoon over a generous amount of sauce. Place the pans under the preheated grill and cook for a few minutes until the omelettes are puffed up and golden brown. Serve hot from the grill with crusty baguettes and plenty of cold French butter.

Preserving

It's hard for most of us to imagine
a time when there were no
refrigerators and freezers to help
prevent fresh food from spoiling.

Since ancient times, when foodstuffs were only available seasonally, all sorts of clever techniques have been devised to prolong the life of food over the course of the leaner winter months. These include salting, air-drying, smoking, pickling in vinegar or alcohol, preserving with sugar, and cooking and preserving in fat.

Perhaps the need to preserve our food in these ways no longer exists, but today these methods are still used and loved because of the delectable ways in which they add different flavours and textures to ingredients. Think of the pleasure we get from an intensely flavoured raspberry jam, or the spicy crunch of pickled vegetables. Or try to imagine life without cured jambon de Bayonne or smoked saucissons. As for me, I think it would be a dark and dreary world without my beloved confits (which are covered in a separate chapter, see pages 135–43) and without the vast range of charcuterie that is so characteristic of provincial French cooking.

For me, the very word 'charcuterie' conjures up memories of sun-kissed holidays in rural France. The word itself means 'cooked meat' and is traditionally based on pork meat or offal (variety meats). It's a vast area of cooking – probably best translated in English as 'small goods' – with nearly every region producing its own specialties.

Most charcuterie butchers will sell a wide variety of fresh and smoked sausages (think andouillettes, boudins blancs and noirs, dried, raw and cooked saucissons), cured meats, rillettes, pâtés and terrines, galantines, ballottines, hams and brawn (known, rather confrontingly in French, as fromage de tête – head cheese!).

Most charcuterie is probably beyond the scope of home kitchens, and let's face it, good delicatessens have a mind-boggling range of these delicacies – even if not to the same extent as in France. But there are some simple and delectable pâtés, terrines and sausages that are easy to make at home and are well worth it for the satisfaction.

Preserves, pickles and chutneys are a natural accompaniment to the rich flavours of charcuterie and there's nothing quite like them for livening up leftovers. They range from the simplicity of fresh garden vegetables pickled in spiced vinegars to mixtures of fruits or vegetables simmered with sugar and vinegar to make sweet-and-sour relishes and chutneys. At the sweet end of the repertoire there is a vast range of spiced fruits, candied fruits, fruits preserved in alcohol, and of course jams and jellies.

Pâté de campagne

This is one of my favourite country-style pâtés. It's rustic, easy to make and very tasty. It's also very versatile; instead of pork, try using rabbit, game, wild boar or veal – all equally delicious. Serve it as a starter or a light lunch with a green salad, plenty of crusty bread and a good dollop of Piccalilli (page 131).

makes 1 terrine

✎ PREP TIME 1 HOUR 🍶 MARINATING TIME OVERNIGHT 🍲 COOK TIME 90 MINUTES

50 ml (2 fl oz) vegetable oil	550 g (1 lb 4 oz) hard pork back fat
2 onions, roughly diced	1 sprig rosemary, finely chopped
80 ml (3 fl oz) port	3 sprigs thyme, finely chopped
80 ml (3 fl oz) Madeira	pinch ground mace
¼ teaspoon pepper	6 juniper berries, ground
½ teaspoon salt	6 cloves, ground
550 g (1 lb 4 oz) pork shoulder or neck	50 g (2 oz) unsalted shelled pistachio nuts
125 g (4½ oz) smoked bacon	50 g (2 oz) butter
150 g (5½ oz) chicken livers	150 g (5½ oz) wild mushrooms, roughly sliced

Heat the oil in a heavy-based saucepan. Fry the onions over a moderate heat until caramelised a deep golden brown, about 15 minutes. Add the port and Madeira and season with salt and pepper. Bring to the boil, then remove the pan from the heat and leave to cool.

Mince (grind) the pork, bacon, chicken livers and 250 g (9 oz) of the back fat through the coarse setting of your mincer/grinder (or ask your butcher to do this for you). Place in a large mixing bowl and add the onion mixture and all the herbs and spices. Use your hands to mix everything together thoroughly then cover with plastic wrap and refrigerate overnight.

The next day, put the pistachio nuts in a saucepan and cover with cold water. Bring to the boil then immediately remove the pan from the heat. Carefully peel off the outer skins, leaving you with the bright green nuts.

Heat the butter in a frying pan until it foams. Add the mushrooms, season with salt and pepper and sauté for a few minutes until golden brown. Remove from the heat and drain.

Add the pistachio nuts and mushrooms to the minced (ground) meats and combine thoroughly. At this point I like to check on the flavour. The best way to do this is to take a teaspoon of the mix, wrap it in plastic wrap and poach it gently in simmering water for a couple of minutes. Taste the cooked mix and adjust the balance of seasoning in the mix according to your liking.

Preheat the oven to 150°C (300°F). Line a 1.5 litre (51 fl oz) terrine mould with 2 sheets of plastic wrap, making sure there is plenty of overhang. Use a sharp knife to cut the remaining piece of back fat into thin long slices.

Line the terrine with sliced back fat, overlapping each piece slightly – they should overhang the sides too. Spoon in the mix, pressing it firmly into the sides and corners. Bang the terrine on the bench to disperse any air pockets. Smooth the surface of the terrine and fold the slices of back fat up over the top. Pull up one side of the plastic wrap, stretching it firmly over the top. Repeat with the other side and then fold up the short ends in the same way.

Bake the terrine in a bain-marie (page 237) for 1½ hours, until the internal temperature reaches 78°C (170°F), or the juices run clear when the terrine is pierced with a skewer. Remove the terrine from the bain-marie and set it in a sink filled with ice for 20 minutes. Once cold, refrigerate for 3 days before using. The terrine will keep in the refrigerator for up to 10 days.

Roast venison sausages

These are fantastic pure meat sausages, free of the preservatives and 'filler' that even many 'gourmet' sausages contain. The venison can be replaced with wild boar, Wagyu beef, rare-breed pork, rabbit or even veal.

makes just under 1 kg (2 lb 3 oz), enough for 4 serves

⁄⁄ PREP TIME 30 MINUTES 🍶 MARINATING TIME OVERNIGHT 🍳 COOK TIME 10 MINUTES

4 tablespoons cooking oil	450 g (1 lb) venison meat or trimmings
2 medium onions, roughly diced	125 g (4½ oz) pancetta
salt and pepper	225 g (8 oz) hard pork back fat
100 ml (3½ fl oz) red wine	50 g (2 oz) fine breadcrumbs
50 ml (2 fl oz) brandy	2 whole eggs
1 tablespoon thyme leaves	100 g (3½ oz) sausage casings

For the perfect supper dish serve with horseradish-flavoured Potato Purée (page 212), Tomato Chutney (page 130) and a little watercress salad.

Heat half the oil in a heavy-based saucepan. Add the onions, season with salt and pepper and sauté over a moderate heat until caramelised a deep golden brown, about 15 minutes. Add the wine and simmer until reduced by a third. Add the brandy, bring back to the boil, then add the thyme leaves and remove the pan from the heat to cool.

Mince (grind) the venison, pancetta and back fat through the coarse setting of your mincer/grinder (or ask your butcher to do this for you). Place in a large mixing bowl and add the onion mixture. Use your hands to mix everything together thoroughly then cover with plastic wrap and refrigerate for 24 hours.

The next day, mix in the breadcrumbs and eggs and season well. At this point I like to check on the flavour. The best way to do this is to take a teaspoon of the mix and fry it for a minute or two on each side. Taste and adjust the balance of seasoning in the mix according to your liking.

The easiest way to fill the sausage casings (if your electric mixer doesn't have a special sausage-filling attachment) is to use a piping bag. Spoon the mix in and squeeze it carefully into the casings. Use your hands to gently squeeze along the length of the casing, to make sure the mix is evenly distributed and there are no air pockets. Cut and tie to your preferred lengths.

Preheat the oven to 160°C (320°F). Heat the rest of the oil in a heavy-based frying pan. Fry the sausages over a moderate heat, turning so they are evenly coloured. Transfer to the oven and bake for 8 minutes. Remove from the oven and allow to rest for a minute before serving.

If you don't want to eat them straight away, the sausages will keep in the refrigerator for a week and up to 2 months in the freezer.

Cured duck ham

Air-drying meat or fish is one of the most ancient preserving methods. It's very easy, requiring only a bit of time and none of your attention! The end result is very similar to prosciutto. The flavour is both sweet and earthy and slightly musty, and the meat has a lovely firm texture. Serve as part of an hors d'oeuvre selection, scatter thin slices over salads or even add to egg dishes (page 112).

makes 4 cured breasts

⫽ PREP TIME 10 MINUTES ⬥ MARINATING TIME 24 HOURS ✺ CURING TIME 7 DAYS

4 duck breasts

50 g (2 oz) Aromatic Confit Salt (page 19)

Trim the breasts of any excess skin and fat. Rub the salt in thoroughly. Place in a bowl, cover with plastic wrap and refrigerate overnight while they marinate. As well as adding flavour, the aromatic salt starts the curing process by drawing out moisture, and helps prevent bacterial growth.

The next day, rinse the duck breasts briefly and pat dry. Wrap each one in a piece of muslin or cheesecloth and hang in a cool dry place with good air circulation. Leave to dry cure for about 7 days, until much of the moisture has evaporated and the meat is firm and the flavour concentrated.

Once cured the duck will keep for 1 month in the refrigerator.

Salt cod – the modern way

A technique that originated in Norway, salt cod spread to become staple fare all around Europe because the heavy salting ensures it keeps for months – even years. In Australia you can buy imported salt cod from delicatessens; it's as stiff as a board, hard as a rock and needs to be soaked for hours to remove the salt and make it suitable for cooking. These days, on-boat refrigeration means we are no longer as dependent on this method of preservation. In my view this is a good thing, as I think it destroys all the natural flavour of the fish. Here's my modern method of salting; it just takes a few hours and I also add lemon and thyme to subtly enhance the delicate flavour of the fish. To cook, I poach it in aromatic milk until it is just cooked, but still translucent in the centre. Naturally you can also use this to make brandade. True North Atlantic cod is not available fresh in Australia, but you can use similar flaky, firmly textured fish such as blue eye, hapuka, warehou, bass grouper or mahi mahi.

makes 500 g (1 lb 2 oz)

PREP TIME 10 MINUTES MARINATING TIME 2 HOURS COOK TIME 6 MINUTES

100 g (3½ oz) sea salt

freshly ground white pepper

zest of 1 lemon

4 sprigs thyme

1 bay leaf, split in half

2 garlic cloves

500 g (1 lb 2 oz) North Atlantic cod or blue eye fillet, skin removed

600 ml (20½ fl oz) milk

Put the salt in a mortar with a generous grind of pepper, the lemon zest, half the thyme, half the bay leaf and 1 garlic clove. Pound thoroughly then rub the salt mixture all over the cod. Cover with plastic wrap and refrigerate for 2 hours.

In a heavy-based saucepan, heat the milk to a gentle simmer with the remaining herbs and garlic clove. Rinse the cod gently then add to the pan and poach gently for 6 minutes. If using straight away, remove from the poaching liquor and break into rough flakes. Use the salt cod to make brandade or as a garnish for salads or egg dishes (page 113). Otherwise allow the cod to cool in the poaching liquor then cover and store in the refrigerator for up to 5 days.

Savoury pickles and preserves

Fennel escabèche

makes 300 g (10½ oz)

PREP TIME 15 MINUTES   COOK TIME 30 MINUTES

1 onion

1 large or 2 medium fennel bulbs

150 ml (5 fl oz) olive oil

pinch saffron

10 coriander seeds

salt and pepper

50 ml (2 fl oz) chardonnay vinegar

few drops lemon juice

Use a mandoline or very sharp knife to slice the onion and fennel as finely as you can.

Heat 50 ml (2 fl oz) of the olive oil in a heavy-based saucepan. Add the onion, fennel and spices and season with salt and pepper. Simmer gently for 20 minutes until the onion and fennel are translucent. Add the vinegar and return to the boil for a few minutes. Remove from the heat, stir in the remaining olive oil, season again and finish with the lemon juice.

The escabèche will keep in a sealed container in the refrigerator for 1 week.

Spiced pear chutney

makes 500 g (1 lb 2 oz)

PREP TIME 20 MINUTES   COOK TIME 1 HOUR 40 MINUTES

1 onion, diced to a small brunoise (page 208)

2 Granny Smith apples, peeled, cored
   and roughly diced

3 Tomatoes Concasse (page 219)

1 orange

1 teaspoon salt

60 g (2 oz) sultanas (golden raisins)

100 g (3½ oz) sugar

½ teaspoon ground cinnamon

½ teaspoon ground nutmeg

1 level tablespoon grated fresh ginger

150 ml (5 fl oz) white wine vinegar

pinch saffron

375 g (13 oz) Beurre Bosc pears, peeled, cored
   and roughly diced

Put the onion, apples and tomatoes in a large heavy-based saucepan. Grate the orange over the pan to capture all the spray and oils then squeeze in the juice. Add all the remaining ingredients, except for the pears, stir well and simmer gently, uncovered, for 1 hour.

Prepare the pears and add them to the pan. Return to a gentle simmer and cook for a further 40 minutes. Ladle the chutney into sterilised jars and seal well. The chutney may be eaten straight away, but definitely benefits from a few days' maturing. It will keep for up to a month in the refrigerator once opened.

Tomato chutney

makes 600 g (1 lb 5 oz)

⟋ PREP TIME 20 MINUTES ⌁ COOK TIME 2 HOURS

20 ml (¾ fl oz) vegetable oil

2 onions, finely sliced

40 g (1½ oz) sugar

50 ml (2 fl oz) sherry vinegar

200 ml (7 fl oz) white wine

1 kg (2 lb 3 oz) vine-ripened tomatoes, roughly chopped

4 star anise

8 coriander seeds

6 sprigs thyme

1 small red chilli

4 garlic cloves

Heat the oil in a heavy-based saucepan. Add the onion and simmer gently for 5 minutes until it is translucent. Sprinkle on the sugar and cook for another few minutes until it caramelises. Add the vinegar and wine and bring to the boil. Cook for a minute, then add the tomatoes and stir well.

Place the star anise, coriander seeds, thyme, chilli and garlic in a mortar and crush lightly. Scrape into a square of muslin (cheesecloth) and tie securely. Tuck the spice bag in amongst the tomatoes, tying the string to the handle. Cook at a very gentle simmer for 2 hours, stirring regularly, until the chutney is thick.

Ladle the chutney into sterilised jars and seal well. It will keep in the refrigerator for 2 weeks.

Baby pickled onions

makes 1 kg (2 lb 3 oz)

⟋ PREP TIME 30 MINUTES ◗ MARINATING TIME 24 HOURS
⌁ COOK TIME 10 MINUTES ✦ MATURING TIME 1 MONTH

1 kg (2 lb 3 oz) pickling (pearl) onions

100 g (3½ oz) salt

700 ml (23½ fl oz) balsamic vinegar

300 ml (10 fl oz) cider vinegar

1 tablespoon mustard seeds

10 cloves

8 black peppercorns

1 cinnamon stick

12 coriander seeds

few sprigs rosemary and thyme (optional)

Bring a large pan of salted water to the boil. Add the onions and blanch for 2–3 minutes. Drain and rinse in cold water, then peel.

Sprinkle the onions with the salt, rolling them around to ensure they are well coated. Leave to dry-marinate in the refrigerator for 24 hours.

Rinse the onions thoroughly. Place all the remaining ingredients in a large non-reactive saucepan and bring to the boil. Add the onions and boil for 6–8 minutes.

Ladle the onions into sterilised jars then pour on enough vinegar to cover them completely. Tuck in a few sprigs of herbs if you like. Set aside for 1 month to mature. Once opened, the onions will keep in the refrigerator for up to 1 year.

Piccalilli

makes 2 large jars

PREP TIME 1 HOUR ▮ MARINATING TIME 24 HOURS ⌁ COOK TIME 20 MINUTES ✸ MATURING TIME 1 MONTH

1 cauliflower, cut into small florets

6 onions, cut into 1 cm (½ in) dice

100 g (3½ oz) salt

1 cucumber, peeled, deseeded and cut into 1 cm (½ in) dice

600 ml (20½ fl oz) white wine vinegar

300 ml (10 fl oz) malt vinegar

½ teaspoon dried chilli flakes

200 g (7 oz) sugar

50 g (2 oz) English mustard powder

25 g (1 oz) ground turmeric

2 tablespoons cornflour (cornstarch)

salt and pepper

Mix the onions and cauliflower in a bowl and sprinkle liberally with most of the salt. Cover with plastic wrap and leave for 24 hours.

The next day, salt the cucumber dice lightly and leave for 10 minutes. Rinse all the salted vegetables under cold running water. Tip into a colander to drain, then pat dry.

Combine the two vinegars in a large non-reactive saucepan. Add the chilli and bring to the boil, then remove from the heat and leave to infuse for 30 minutes. Strain the vinegar and discard the chilli. Leave to cool slightly.

Mix the sugar, mustard, turmeric and cornflour with a few tablespoons of the cooled vinegar to make a paste. Boil the rest of the vinegar and whisk it into the paste, then return to the pan. Boil for 3 minutes until thickened.

Combine all the vegetables in a mixing bowl then pour on the spiced vinegar. Season and stir well. Ladle into sterilised jars and set aside for 1 month to mature. Once opened, the piccalilli will keep in the refrigerator for up to 6 months.

Seville orange marmalade

makes around 500 ml (17 fl oz)

⁄ PREP TIME 10 MINUTES ⊨ RESTING TIME 24 HOURS ⊏ COOK TIME 3 HOURS

2 kg (4 lb 6 oz) Seville oranges
7 litres (238 fl oz) water
1 teaspoon salt
sugar

Slice the oranges very finely, removing the seeds and central membrane. These contain a lot of pectin, which helps the marmalade to set, so place them on a square of muslin (cheesecloth), tie it into a bag and set aside.

Pour the water into a large preserving pan. Add the sliced oranges and salt and bring to the boil. Lower the heat and simmer for 1–2 hours, until the oranges are soft and easily squashed between your fingers. Remove the pan from the heat and allow to cool. Hang the muslin bag from a wooden spoon balanced on the rim of the pan, so that the bag is submerged in the liquid. Transfer to the refrigerator and leave for 24 hours.

The next day remove the muslin bag and tip the orange mixture into a bowl to weigh it. Weigh out an equal measure of sugar. Return the orange mixture to the saucepan and bring it to the boil. Add the sugar and bring to the boil, then lower the heat and simmer for 1½ hours.

To test if the marmalade has reached its setting point, place a couple of saucers in the freezer to chill. Spoon a little marmalade onto a cold saucer and place it in the fridge to cool. You'll see if you have a set by pushing the surface of the marmalade with your finger: if it is thick with a crinkly skin it's set. Otherwise, continue to boil and test at 10-minute intervals until it does set.

Remove the pan from the heat and skim off any surface scum. Leave to settle for around 15 minutes before spooning into sterilised jars. Seal while still hot. The marmalade will keep up to 12 months in a cool place.

Jam

The same cooking method is used for
all sorts of jams, such as strawberry,
blueberry, blackberry, cherry or apricot.

makes around 500 ml (17 fl oz)
☞ COOK TIME 45 MINUTES

1 kg (2 lb 3 oz) fruit of your choice

1 kg (2 lb 3 oz) sugar

Combine the fruit and sugar in a large preserving
pan. It's important that you do use a pan with a large
surface area as this helps the evaporation process,
ensuring the fruit cooks down to an intensely
concentrated flavour and that it sets at a good
consistency. Cook for about 45 minutes, stirring from
time to time to ensure the fruit doesn't stick and
burn. The jam should reach setting point at about
106°C (223°F). To test, place a couple of saucers in
the freezer to chill. Spoon a little jam onto a cold
saucer and place it in the fridge to cool. You'll see if
you have a set by pushing the surface of the jam with
your finger: if it is thick with a crinkly skin it's set.
Otherwise, continue to boil and test at 10-minute
intervals until it does set.

Remove the pan from the heat and skim off any
surface scum. Leave to settle for around 15 minutes
before spooning into sterilised jars. Seal while still hot.
The jam will keep up to 12 months in a cool place.

Confit citrus rind in syrup

Use any citrus rind or any combination
of rinds. I like to use this as a garnish for
citrus tarts, but it's also lovely folded
through ice creams or added to brioche
or cakes to add a sweet lemony zing.

makes 750 ml (25 fl oz)
✎ PREP TIME 10 MINUTES ☞ COOK TIME 1 HOUR

1 kg (2 lb 3 oz) citrus fruit

500 ml (17 fl oz) water

625 g (1 lb 6 oz) sugar

Peel the citrus fruit and remove as much pith as you
can from the peelings. You can either leave it in long
lengths, or shred it into thin strips. Bring a small pan
of water to the boil and blanch the peel three times to
remove any bitterness.

Combine the water and sugar in a preserving pan.
Heat slowly until the sugar has completely dissolved,
then increase the heat and bring to the boil. Add the
citrus rind and cook at 65°C/149°F (just below a
simmer), for about 30 minutes, until the rind is soft.

Remove the pan from the heat and ladle rind into
sterilised jars. Pour on enough syrup to cover
completely and seal while still hot. The confit citrus
rinds will keep up to 12 months in a cool place.

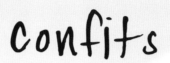

confits

The French word 'confit' means
preserved, and is perhaps best known
as a specialty of south-western France.
Originally this ancient method was used
to cook and, more specifically, to preserve
meats such as pork, goose or duck in
their own rendered fat.

Confit meats were stored in earthenware jars or pots to be eaten during the long winter months when fresh meat was less readily available. Its appeal is in the exquisite, melting texture – far closer to fresh meat than other preserving techniques, such as pickling, drying or smoking.

In contemporary cooking the definition of a confit has broadened, and it no longer specifically refers to preserved foods. Instead all kinds of foodstuffs – even seafood and vegetables – may be slow-cooked in rendered fat or even certain oils, to a divine tenderness.

Confit dishes are fairly straightforward to prepare, although the specifics will vary depending on the nature of the ingredient. Dense cuts of meat such as pork belly, neck or shoulder of veal and lamb, poultry legs and wings are first rubbed in an aromatic salt and left to cure overnight. The pieces of meat are then completely submerged in liquid fat and baked in the oven, long and slow, until soft as butter. Once cooked, the meat is covered in liquid fat which sets around it in a white blanket.

Less robust ingredients, such as fish, seafood or vegetables, need only to be salted for a few hours, ideally in a light citrus-flavoured salt. They are better suited to cooking in a neutral-flavoured fat or oil that doesn't overpower their more delicate flavour.

Good-quality rendered goose and duck fat can be bought from specialty food stores and even from some butcher's shops. You can also render your own confit fat at home simply by purchasing pieces of raw duck, goose or chicken fat from the butcher and cooking it for a few hours over a very low heat with a little water and a few aromatics. Once rendered, sieve and store it in a sterilised container in the refrigerator.

Confit belly of pork

serves 4

⟋ PREP TIME 10 MINUTES   ☖ MARINATING TIME 24 HOURS
☐ COOK TIME 3–4 HOURS

---

800 g (1 lb 12 oz) pork belly

100 g (3½ oz) Aromatic Confit Salt (page 19)

2 litres (68 fl oz) rendered duck fat

½ garlic bulb

6 sprigs thyme

1 bay leaf

20 ml (¾ fl oz) vegetable oil

Follow the same method as for the Confit Chicken (page 138). The pork belly will need to marinate for 24 hours and will take 3–4 hours to cook. When it is done, you should be able to push the handle of a spoon through the meat with little resistance. Allow the pork belly to cool a little then carefully turn it skin-side down and remove any pieces of cartilage. Weight the pork belly down between 2 baking trays and refrigerate for 2–3 hours.

Preheat the oven to 180°C (350°C). Remove the pork belly from the fridge and cut into neat squares. Heat the oil in a heavy-based frying pan and fry until the skin starts to colour. Transfer to the preheated oven and cook for 5–10 minutes until the meat has warmed through and the skin is crisp and golden. Serve immediately with your chosen accompaniments.

This is absolutely delicious served with Caramelised Sweet and Sour Turnips (page 225) and Vanilla and Apple Cider Reduction (page 22).

Confit chicken

This recipe can also be used for duck leg quarters and for other game birds such as pheasant and guinea fowl. You can even confit chicken or duck thighs or wings, although you'll need to reduce the cooking time by half for the wings.

serves 4

⟋ PREP TIME 10 MINUTES ▯ MARINATING TIME 6 HOURS ⌣ COOK TIME 3 HOURS

50 g (2 oz) Aromatic Confit Salt (page 19)

4 x 250 g (9 oz) chicken leg quarters

1 litre (34 fl oz) rendered duck fat

3 garlic cloves, roughly crushed

4 sprigs thyme

1 bay leaf

Serve with a simple mixed salad, Roasted Baby Carrots or Parsnips (page 224) or Caramelised Parsnips (page 211) and just about any potato dish you fancy.

Rub the aromatic salt all over the chicken pieces, wrap them in plastic wrap and refrigerate for 6 hours while they marinate.

Preheat the oven to 110°C (230°F). Rinse the chicken pieces briefly and pat dry. Slowly heat the rendered duck fat in a heatproof braising pan, then add the chicken pieces, garlic cloves and herbs, ensuring the meat is completely submerged. Cut a piece of baking paper to the size of the pan to make a cartouche and place on the surface. Do not cover the pan.

Bake for 3 hours, turning the chicken pieces around in the fat every half hour or so. It is important that the temperature be low and even – just a very gentle blip. At the end of the cooking time the meat should come away from the bone easily. Remove from the oven, drain the chicken pieces in a colander and allow to cool.

Strain the fat through a fine colander into a clean dish. Arrange the chicken pieces in the dish and pour on the fat to cover them. Allow to cool then chill until ready to use.

If using straight away, preheat the oven to 180°C (350°F), then fry the drained chicken pieces in a heavy-based pan until the skin starts to colour. Transfer to the oven for 5–10 minutes, until the meat has warmed through and the skin is crisp and golden.

Confit rolled chicken thighs with prosciutto and cep mushrooms

You could also use duck, pheasant or guinea fowl thighs, which work equally well. As they are all more or less the same size, the marinating and cooking times will be the same. Ask your butcher to bone the thighs for you, but keep the skin intact.

serves 4

PREP TIME 30 MINUTES ▯ MARINATING TIME 4 HOURS ▭ COOK TIME 2 HOURS

4 x 250 g (9 oz) boned chicken thighs

20 g (¾ oz) dried cep (porcini) mushrooms

50 ml (2 fl oz) Madeira

8 thin slices prosciutto

salt and pepper

1 litre (34 fl oz) rendered duck fat

I like to serve these with Bread Sauce (page 83), Pommes Fondant (page 218) and Roasted Baby Carrots or Parsnips (page 224).

Open out the thighs and lay them on a tray, skin side down. Lay a few cèpes on each thigh, then drizzle on the Madeira. Cover with plastic wrap and refrigerate for 4 hours while they marinate.

Preheat your oven to 100°C (210°F). Uncover the chicken thighs and place a slice of prosciutto on top of each one. Roll each into a neat cylinder and secure with butcher's twine. Slowly heat the rendered duck fat in a heatproof braising pan, then add the chicken thighs, ensuring the meat is completely submerged. Cut a piece of baking paper to the size of the pan to make a cartouche and place on the surface. Do not cover the pan. Bake for 2 hours, turning the thighs around in the fat every half hour or so.

Remove the chicken thighs from the oven and drain in a colander. Fry the chicken thighs in a heavy-based pan, turning so the skin colours golden brown all over. Transfer to a chopping board and snip away the twine. Use a sharp knife to cut each thigh into 3 medallions. Lift onto your serving plates and serve immediately with your chosen accompaniments.

Chicken wings with seared scallops, peas and Albufera sauce

For neat presentation I remove the wing tips first. After cooking I carefully remove the remaining bones – they come out very easily – and weight the meat down between 2 baking trays overnight. This ensures they are nice and flat when you fry them. If you want to be really clever, bone the wings out before cooking them, leaving one small bone in so they look like a small drumstick. This is a great way of serving them as a canapé.

serves 4

✐ PREP TIME 20 MINUTES 🍾 MARINATING TIME 3 HOURS 🍲 COOK TIME 90 MINUTES

10 ml (¼ fl oz) vegetable oil

12 confit chicken wings (see page 138)

12 fresh scallops

30 g (1 oz) butter

salt and pepper

few drops lemon juice

200 g (7 oz) Buttered Peas (page 227)

200 ml (7 fl oz) Albufera Sauce (page 82)

Heat the oil in a heavy-based frying pan. Fry the chicken wings on each side until golden brown. Remove from the pan and keep warm. Add the scallops to the pan and season. Cook for 1 minute then add the butter to the pan and allow to foam. Cook for another minute, then turn the scallops, add the lemon juice and remove them from the pan. Reserve the pan juices.

To serve, place 3 scallops and 3 chicken wings on each plate. Scatter on the buttered peas. Use a hand-blender to lightly aerate the Albufera sauce and spoon it over the scallops and chicken wings. Finish with a drizzle of the reserved pan juices and serve immediately.

Plump juicy chicken wings are often overlooked as being cheap and dull. But try them cooked in a confit and then fried until golden and crisp.

Warm citrus-marinated ocean trout confit

Confit salmon and trout have been in the classic French repertoire for decades, in one form or another. In my favourite version the fish is marinated first to infuse the flesh with a lovely citrus flavour. I add a little olive oil to the duck fat, which gives it a more fruity, peppery dimension. The neutral grapeseed oil acts to fuse these flavours together so that neither overpowers the other. Confit fish is divine as the extremely gentle heat is just enough to set the protein to a wobbly, tender, jelly-like consistency that melts in the mouth.

serves 4

PREP TIME 15 MINUTES   MARINATING TIME 2 HOURS
COOK TIME 30 MINUTES

600 g (1 lb 5 oz) fillet of ocean trout, skinned,
    pin bones, belly and blood line removed

50 g (2 oz) Wet Citrus Salt (page 19)

200 ml (7 fl oz) rendered duck fat

200 ml (7 fl oz) olive oil

200 ml (7 fl oz) grapeseed oil

Rub the aromatic salt all over the fish, wrap it in plastic wrap and refrigerate for 2 hours while it marinates.

Preheat the oven to its lowest setting. Rinse the fish briefly and pat dry. Cut into 4 neat portions, each about 150 g (5½ oz). Combine the rendered duck fat and oils in a heatproof braising pan, and heat very gently to about 45°C (110°F). Add the fish pieces, ensuring they are completely submerged. Cook for 30 minutes until soft – they should still look raw, but will have cooked in the fat to a lovely wobbly pinkness. Serve immediately with your chosen accompaniments.

Confit tomatoes

Although not really a confit in the literal sense of the word, the end result is similar in that the tomatoes achieve a delectable soft consistency and a rich salty-sweet flavour. They make a delicious addition to salads instead of the usual sun-dried variety!

serves 4

PREP TIME 15 MINUTES   COOK TIME 15 MINUTES

10 vine-ripened tomatoes

50 g (2 oz) Aromatic Confit Salt (page 19)

1 cup Herbes de Provence (page 14)

30 ml (1 fl oz) Lemon and Garlic Oil (page 75)

Preheat the oven to 180ºC (350°F). Cut the tomatoes in half and squeeze out the seeds. Scatter the aromatic salt and the herbs onto a baking tray and arrange the tomatoes on top. Sprinkle on the oil and cover loosely with foil.

Bake for 15 minutes then remove from the oven. Carefully peel away the skins while the tomatoes are still warm. Hang them in muslin (cheesecloth) squares in small batches overnight. Make sure you retain the juices that drip through.

Serve the confit tomatoes as an accompaniment to grilled lamb cutlets or roasted fish or poultry. They are also delicious scattered into salads. If you don't plan on using them straight away, store them in an airtight container with about 250 ml (8½ fl oz) of the reserved juices and top them up with olive oil to cover completely.

Serve the trout with Fennel Escabèche (page 129), Fennel Coulis (page 74) and a salad of mixed herbs and baby cress.

Steaming, poaching and sous-vide

I am often drawn to the simplicity of these most ancient of cooking techniques.

Archaeologists tell us that boiling, poaching and steaming predate the discovery of fire. It seems that ancient man's first go at 'cooking' raw ingredients to make them more palatable involved using hot stones and water from naturally occurring hot springs. And once he had learned how to fashion cooking pots, this primitive technique evolved into a sophisticated and varied art. These methods have become popular in recent times because they are delicate, maintain the natural flavour of the food and have natural health benefits from not using cooking fats.

Cooking with hot water is a real no-fuss method that is ideal for many ingredients – both savoury and sweet. It's probably best suited to foods that have a delicate texture, such as fish, seafood, poultry, vegetables and fruit. With these techniques it's all about preserving and intensifying the natural flavours of the foods, so it is vital to use super-fresh and top-notch produce. The water may be kept plain or it can be lightly salted, flavoured with herbs and aromatic vegetables or with sweet spices, citrus, vanilla or even wine, all of which cleverly draws out and intensifies the natural flavours.

The difference between the various techniques revolves around the speed and temperature at which they are cooked. The quickest method, blanching, is really more of a preparation for further use: it's used to loosen the skins of nuts, to reduce strong flavours and to 'set' delicate offal. It's perhaps most commonly used for green vegetables, which are dunked into rapidly boiling salted water and cooked as quickly as possible to preserve the vividness of colour and flavour.

Apart from this technique, though, not many ingredients benefit from actually being boiled, as this tends to break-up or over-cook them. In fact, most foods need to be poached, a slower, gentler cooking method that enables them to cook through completely without disintegrating.

Poaching – by which we mean simmering gently at around 80–90°C (175–195°F) (the cooking liquid should only 'shiver' in the pot) – is ideal for very delicate foods and also for those that are naturally tough and fibrous (like certain cuts of meat) and need to be cooked for a long time to become tender. One of the reasons for poaching, rather than steaming, is because you end up with a flavoursome poaching liquor that can be made into a sauce. You really need to have a heavy-based saucepan for successful poaching, so as to maintain the low, constant temperature.

Steaming is an even gentler method of cooking than poaching, because the ingredients don't come into direct contact with the cooking medium or heat source. Curiously, steaming actually cooks food at higher temperatures than poaching, which means it seals in the flavour and results in a wonderfully tender and moist texture. With ingredients like fish or poultry, the heat also renders out some of the natural fats, but recycle their natural flavour back into the food. Steaming has the added advantage of keeping more of the vitamins and minerals in the foods themselves, rather than leaching them out into the cooking water.

Another steaming method that I especially love is cooking 'en papillotte'. It's well suited to small whole fish or to fillets of fish, which are wrapped up in a piece of baking paper or foil with a little liquid, herbs and aromatic vegetables and baked in the oven. The paper puffs up in the heat to create a sort of mini steamer that locks in and magically intensifies the flavours. It's also a great way of creating a bit of theatre at the dining table, as people love breaking open their own individual parcels to release the wonderful aromas.

The gentlest cooking method of all, sous-vide (literally, 'under vacuum'), is also one of the most modern, and is a brilliant example of the way current thinking has built upon and improved the more traditional approach. In sous-vide

Previous spread: Coral trout with lemon verbena (page 155)

cooking, ingredients are sealed and vacuumed in heat-resistant bags, and are cooked at very low and precise temperatures. Until recently, it was really only undertaken in professional kitchens that had expensive machines and its main use was to extend the storage life of foodstuffs. Thanks to modern-masters, such as American chef Charlie Trotter, the sous-vide approach is now filtering into domestic kitchens. Relatively inexpensive sealing machines are more readily available, and you can even achieve acceptable results using a sealable plastic bag. The beauty of sous-vide cooking is that it results in extraordinarily flavoursome food and virtually no nutrients are lost in the cooking process.

Steamed snapper

serves 4

✎ PREP TIME 5 MINUTES ☐ COOK TIME 8 MINUTES

4 x 150 g (5 ½ oz) snapper fillets
50 ml (2 fl oz) olive oil
salt and pepper
few drops lemon juice

Arrange a steamer or double boiler over a moderate heat. Skin the snapper fillets if you like, but this is not essential. Brush each with olive oil, season and sprinkle on the lemon juice. Cut 4 squares of baking paper and arrange a snapper fillet on each. Place in the steamer, one at a time, and cook, covered, for 8 minutes. The snapper is cooked when tender, just giving way if you gently prod the flesh with a knife. It should still be transparent in the middle. Keep warm while you steam the remaining fillets.

Steaming

Steamed baby clams, squid and baby gem

Serve this wonderful lemon-scented seafood with the steamed snapper – or even as a delicate pasta sauce.

serves 4

✎ PREP TIME 15 MINUTES ☐ COOK TIME 5 MINUTES

200 ml (7 fl oz) Lemon-scented Clam Jus (page 83)
1 kg (2 lb 3 oz) clams
2 x 200 g (7 oz) cleaned squid tubes, cut into small pieces
1 head baby/little gem lettuce, cut into small pieces
2 tablespoons finely chopped chives

Heat the clam jus in a saucepan over a high heat, add the clams and cover. Steam for 2 minutes until the clams open, then add the squid to the pan. Steam for a further minute then remove the pan from the heat, stir in the lettuce and chives and toss everything together well. Serve immediately. Divide the clam mixture between 4 serving bowls and top with a piece of steamed fish.

Red mullet 'en papillote' with
fennel and aromatics (page 150)

Steamed zucchini flowers and scallop mousse
with Noilly Prat and chervil velouté (page 151)

Red mullet 'en papillote' with fennel and aromatics

serves 4

PREP TIME 20 MINUTES   COOK TIME 15 MINUTES

50 ml (2 fl oz) olive oil

4 shallots, finely sliced

1 fennel bulb, finely sliced

1 pinch saffron

salt and pepper

4 fennel seeds

6 coriander seeds

2 star anise

8 small whole red mullet or small red snapper, cleaned

sea salt

1 lemon, finely sliced

50 ml (2 fl oz) Clarified Butter (page 91)

Serve with Crushed Potatoes (page 218) to soak up all the wonderful juices.

Preheat the oven to 190°C (375°F). Heat the oil in a heavy-based saucepan. Add the shallots, fennel and saffron and sweat over a low heat until soft and translucent, about 5 minutes. Season well.

In a small frying pan toast the fennel seeds, coriander seeds and star anise for a few minutes until aromatic. Tip into a mortar and use the pestle to crush them roughly.

Cut out 4 rectangles of baking paper, around 21 cm x 30 cm (8½ in x 12 in). Spoon some of the shallot-fennel mixture onto each piece and top with 2 red mullet. Sprinkle on the crushed spices, season and arrange a few lemon slices on each fillet.

And now for the origami. Bring the 2 longest sides of the paper to the centre over the fish and fold together neatly a few times. Fold up the two short ends. Flip the parcels over onto a baking tray to make neat parcels, with the folds underneath. Brush with clarified butter and bake for 15 minutes. The bags will puff up and become golden and glazed.

Remove from the oven and carefully lift the parcels onto serving plates. For maximum effect, serve straight away; the bags will start to deflate as soon as they are removed from the oven.

Encourage each diner to make an incision with kitchen scissors down the centre of the paper bags and peel the paper back to reveal the colourful and aromatic surprise within.

Steamed zucchini flowers and scallop mousse with Noilly Prat and chervil velouté

serves 4

PREP TIME 15 MINUTES · COOK TIME 6 MINUTES

250 g (9 oz) Scallop Mousse (page 113)

8 zucchinis (courgettes) with the flowers attached

olive oil

sea salt

pepper

few drops lemon juice

Noilly Prat and Chervil Velouté (page 82)

2 tablespoons chopped chervil

½ cup chervil sprigs

Arrange a steamer or a double boiler over a moderate heat.

Spoon the scallop mousse into a piping bag and carefully fill the zucchini flowers. Twist the ends of the flowers to seal. Brush the stuffed flowers with a little oil, season and sprinkle with lemon juice.

Warm the velouté over a gentle heat then stir in the chopped chervil and adjust the seasoning to taste.

Arrange the zucchini flowers on a piece of baking paper cut to the size of the steamer basket. You will probably fit 4 in at a time. Cover and steam for 6 minutes. The zucchinis will swell and puff up like a soufflé. Remove from the steamer and arrange on serving plates.

Pour on a little of the velouté and serve garnished with sprigs of chervil.

Poaching

Marinière of shellfish with basil

serves 4

🔪 PREP TIME 15 MINUTES 🍲 COOK TIME 6 MINUTES

1 leek, tough outer leaves discarded

200 ml (7 fl oz) Fish Velouté (page 82), or mix together 100 ml (3½ fl oz) each of white wine and cream

12 mussels

12 clams

12 prawns (shrimp)

12 scallops

salt and pepper

few drops lemon juice

1 cup basil leaves, roughly torn

I like to serve this delicate stew of poached seafood with a little drizzle of Herb or Basil Oil (page 75).

Use a sharp knife to cut the leek to neat dice.

Place the fish velouté in a heavy-based saucepan over a moderate heat and bring to a gentle simmer. Add the diced leek, mussels and clams and gently poach for 2 minutes until the shells just open. Add the prawns and cook for 1 minute, then turn them over in the poaching liquid and poach for a further minute. Add the scallops and poach for 30 seconds on each side.

Remove the pan from the heat, season and add the lemon juice. Scatter on the basil leaves and swirl around gently so that everything is well mixed. Spoon into hot serving bowls and serve straight away.

Quails poached in consommé

This dish is elegant and simple. I like to serve it with Caramelised Parsnips (page 211) and Morel and Parmesan Gnocchi (page 216). For a more fragrant, sweeter flavour, infuse the consommé with a little Earl Grey tea and Date Purée (page 245) before you poach the quails.

serves 4

🔪 PREP TIME 5 MINUTES 🍲 COOK TIME 30 MINUTES

4 x 250 g (9 oz) whole quails

1 litre (34 fl oz) Game Consommé (page 48)

salt and pepper

Remove the wishbone from the quails, cut off the wing tips and clean the wing bones.

Place the consommé in a heavy-based saucepan and heat gently to 80°C (175°F), just under a gentle simmer. Taste and season to your liking. Gently place the quails in the consommé, ensuring they are completely submerged. Poach gently for 30 minutes, which will cook them medium-rare.

Serve the quails whole, or divide them into legs and breasts. Either way, arrange them in serving bowls and ladle on a generous amount of consommé. Serve straight away.

Sous—vide

Aiguillettes of chicken with lemon thyme beurre blanc, pine nuts and black olives

Aiguillette is the French word for 'needle' and this is what these are: long fine slivers cut from the breast fillet. The finished dish looks so pretty and delicate, and the gentle sealed cooking method keeps the chicken exquisitely moist and full of flavour.

serves 4

PREP TIME 20 MINUTES   COOK TIME 25 MINUTES

Serve with a Salade Simple (page 97).

4 medium chicken breasts, skins left on

salt and pepper

1 bunch lemon thyme

200 ml (7 fl oz) Beurre Blanc (page 93)

½ cup black olives, pitted and finely chopped

80 ml (3 fl oz) extra-virgin olive oil

20 ml (¾ fl oz) vegetable oil

½ cup pine nuts

Heat a large saucepan of water to just below a very gentle simmer – 65°C (150°F) if you have a thermometer.

Place each chicken breast in a vacuum bag (or at a pinch, a sealable plastic bag), season well and add a sprig of lemon thyme to each bag (reserve the best leaves and flowers for garnish and the stalks for infusing). Press all the air out of the bags then seal tightly shut. Immerse the bags in the hot water and bring it back to temperature. Cook at a constant 65°C (150°F) for 20 minutes.

In another saucepan, heat the beurre blanc gently. Add the stalks from the lemon thyme and set aside for 10 minutes to infuse. Strain through a fine sieve and keep warm. Mix together the finely chopped olives and the olive oil. Season lightly and set aside. Heat half the vegetable oil in a frying pan and fry the pine nuts until golden brown. Drain on paper towels, season and set aside.

Remove the bags of chicken from the water. When cool enough to handle, open the bags and carefully remove the chicken breasts. Heat the remaining vegetable oil in the frying pan and fry the chicken breasts, skin side down, until coloured a delicate golden brown. Slice the breasts very finely lengthwise and arrange them on your serving plates. Spoon a little of the beurre blanc and the olive dressing around each plate. Garnish the chicken slivers with toasted pine nuts and a scattering of the reserved lemon thyme flowers and leaves, and serve immediately.

If you can't find coral trout, then red emperor, chinook salmon, snapper, morwong or sea bream (porgy) would all be good substitutes. Similarly, you could use lemon balm instead of lemon verbena, and if you don't have any Wet Citrus Salt (page 19) to hand, simply mix together a tablespoon of sea salt with ¼ teaspoon each of grated lemon, orange and lime zest.

When selecting your verjuice choose one that has a nice balance of acidity and sweetness. Some are fairly acidic, and will be quite overpowering once they've been reduced down. If you do find the reduction a bit too sharp, you can dilute it with a little Stock Syrup (page 232) to taste.

Coral trout with lemon verbena

serves 4

✎ PREP TIME 5 MINUTES ⌕ COOK TIME 15 MINUTES

4 x 180 g (6 ½ oz) coral trout fillets

40 ml (1 ½ fl oz) olive oil

salt and pepper

¼ cup lemon verbena leaves

400 ml (14 fl oz) verjuice

Wet Citrus Salt (page 19)

few drops lemon juice

Serve with Buttered Spinach (page 227) and a little Potato Purée (page 212) flavoured with extra-virgin olive oil.

Heat a large saucepan of water to just under a very gentle simmer – 60°C (140°F) if you have a thermometer.

Place each fish fillet in a vacuum bag (or at a pinch, a sealable plastic bag), season well and add a few lemon verbena leaves to each bag. Press all the air out of the bags then seal tightly shut. Immerse the bags in the hot water and bring it back to temperature. Cook at a constant 60°C (140°F) for 15 minutes.

In another saucepan, bring the verjuice to the boil. Lower the temperature and simmer until reduced to a syrupy consistency. Taste and adjust the flavour balance to your liking. Keep warm until ready to serve.

Remove the bags of fish from the water. When cool enough to handle, open the bags and carefully remove the fish fillets. Arrange one on each of your serving plates. Sprinkle each with a little citrus salt and a drop of lemon juice. Drizzle a little of the verjuice syrup around the plate and serve straight away.

Fricassées and ragoûts

These two cooking methods form the backbone to a vast range of French dishes that use everything from poultry and game, red and white meats to vegetables, seafood and even offal (variety meats).

These dishes are simple and tasty, and, best of all, can mostly be made using only one saucepan or frying pan. Both these techniques are actually based on the sauté (see page 186), which means 'to jump' in French, reflecting the way the ingredients are tossed or shaken in a hot pan to lightly seal the surface. But whereas sautés use only a minimal amount of extra liquid, fricassées and ragoûts are closer to what we think of as a casserole.

A fricassée is a rather loose term that includes all kinds of variations on a basic theme. Traditionally speaking, a fricassée uses small pieces of meat, chicken, fish or vegetables that are sautéed over a low heat in butter or oil, dusted with a little flour, then simmered in stock and finished with cream. Contemporary versions of the fricassée tend not to use flour or cream as thickening agents, but instead are finished with a flavoursome stock. They are quick and easy to prepare and are a great way of using up leftovers at home.

Ragoûts tend to be cooked for longer in a larger volume of liquid – making them more like an English stew. As with braised dishes, ragoûts can be brown or white. Brown ragoûts use darker meats, which are browned in the pan before being cooked in a rich brown stock. For white ragoûts, lighter meat – poultry or fish – is not browned first, and it is cooked in a light

stock. Ragoûts are more robust and hearty than a fricassée and are traditionally thickened with flour or a starchy vegetable like potato. In contrast to braised dishes, however, ragoûts tend to be cooked on top of the stove, uncovered, rather than in the oven, so that they reduce and concentrate to become intensely flavoured.

Modern ragoûts, while respecting the traditional principles, have evolved to become lighter and less, shall we say, gluggy than classic versions. As with a fricassée, the focus is on flavour. What I'm looking for is a full-flavoured stew, but with less reliance on heavily reduced creams and certainly no flour or butter. This is achieved by gently searing or sautéing the ingredients, adding a flavoursome stock and substituting some of the cream with milk. I try not to reduce the ragoût too much, to retain the purity and freshness without overconcentrating the flavours.

Neither fricassées nor ragoûts rely on prime cuts of meat. For a fricassée, though, you do need to choose a cut that will cook quickly – loin, rump trimmings, livers and sweetbreads, fish and seafood all work brilliantly. Ragoûts require longer cooking, so cheaper cuts or firm-fleshed fish are preferable. I also like to include grains or pulses (legumes), and vegetables such as onions, shallots or leeks, which are improved by slower cooking.

Previous spread: Fricassée of marron tail and scallops (opposite)

Fricassée of marron tail and scallops

In this fricassée the inherent sweetness of the marron tails and the scallops is really brought to the fore.

serves 4

✎ PREP TIME 20 MINUTES ⌒ COOK TIME 10 MINUTES

4 marron or crayfish tails

10 ml (¼ fl oz) vegetable oil

salt and pepper

12 scallops

100 g (3½ oz) butter

80 ml (3 fl oz) sauternes or sweet white wine

chervil leaves to garnish

I like to serve this fricassée with Parsnip Purée (page 224) or Caramelised Parsnips (page 211), and a splash of Vanilla Gastrique (page 24). It's equally good with a big bowl of Buttered Peas (page 227).

To prepare the marron tails, remove the intestinal tract then use a pair of kitchen scissors to cut each of the marrons into 3–5 medallions, still in the shell.

Heat the oil in a heavy-based frying pan over a high heat. Add the marron medallions, season well and sear for a minute on each side. Add the scallops and sauté for 2 minutes. Add half the butter, allow to froth and cook for a further minute. Add the wine to the pan and bring to the boil. Add the rest of the butter and swirl over the heat so it melts and emulsifies, coating the marrons and scallops with a lovely shiny glaze.

Divide the marron medallions and scallops between 4 warm serving plates and spoon on the pan juices. Garnish with chervil leaves and serve straight away.

Fricassée of chicken with morels and leeks

The fricassée is great served hot straight away but will keep just fine refrigerated for a day or two. I love to serve it with a silky Potato Purée (page 212) to soak up all the juices.

serves 4

PREP TIME 20 MINUTES COOK TIME 20 MINUTES

1.5 kg (3 lb 5 oz) chicken

10 g (½ oz) dried morels

4 medium leeks, tough outer leaves discarded

20 ml (¾ fl oz) vegetable oil

salt and pepper

80 ml (3 fl oz) Madeira

500 ml (17 fl oz) Brown Chicken Stock (page 34)

2 tablespoons finely chopped parsley

50 ml (2 fl oz) cream (optional)

Cut the chicken into 12 pieces as follows: remove the legs and separate into thighs and drumsticks, remove the wings (discarding the tips for making stock), then remove the breasts and cut each into 3 pieces. When you come to serve, make sure each person gets a mixture of white and brown meat. Use the carcass and trimmings for making brown stock; if you don't want to make it straight away, they will keep in a plastic bag in the freezer for up to 3 months.

Soak the morels in a little warm water for 20 minutes. Remove them and strain and discard the liquid. Slice the leeks into thin batons.

Heat the oil in a large casserole or heavy-based frying pan over a high heat. Season the chicken pieces all over and add to the pan skin side down. Sauté on each side for a few minutes until caramelised a deep golden brown. Add the leeks and sauté for a few minutes until coloured. Drain off any excess fat from the pan, then deglaze with the Madeira. Stir well to scrape up any caramelised residue.

Add the morels and the chicken stock to the pan and bring to the boil. Lower the heat and simmer gently for 15 minutes, skimming occasionally to remove any impurities that rise to the surface. Check to see if the chicken is cooked by inserting a skewer or sharp knife into a thigh or drumstick, close to the bone. If the juices run clear, it is cooked. Sprinkle with parsley and stir in the cream, if using. Serve straight away.

Fricassée of duck livers with watercress and roasted hazelnuts

The creamy richness of the duck livers is beautifully cut by the sharp pepperiness of the watercress leaves and the toasty crunch of the hazelnuts. To keep it simple, dress with the pan juices and a splash of hazelnut oil. To make it really special, dress with Hazelnut Emulsion (page 73) and scatter on some slices of Vanilla Poached Apples (page 251).

serves 4

PREP TIME 5 MINUTES   COOK TIME 5 MINUTES

500 g (1 lb 2 oz) duck livers

10 ml (¼ fl oz) vegetable oil

salt and pepper

30 g (1 oz) butter

2 tablespoons red wine vinegar

50 ml (2 fl oz) port

2 tablespoons roasted hazelnuts

2 bunches watercress, washed and leaves picked

2 tablespoons hazelnut oil

To clean the livers, slice away the membranes, any green bits and the sinewy fibres at the centre of each. Cut into small pieces, about the size of a coin.

Heat the oil in a heavy-based frying pan over a high heat. Season the livers then add them to the pan and sear for a minute on each side. Add the butter and allow to froth. Turn the livers over and cook for a further minute, basting with the butter. Add the vinegar and port to the pan and cook for a few minutes until reduced. Swirl the pan to emulsify the liquids and butter. The whole process should take no longer than 5 minutes, which will cook the livers to medium-rare.

To roast the hazelnuts, bake them in an oven preheated to 180°C (350°F) for 5–10 minutes, until the skin is dark and flaky. Tip into a clean tea (dish) towel and rub them vigorously to remove the skins. Cut them in half and season lightly.

Place the watercress leaves in a mixing bowl and pour in the pan juices. Add the hazelnut oil and toss gently to dress the leaves evenly. Arrange a handful of leaves on each of 4 serving plates and top with the duck livers. Scatter on the roasted hazelnut halves and serve immediately.

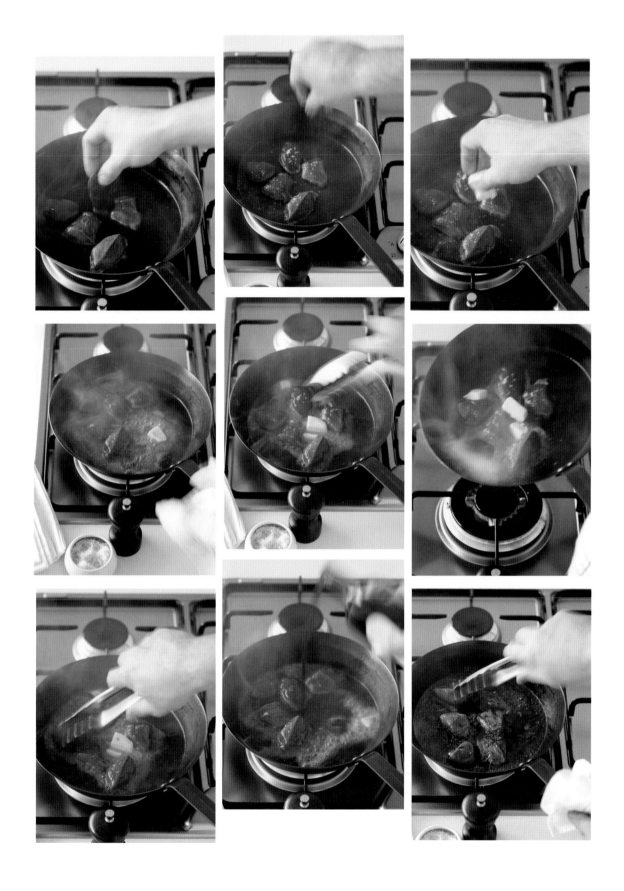

163

Fricassée of duck livers with watercress
and roasted hazelnuts (page 162)

Ragoût of chestnuts, shallots and parsnips

This is a wonderful and unusual ragoût to serve in the autumn months, either as a starter or as an accompaniment to roasted game birds. The sweet mealiness of the chestnuts works beautifully with the parsnips and shallots. If you really want to impress your friends, dollop on a knob of truffled butter as you bring the plates to the table – the sweet, earthy, pungent aromas are to die for.

serves 4

PREP TIME 15 MINUTES COOK TIME 30 MINUTES

2 parsnips, peeled and cored

10 ml (¼ fl oz) vegetable oil

24 shallots, peeled but left whole

24 peeled chestnuts

salt and pepper

10 ml (¼ fl oz) sherry vinegar

500 ml (17 fl oz) Brown Chicken Stock (page 34)

100 g (3 ½ oz) Truffle Butter (page 78) (optional)

2 tablespoons finely chopped parsley leaves

Cut the parsnips into large batons. Heat the oil in a casserole or earthenware braising dish over a high heat. Add the shallots, chestnuts and parsnips, season well and sauté until coloured a deep golden brown.

Add the sherry vinegar and then the chicken stock. Bring to the boil and skim well, then lower the heat to a gentle simmer. Cut a piece of baking paper to the size of the pan to make a cartouche and place on the surface. Simmer the ragoût for about half an hour until the liquid has thickened and concentrated to form a rich sauce.

Ladle into 4 serving bowls and serve immediately, topped with a knob of truffle butter, if using, and a scattering of parsley.

Ragoût of pearl barley

Similar in style to a risotto, but pearl barley is more robust and has an unusual chewy texture. It needs to be soaked in cold water for 12 hours before cooking. I love to serve this ragoût with Confit Duck (page 138). Shred the meat from 2 duck legs and fold through the ragoût just before serving. It is also delicious with barramundi or sea bass/porgy (cooked in the same way as Roasted Mulloway, page 204), Braised Shallots (page 227) and Red Wine Sauce (page 85) for a tasty winter fish dish.

serves 4

PREP TIME 10 MINUTES   COOK TIME 45 MINUTES

20 g (¾ oz) butter

½ onion, roughly diced

50 ml (2 fl oz) Madeira

80 g (3 oz) pearl barley, soaked for 12 hours in cold water

500 ml (17 fl oz) Brown Chicken Stock (page 34)

3 sprigs thyme

½ bay leaf

2 garlic cloves, roughly crushed

2 tablespoons finely chopped parsley

Heat the butter in a small casserole or braising pan over a medium heat. Add the diced onion and sauté until caramelised a light golden brown. Add the Madeira and simmer until slightly reduced. Add the pearl barley, chicken stock, herbs and garlic. Bring to the boil, then lower the heat to a gentle simmer. Cut a piece of baking paper to the size of the pan to make a cartouche and place on the surface. Simmer the ragoût for about 45 minutes, adding a little more stock if the barley seems to be drying out.

At the end of the cooking, the pearl barley should be soft and tender, but still retain its shape and a slight chewiness. Serve sprinkled with parsley and with your choice of accompaniments.

Ragoût of mussels, leeks and saffron with croutons and aioli

serves 4

PREP TIME 10 MINUTES · COOK TIME 20 MINUTES

4 potatoes	200 ml (7 fl oz) milk
2 leeks, tough outer leaves discarded	1 baguette
1 fennel bulb, core removed	1 garlic clove
20 ml (¾ fl oz) vegetable oil	20 ml (¾ fl oz) olive oil
1 teaspoon grated fresh ginger	1 kg (2 lb 3 oz) mussels, scrubbed and beards removed
pinch saffron	
salt and pepper	½ cup chopped chives
200 ml (7 fl oz) riesling	few drops lemon juice
800 ml (27 fl oz) cream	Aioli (page 72)

Preheat your oven to 160°C (320°F). Peel the potatoes and cut them to a macedoine (page 208). Slice the leeks into thick slices on a slight angle, and finely slice the fennel.

Heat the oil in a casserole or earthenware braising dish over a high heat. Add the leeks and fennel and sweat for 5 minutes until soft and translucent. Add the potatoes, ginger and saffron and season well. Add the riesling and cook until reduced by half. Add the cream and milk and return to the boil. Lower the heat and simmer gently for 15 minutes.

Meanwhile, slice the baguette into thin rounds and arrange on a baking tray. Rub each slice with the garlic clove and brush with a little oil. Bake for 8 minutes until crisp and golden.

Add the mussels to the pan, cover and cook for 5 minutes until the mussels have opened (discard any that refuse to open). Remove the pan from the heat, taste and adjust seasoning to your liking then sprinkle on the chives and lemon juice.

Ladle the ragoût into warm serving bowls and top with a couple of garlic croutons. Serve with a big bowl of aioli so everyone can help themselves.

Braising and slow cooking

The modern world is all about speed: we want everything quickly – and that includes our dinner! This approach is completely at odds with braising and slow cooking, and it means that we miss out on the vast range of blanquettes, daubes and other braises that are the mainstay of French country cooking.

There are subtle differences in each method, but generally speaking all involve simmering meat in a covered pot with vegetables and other aromatics, such as herbs, wine and stock, so that the flavours fuse and deepen with time.

In the way of all good country fare, this is economical cooking too. It calls for mature, secondary cuts of meat whose tougher texture is riddled with connective tissue, sinew and gristle – which sounds rather unappealing. But this is the whole point. During the long slow cooking this all breaks down: the texture of the meat softens and it releases gelatinous juices that create a deep-flavoured, rich syrupy sauce.

In a braise, the meat is usually cut into large pieces – or even a single large piece – and will often be marinated in wine and aromatic herbs before cooking. The meat is seared first – sometimes to a dark brown, sometimes just enough to seal the surface – before cooking with a mirepoix of vegetables (see page 208) in just enough liquid to cover it. This initial frying seals the meat and concentrates the flavours. Because braises are always cooked in a tightly covered pan, as the meat cooks, liquid is drawn out to create a fragrant steam, which then condenses and is reabsorbed back into the meat.

As with sauces, braises can be divided into brown and white. Brown braises tend to use darker meats, such as beef, lamb or game birds cooked in brown stock and red wine. White braises use white wine and light stock, and the meat – or even fish – is not well browned before cooking.

Tougher-textured secondary cuts of meat are ideal for this method of cooking. Choose anything from neck, shoulder or belly brisket, oyster blade (flat iron/butler's), skirt, shanks, tail or cheeks. With poultry, choose leg quarters or thighs. Whichever cut you choose, you do need to make sure there is a good marbling of fat, which creates flavour and the desired soft, gelatinous texture.

Although this style of dish does take time – both in the marinating and in the actual cooking – it is hardly difficult. Most of that time can be spent doing something else entirely! And the beauty of braised dishes is that once made, they don't have to be eaten straight away. In fact they improve with time as the flavours mature and develop. This makes them ideal dishes for dinner parties as they can be cooked well ahead of time and simply reheated in time to serve your guests.

Braising

Daube of beef

Beef cheeks are available from good butchers. You can also use brisket, short ribs or oxtails for this daube, all of which have a wonderful gelatinous quality. Wagyu beef, although rather extravagant, gives an amazing depth of flavour.

serves 4

/ PREP TIME 20 MINUTES ▯ MARINATING TIME 24 HOURS ☞ COOK TIME 4 HOURS

4 x 300 g (10½ oz) beef cheeks

1 onion

1 carrot

1 celery stalk

½ garlic bulb, cloves left whole

4 sprigs thyme

1 bay leaf

1.5 litres (51 fl oz) red wine

500 ml (17 fl oz) port

flour for dusting

50 ml (2 fl oz) vegetable oil

2.5 litres (85 fl oz) Brown Veal Stock (page 35)

salt and pepper

Serve with Roasted Baby Carrots (page 224) and Horseradish Potato Purée (page 212).

Put the cheeks in a large bowl or plastic container. Cut the vegetables to a rough mirepoix (page 208) and scatter them over the beef with the garlic cloves and herbs.

Heat the red wine and port in a heavy-based saucepan over a high heat. Bring to the boil, then lower the heat and simmer until reduced by half. Allow to cool a little then pour over the beef and vegetables. (Make sure the marinade is still warm, which helps all the flavours to penetrate the meat.) Leave to cool at room temperature, then cover and refrigerate. Leave to marinate for 24 hours.

When ready to cook, preheat your oven to 110°C (230°F). Tip the beef and vegetables into a colander to drain, reserving the marinade. Set aside the vegetables and herbs. Lightly dust the beef cheeks with flour, patting to remove any excess. The flour is not used to thicken the sauce, but helps to prevent the cheeks from burning when you brown them.

Heat the oil in a large casserole or braising pan over a moderate heat. Season the beef cheeks and add them to the pan. Fry one at a time, until browned evenly all over. Drain on paper towels. Add the reserved vegetables to the pan and fry until browned all over. Add the marinade to the pan and bring to the boil. Lower the heat and simmer until reduced by half.

>

Meanwhile, bring the veal stock to a gentle simmer in another pan. Add the beef and reserved herbs to the braising pan then add the hot stock. Bring it all to a gentle simmer then skim, taste and adjust the seasoning to your taste. Cut a piece of baking paper to the size of the pan to make a cartouche and place on the surface. Cover tightly with a lid and transfer to the oven. Braise for 4 hours, checking and turning every 30 minutes or so. At the end of the cooking time the beef cheeks should be soft and tender.

Remove the beef cheeks from the pan and keep warm. Strain the braising liquor through a fine sieve then bring to the boil over a high heat. Cook until reduced to a syrupy sauce consistency. To serve, place a beef cheek on each plate and ladle over the hot sauce. Serve with your choice of accompaniments.

If you don't want to serve the beef immediately, allow it to cool then transfer everything to a container with a tight-fitting lid and refrigerate. The daube will keep in a sealed container in the refrigerator for up to 5 days.

Blanquette of veal

A blanquette is a white braise, and a classic of French provincial cuisine. For this recipe you can use veal shoulder, neck, breast, shanks or cheeks. This blanquette has a delicate flavour and a wonderful gelatinous, soft texture.

serves 4

PREP TIME 20 MINUTES   COOK TIME 3 HOURS

1 kg (2 lb 3 oz) veal shoulder, boned and cut into 4 even-sized pieces

1 onion

2 celery stalks

½ leek, tough outer leaves removed

½ garlic bulb, cloves left whole

20 ml (¾ fl oz) vegetable oil

60 g (2 oz) butter

6 sprigs thyme

1 bay leaf

200 ml (7 fl oz) white wine

2 litres (68 fl oz) White Veal Stock (page 30)

salt and pepper

Serve it with a big bowl of Potato Purée (page 212) and perhaps some Braised Borlotti Beans (page 221) on the side.

Preheat your oven to 110°C (230°F). Cut the vegetables to a rough mirepoix (page 208).

Heat the oil in a large casserole or braising pan over a moderate heat. Add the veal pieces, one at a time, and cook gently, until just seared all over. As this dish is a white braise you don't really want the meat to colour. Remove from the pan and set aside.

Add the butter and allow to foam without colouring. Add the vegetables and sweat gently for about 8 minutes, until soft and translucent, but not coloured. Add the herbs and the white wine to the pan and bring to a gentle simmer. Cook until almost completely reduced, then return the veal pieces to the pan.

In another pan, bring the veal stock to a gentle simmer, then pour it onto the veal and vegetables. Season to taste. Cut a piece of baking paper to the size of the pan to make a cartouche and place on the surface. Cover tightly with a lid and transfer to the oven. Braise for 3 hours, checking and turning every 30 minutes or so. At the end of the cooking time the veal should be soft and gelatinous.

To serve, place the casserole dish in the middle of the table with your selection of accompaniments, for everyone to help themselves. If you don't want to serve the veal immediately, allow it to cool then transfer everything to a container with a tight-fitting lid and refrigerate. The blanquette will keep in a sealed container in the refrigerator for up to 5 days.

Braised boneless lamb neck (page 180)

Duck legs braised with port, orange and thyme (page 181)

Braised boneless lamb neck

serves 4

PREP TIME 20 MINUTES   MARINATING TIME 12 HOURS   COOK TIME 3 HOURS

Serve with Crushed Potatoes (page 218) and Piperade Sauce (page 85).

50 g (2 oz) Aromatic Confit Salt (page 19)	2 tomatoes
2 boneless lamb necks	4 sprigs thyme
1 onion	2 sprigs rosemary
1 carrot	150 ml (5 fl oz) white wine
2 celery stalks	2.5 litres (85 fl oz) Brown Lamb Stock (page 37)
½ garlic bulb	salt and pepper
20 ml (¾ fl oz) vegetable oil	

Rub the aromatic salt into the lamb necks, cover with plastic wrap and refrigerate for 12 hours to marinate.

Preheat your oven to 110°C (230°F). Cut the vegetables to a rough mirepoix (page 208). Rinse the pieces of lamb and pat them dry.

Heat the oil in a large casserole or braising pan over a moderate heat. Add the lamb pieces, one at a time, and fry until browned evenly all over. Drain on paper towels. Add the diced vegetables to the pan and fry until browned all over. Add the tomatoes, herbs and white wine to the pan and bring to a gentle simmer. Cook for 2 minutes.

Meanwhile, bring the lamb stock to a gentle simmer in another pan. Return the pieces of lamb to the braising pan then add the hot stock. Bring it all to a gentle simmer then skim, taste and adjust the seasoning to your taste. Cut a piece of baking paper to the size of the pan to make a cartouche and place on the surface. Cover tightly with a lid and transfer to the oven. Braise for 3 hours, checking and turning every 30 minutes or so. At the end of the cooking time the lamb should be soft and tender.

Remove the lamb pieces from the pan and keep warm. Strain the braising liquor through a fine sieve then bring to the boil over a high heat. Cook until reduced to a syrupy sauce consistency. (Alternatively, use the braising liquor to make a Piperade Sauce, page 85.)

To serve, slice each neck in half and arrange a portion on each plate. Ladle over the hot sauce and serve with your choice of accompaniments. If you don't want to serve the lamb immediately, allow it to cool then transfer everything to a container with a tight-fitting lid and refrigerate. The lamb will keep in a sealed container in the refrigerator for up to 5 days.

Duck legs braised with port, orange and thyme

serves 4

PREP TIME 20 MINUTES   MARINATING TIME 24 HOURS   COOK TIME 3 HOURS

Rich and zesty, this duck braise is delicious served with Sarladaise Potatoes (page 214) and Sweet and Sour White Turnips (page 225).

½ onion	6 sprigs thyme
1 carrot	4 duck leg quarters
1 celery stalk	20 ml (¾ fl oz) vegetable oil
3 garlic cloves, roughly crushed	salt and pepper
200 ml (7 fl oz) port	1.5 litres (51 fl oz) Brown Duck Stock (page 34)
zest and juice of 2 oranges	

Cut the vegetables to a rough mirepoix (page 208) and put them in a saucepan with the port, orange zest and juice and thyme. Bring to the boil, then remove from the heat and allow to cool slightly. Pour over the duck legs and mix well. Allow to cool at room temperature, then cover and refrigerate. Leave to marinate for 24 hours.

When ready to cook, preheat your oven to 110°C (230°F). Tip the duck pieces and vegetables into a colander to drain, reserving the marinade. Set aside the vegetables and herbs and pat the duck pieces dry. Heat the oil in a heavy-based casserole or braising pan and fry the duck until browned evenly all over. Remove from the pan and set aside. Add the reserved vegetables to the pan and fry until browned all over. Add the marinade to the pan and bring to the boil. Return the duck legs to the pan and season.

Meanwhile, bring the duck stock to a gentle simmer in another pan. Add the hot stock to the braising pan and bring it all to a gentle simmer. Skim, taste and adjust the seasoning to your taste. Cut a piece of baking paper to the size of the pan to make a cartouche and place on the surface. Cover tightly with a lid and transfer to the oven. Braise for 3 hours, checking and turning every 30 minutes or so. At the end of the cooking time the duck should be tender and should come away from the bone easily.

Remove the duck pieces from the pan and keep warm. Strain the braising liquor through a fine sieve then bring to the boil over a high heat. Cook until reduced to a syrupy sauce consistency. To serve, place the duck pieces in warm bowls and ladle over the hot sauce. Serve with your choice of accompaniments. The duck is best served immediately, but it will keep in a sealed container in the refrigerator for up to 5 days.

Braised blue eye

People don't often think of braising fish, but this is a wonderful hearty dish, and can be made with any dense, meaty white-fleshed fish, such as hapuku, bass, groper or bar cod.

serves 4

/ PREP TIME 15 MINUTES ☐ COOK TIME 20 MINUTES

4 x 180 g (6½ oz) blue eye fillets

30 ml (1 fl oz) vegetable oil

8 shallots, finely sliced

12 button mushrooms, finely sliced

4 garlic cloves, finely sliced

salt and pepper

100 ml (3½ fl oz) Noilly Prat

200 ml (7 fl oz) white wine

200 ml (7 fl oz) cream

50 g (2 oz) butter

2 tablespoons chopped chives

few drops lemon juice

I recommend serving this with Pommes Boulangère (page 215) and Petit Pois à la Française (page 219).

Preheat your oven to 150°C (300°F). Clean the blue eye, removing skin, pin bones and any bloodline.

Heat the oil in a braising pan over a moderate heat. Add the sliced vegetables, season well and sweat gently for 8 minutes until soft and shallots are translucent. Add the Noilly Prat and wine, bring to the boil and cook for 2 minutes.

Season the fish fillets and add them to the pan. Cover and bake in the preheated oven for 8 minutes.

Remove the fish fillets from the pan and keep warm. Strain the braising liquor through a fine sieve then bring to the boil over a high heat. Add the cream, return to the boil and cook for a minute. Whisk in the butter, chives and lemon juice, then taste and adjust the seasoning to your liking.

To serve, place the fish on warmed plates and ladle over the hot sauce. Serve with your choice of accompaniments.

Hapuku Provençale

serves 4

PREP TIME 20 MINUTES   COOK TIME 20 MINUTES

4 x 180 g (6 ½ oz) hapuku or cod fillets

200 ml (7 fl oz) olive oil

1 Spanish (red) onion, finely sliced

4 garlic cloves, finely sliced

salt and pepper

6 tomatoes, roughly chopped

zest of 1 lemon

½ cup green olives, pitted and halved

100 ml (3 ½ fl oz) white wine

20 mussels, scrubbed and beards removed

½ cup basil leaves

As for the braise opposite, use any dense, meaty white-fleshed fish, such as bass, groper or bar cod. Serve with Confit Kipfler Potatoes (page 217).

Preheat your oven to 150°C (300°F). Clean the hapuku, removing skin, pin bones and any bloodline.

Heat half the oil in a braising pan over a moderate heat. Add the sliced vegetables, season well and sweat gently for 4 minutes until soft and onion is translucent. Add the chopped tomatoes, lemon zest and olives to the pan. Pour in the white wine, add the rest of the olive oil and cook for 5 minutes until the tomatoes have broken down to a sauce-like consistency.

Season the fish fillets and add them to the pan. Cover and bake in the preheated oven for 4 minutes. Add the mussels to the pan, cover and return to the oven for another 4 minutes until the fish has cooked through and the mussels have opened.

Taste the sauce, which should be rich and tomatoey. Adjust the seasoning to your liking and scatter on the basil leaves. To serve, place the fish on warmed plates and ladle over the hot sauce. Serve with your choice of accompaniments.

Grilling and frying

Close your eyes and imagine a piece of steak, hot from the grill: it's beautifully brown on the outside, and as you cut into the meat, it's pink and juicily tender within. Or think about a fine piece of John Dory, sealed in a hot frying pan with a knob of butter: on the underside the skin is crisp and golden, while the surface is speckled a delicate light brown. Irresistible, aren't they?

Grilling and frying use fierce heat to brown and caramelise the surface of food, and it's this browning and caramelising that makes it smell and taste so delicious. To be technical just for a minute, what's going on here is something called the Maillard reaction: as the natural sugars and amino acids in the food are heated, they interact with each other to form new aromas and flavours and to brown the surface of the food. It's a flavour maximiser.

Grilling and frying are best suited to what we call prime cuts of meat – that is, lean and tender meats with little tough connective tissue or sinew. Many of these prime cuts are bred to appeal to the health-conscious, with minimal fat. And yet fat is the other key factor in developing flavour – the Maillard reaction – in meat. Without fat, meat will always taste disappointingly bland. So whether you're cooking a lean chicken breast, a fillet (tenderloin) steak or a piece of King George whiting, you'll always need to moisten the meat with a little oil or butter.

Strictly speaking, food is 'grilled' by exposure to a radiant heat. The heat source may come from below, as in the case of the barbecue (char-grilling simply means using a solid fuel such as charcoal or wood) or on a cast-iron grill plate. Most domestic ovens have an internal grill (broiler), and in this instance food is placed directly beneath it to grill. Overhead grills (sometimes called salamanders) are also used to make gratins, those delectable bubbling dishes, topped with grated cheese or breadcrumbs.

Grilling is one of the simplest methods of cooking, and there are only a few rules to ensure success. First, make sure your grill is well cleaned – that way your food won't be tainted by old, burnt flavours. Second, the grill must always be preheated, or the food won't brown properly. Third, lightly brush the surface of your meat with a little oil before cooking – if the meat is very lean, you might need to baste with a little extra oil as it cooks.

Frying is known as sautéing in French, which refers to the way the food is tossed around in the pan, making it 'jump'. It is a quick method of cooking smallish cuts of meat, poultry or fish, and again relies on a little added fat to brown and caramelise the surface. A good-quality frying pan will have a heavy base – this is essential to withstand the high heat that's needed to brown food properly.

Variations on the frying theme, such as shallow-frying or deep-frying, simply refer to the quantity of oil or other fat that is used, and also to the way in which the food is moved around in the pan. As we learned above, sautéed foods are tossed quickly and frequently in the pan; shallow-fried foods are usually only turned once in the pan, whereas deep-fried food is usually suspended in a much larger amount of oil.

With all frying, it is critical to use the right kind of fat or oil for the job. Generally, grapeseed or canola oils are best for shallow-frying. Olive oil is also good, but it has a lower smoking point, so you'll need to watch it carefully. If you want the flavour of butter, then it's best to mix it with oil, as the milk solids will burn at a high heat.

When deep-frying foods, I prefer to use a neutral-flavoured vegetable oil which can withstand high temperatures without burning. Frying temperatures will vary slightly depending on the items being cooked, but in general, 180°C (350°F) will give a crisp, golden coating, without making it too greasy. If you don't have a thermometer, test to see if the oil is hot enough by dropping in a cube of bread: if it sizzles and floats to the surface and browns in about 10 seconds, the fat is hot enough.

Another pleasing thing about frying in oil is that food can be coated in flour, crumbs or batter, all of which make a delectable crisp, crunchy crust.

Grilled entrecôte steak

Use this technique for baby lamb cutlets and serve with Gremolata (page 70), Slow-roasted Garlic (page 219) and Potato Dauphinoise (page 214).

serves 4

PREP TIME 5 MINUTES COOK TIME 8 MINUTES

4 x 250 g (9 oz) sirloin steaks

50 ml (2 fl oz) vegetable oil

salt and pepper

Heat a char-griller or your barbecue to medium-high. Rub the steaks all over with the oil and season.

Place on the grill at a 45° angle to the ridges. Cook for 2 minutes then move the steaks around on the ridges to form the standard criss-cross markings on the underside. Cook for a further 2 minutes. Turn the steaks over and repeat this process on the other side, then remove from the heat and leave in a warm place to rest for at least 5 minutes. This allows all the juices to settle back into the meat and will give you a steak cooked to medium-rare perfection.

Serve the steaks as they are, or carve them on an angle into thickish slices. Serve immediately with your choice of accompaniments.

Serve with a salad and Pommes Anna (page 214) and the classic condiments, Café de Paris Butter (page 78) or Béarnaise Sauce (page 92).

Butterflied quail grilled with garlic and rosemary butter

Butterflying simply means that the quail is boned and flattened, which helps it to cook quickly and evenly on the grill.

serves 4

PREP TIME 10 MINUTES COOK TIME 6 MINUTES

8 quails, boned and butterflied

50 ml (2 fl oz) vegetable oil

salt and pepper

100 g (3½ oz) Garlic and Rosemary Butter (page 76)

Heat a char-griller or your barbecue to medium-high.

Trim the wing tips from the quail, then rub them all over with the oil and season. Place on the grill, skin side down, at a 45° angle to the ridges. Cook for 2 minutes then move the quails around on the ridges to form the standard criss-cross markings. Cook for a further 2 minutes. Turn the quails over and cook for another 2 minutes (there's no need for the criss-cross marking on this side). Once you've turned the quail, place a slice of herb butter on top of each, so it will melt and flavour the quails. Serve hot from the grill with your choice of accompaniments.

Serve with Choucroute (page 220) and Spiced Cherry Jus (page 89). And feel free to ring the changes with the herb butter if you like!

Grilled scampi tails with lemon and parsley butter

Here the scampi (langoustines) are grilled (broiled) underneath a heat source, instead of directly on a char-grill or barbecue. Shellfish lends itself particularly well to this method of cooking, especially when brushed with a flavoured oil or butter that melts under the heat and bastes and infuses the delicate meat with flavour.

serves 4

PREP TIME 5 MINUTES   COOK TIME 4 MINUTES

8 large whole scampi (langoustines)

150 g (5½ oz) Lemon and Parsley Butter
   (page 77)

sea salt

Heat your overhead grill (broiler) to the highest setting.

With a large sharp knife split the scampi lengthwise straight down the middle. Turn them so the flesh is uppermost and lay them out on a baking tray.

Finely dice the butter and scatter it over the surface of the scampi. Place under the hot grill and cook for 4 minutes until the butter is melted and bubbling and the scampi meat is just cooked.

This needs nothing more than a Salade Simple (page 97) as accompaniment.

Pan-fried John Dory

There are few things better than tender fillets of white flat fish, fried in butter to a crisp golden brown and served with a wedge of lemon. But if you want to go one step further, try serving this Dory with Confit Kipfler Potatoes (page 217), a chunky Caponata Dressing (page 69) and the Sweet and Sour Capsicum Emulsion (page 74).

serves 4

PREP TIME 5 MINUTES   COOK TIME 8 MINUTES

4 x 200 g (7 oz) John Dory or sole fillets, skin on

salt and pepper

20 ml (¾ fl oz) grapeseed or canola oil

60 g (2 oz) butter

few drops lemon juice

Season the fish fillets lightly on the fleshy side. Heat the oil in a heavy-based frying pan on a medium-high heat. Add the fish to the pan, seasoned side down, and fry for 3 minutes. Season the skin side. Add the butter to the pan and cook to a light brown foam. Lift the fish carefully to check its colour, and when it is a light golden brown turn onto the skin side. Add the lemon juice and continue to fry for another couple of minutes, basting continuously. Use a sharp knife to check the fish at its thickest place; it should still be slightly translucent.

Serve straight away, skin side down, on warm serving plates.

Pan-fried tuna

Both tuna and swordfish are fairly meaty, and are well suited to pan-frying.

serves 4

PREP TIME 5 MINUTES   COOK TIME 5 MINUTES

4 x 200 g (7 oz) tuna or swordfish loins

salt and pepper

20 ml (¾ fl oz) olive oil

60 g (2 oz) butter

few drops lemon juice

Season the fish pieces lightly on one side. Heat the oil in a heavy-based frying pan on a medium-high heat. Add the fish to the pan, seasoned side down, and fry for 1 minute. Season the uppermost side. Add the butter to the pan and cook to a light brown foam. Lift the fish carefully to check its colour, and when it is a light golden brown turn over. Add the lemon juice and continue to fry for another couple of minutes, basting continuously. Use a sharp knife to check the fish at its thickest place; tuna should still be pink and rare, swordfish should be translucent.

Serve straight away, skin side down, on warm serving plates.

Serve with Crushed Potatoes (page 218) and Verbena Tea Vinaigrette (page 67).

Pan-fried calves liver

Calves liver is perfectly suited to this high-heat, quick-cook method. It should only be cooked to a tender pink, so you do need to make sure you get the best-quality, freshest liver you can find from a reputable butcher.

serves 4

PREP TIME 5 MINUTES   COOK TIME 5 MINUTES

4 x 150 g (5 ½ oz) escalopes of calf's liver

salt and pepper

50 ml (2 fl oz) grapeseed or rice bran oil

50 g (2 oz) butter

10 ml (¼ fl oz) sherry vinegar

2 tablespoons finely chopped capers

2 tablespoons finely chopped parsley

Make sure the liver has been trimmed of all membranes and sinewy bits and season it lightly on one side only.

Heat the oil in a heavy-based frying pan on a medium-high heat. Add the liver pieces to the pan, seasoned side down, and fry for 2 minutes until it begins to caramelise. Add the butter to the pan and cook to a light brown foam. Season the uppermost side of the liver and turn it over. Fry for another 2 minutes, basting continuously. Deglaze the pan with the vinegar, swirling all the pan juices around so they emulsify.

Remove the pan from the heat and add the capers and parsley. Serve immediately with your choice of accompaniments. Remember, the liver should still be pink in the middle.

My favourite accompaniments are Potato and Bacon Roesti (page 215) and a tangy Lime Jus (page 87).

189

Grilled scampi tails with lemon and parsley butter (page 188)

Pan-fried John Dory (page 188)

Deep-frying is such a popular way to cook seafood and you can use a simple beer batter for all sorts of small pieces of fish, as well as prawns (shrimp), scallops, marron or crayfish tails or even lobster.

Deep-fried king prawn beignets with lemon and chervil mayonnaise

serves 4

✎ PREP TIME 20 MINUTES ⌒ COOK TIME 10 MINUTES

2 litres (68 fl oz) cooking oil

24 large king prawns (jumbo shrimp), shelled and deveined

salt and pepper

Beer batter

375 ml (12½ fl oz) bottle lager

160 g (5½ oz) plain (all-purpose) flour

1 tablespoon salt

Lemon and chervil mayonnaise

500 ml (17 fl oz) mayonnaise (page 72)

zest and juice of 2 lemons

½ cup chopped chervil

Serve with a big bowl of lemon and chervil mayonnaise so everyone can dip in to their heart's content.

To make the beer batter, put the lager in a mixing bowl and gradually whisk in the flour. The batter should be a thin consistency. Add salt. Leave to rest for 30 minutes before using.

Make the mayonnaise and stir in the lemon zest and juice and the chopped chervil.

Heat the oil in a deep-fryer or a large heavy-based saucepan to 180°C (350°F).

Season the prawns well. Dip them in beer batter, 6 at a time, allowing any excess batter to fall back into the bowl. Add them carefully to the hot oil and deep-fry for about 2 minutes. Move them around in the oil so they cook evenly and are crisp and a light golden brown.

Remove with a slotted spoon and drain on paper towels while you cook the remaining prawns. Serve immediately with the mayonnaise while still piping hot.

Roasting

There are few sights to
rival a gloriously bronzed roast
emerging from the oven in a
cloud of savoury steam.

From a humble chicken to a magnificent rib of beef, roast meats are the meal of choice to celebrate festive occasions, holidays, birthdays – or even just the traditional day of rest.

Roasting is one of the simplest culinary techniques in the French kitchen. Strictly speaking, it's a method of cooking a piece of meat – or poultry or fish – by exposing it to a naked flame (which we call spit-roasting) or to the radiant heat of an oven. These days spit-roasting tends to be seen as a bit of a fun gimmick for parties and most discussion of modern roasting centres on oven-roasting.

This is one of the most fundamental skills learned by apprentice chefs and really hinges upon an understanding of timing and temperature, rather than any complex techniques. These factors depend upon the weight of the meat and how well cooked you want it to be. But irrespective, you should always make sure the meat is at room temperature before you start cooking. If the meat is cold it will take longer to cook and will tend to steam, rather than roast. It's also essential to preheat your oven to the appropriate temperature.

The meat should be well seasoned with salt and pepper and set on a rack or trivet in your roasting pan. This makes it easy to spoon the roasting juices back onto the meat as it cooks, a technique known as basting, which helps keep it moist.

One of the characteristics of this method of cooking is the high temperature. The French approach starts the meat off in a blast of high heat. This method causes the inherent sugars to caramelise and the surface of the meat to brown, and that's what makes it so tasty. After around 15–20 minutes the temperature is reduced for the remainder of the cooking time.

Assessing when the meat is done is perhaps the trickiest thing for the home cook. A meat thermometer certainly takes most of the guesswork out of assessing when it is done, but you can also do what we chefs do: insert a giant skewer right to the centre of the meat, or to the thickest part of a bird's thigh, and leave it for 20 seconds. Remove it and hold it to the back of your hand. If the skewer feels cold, the meat is not yet cooked through to the centre. If it is warm, the meat is rare, if it feels hot it is medium-rare, and if it burns and you end up with a blister it's well done!

When the meat is cooked to your liking it is very important to allow it to rest before carving. Transfer it to a carving board, cover it loosely with a large piece of foil and leave it in a warm place for 15–20 minutes. I can't stress how important this resting is: it allows the muscles to relax and all the juices (and the flavour) to settle back down into the meat. Don't worry about the meat getting cold. As long as you don't cut into it, and you leave it in a warm spot, it will stay hot inside. And remember, this resting time is the perfect opportunity for you to make the gravy from all the tasty bits of sticky sediment and flavoursome pan juices that have collected in the bottom of the roasting pan (see page 84).

You need to choose prime-quality cuts for this high-heat method of cooking. When it comes to poultry or game, try to choose free-range, corn-fed or organic birds and not battery-farmed birds. The difference in flavour really is worth the extra few dollars.

With beef, fillet (tenderloin) is the most expensive cut, of course, but to my mind it is not as flavoursome as other joints and the softer texture often verges on being mushy. Personally I like a roast that you can really get your teeth into! Top of my list would be rib roasts, as I find that meat cooked on the bone has a wonderful depth of flavour and juiciness. Next, I'd choose rump, rump tip or sirloin, all of which have a good covering of fat and nice internal marbling. And if you want to go all-out, try roasting a piece of Wagyu sirloin, dry-aged for 6 weeks.

Previous spread: Whole roasted baby chicken (page 199)

Take a similar approach with veal and lamb – roasted leg, loin, sirloin or rump are all outstanding choices. With pork, do make sure you buy from a good butcher and, above all, avoid the flabby, lean-bred, mass-produced supermarket pork. Thankfully rare-breed and organic pork is making a bit of a comeback – and with it, flavour returns to the Sunday roast!

Roast rib of dry-aged beef

This is a classic roast, starting at a high temperature to caramelise and brown the surface of the meat, then cooking further at a lower temperature. I like to rest the beef inside the oven, after it's been turned off. The residual heat keeps the meat warm without further cooking. The times specified are for medium-rare.

serves 4

PREP TIME 5 MINUTES   COOK TIME 60 MINUTES

2 kg (4 lb 6 oz) beef rib roast, at room
    temperature

salt and pepper

80 ml (3 fl oz) vegetable oil

Preheat the oven to 220°C (430°F). Season the beef all over with salt and pepper and rub the surface of the meat and fat with oil.

Place the beef on a rack or trivet in a roasting tray. Roast for 20 minutes, then lower the temperature to 180°C (350°F) and roast for a further 30 minutes.

Turn off the oven and leave the beef in the oven for a further 10 minutes to rest.

Remove from the oven, carve and serve with your choice of accompaniments.

Serve with
Pommes Anna
(page 214) and
Bordelaise Sauce
(page 85).

Roast loin of venison

Venison is a very lean cut with little fat marbling so I prefer not to subject it to a fierce blast of heat in the oven. Instead I brown the meat in a little oil on the top of the stove before roasting. The times specified are for rare.

serves 4

PREP TIME 10 MINUTES   COOK TIME 8 MINUTES

800 g (1 lb 12 oz) venison loin

salt and pepper

50 ml (2 fl oz) vegetable oil

Preheat the oven to 190°C (375°F). Season the venison all over with salt and pepper. Heat the oil in a roasting tray over a high heat. Add the venison and brown it all over until evenly caramelised; this should take about 5 minutes.

Roast for 8 minutes, turning the meat over after 4 minutes. Remove from the oven and cover loosely with foil. Rest for 4 minutes in a warm area. This will give a nice rare cooking degree.

Carve and serve with your choice of accompaniments.

Serve with
Truffle-baked Nicola
Potatoes (page 217),
Sprout and Chestnut
Sauté (page 210)
and Périgueux Sauce
(page 87).

Whole roasted baby chicken

One of the difficulties with roasting chicken and other white meat birds is that the delicate breast meat tends to dry out in the hot temperatures. This area is especially vulnerable if you use the classic approach of roasting at an initial high temperature to caramelise the skin. My method avoids this problem altogether. I caramelise the skin in foaming butter on top of the stove before quickly roasting the bird in the oven at a medium heat. While the bird rests, I prop it upright and pour the roasting juices and butter into the cavity. This allows all the wonderful flavours and juices to be absorbed back into the breast meat. I guarantee that this will be the tenderest, most flavoursome chicken you'll ever eat.

serves 2

PREP TIME 10 MINUTES   COOK TIME 35 MINUTES

Serve it with Truffle Potato Purée (page 212), Confit Cabbage (page 211) and Jus Gras (page 84).

800 g (1 lb 12 oz) poussin or baby/young chicken
salt and pepper
120 g (4½ oz) butter
1 bunch thyme
4 garlic cloves
50 ml (2 fl oz) vegetable oil

Preheat the oven to 190°C (375°F). Rub the chicken inside and out with salt and pepper. Place half the butter inside the cavity with the thyme and garlic.

Heat the oil and remaining butter in a large heavy-based frying pan over a moderate heat. When the oil is hot and the butter foaming, place the chicken in the pan and start to brown it. Baste continuously and turn the bird over in the pan so it caramelises evenly all over. When it's a lovely golden brown – and this should only take a few minutes – lift the chicken onto a rack or trivet in a heavy-based roasting pan. Roast for 25 minutes, basting from time to time with the pan juices.

Remove from the oven and carefully transfer the chicken to another roasting tray, so that the cavity is pointing skywards. Pour all the roasting juices into the cavity, cover loosely with foil and leave in a warm place to rest for 5–10 minutes before carving. Serve with your choice of accompaniments.

Slow-roasted pork rump with crackling

This is a slightly different method of roasting. Instead of the usual process which involves roasting at an initial high heat, and then further roasting at a lower temperature, I like to cook the pork more slowly at an even temperature. This always ensures a delectably juicy and tender roast. To make sure you get good crackling, salt and dry the skin first and then fry it in hot oil before roasting the joint in the oven. That way you still get the lovely puffy, crunchy crackling that everyone loves.

serves 4

PREP TIME 20 MINUTES SALTING TIME 4 HOURS COOK TIME 50 MINUTES

1 kg (2 lb 3 oz) pork rump or loin, with fat and skin intact

30 g (1 oz) salt

30 ml (1 fl oz) vegetable oil

Use a very sharp kitchen knife or a Stanley (utility) knife to score the rind. Work from one end to the other, making parallel incisions about 1 cm (½ in) apart. Massage the salt into the skin, making sure you get into all the cuts. Place in a shallow dish and refrigerate, uncovered, for at least 4 hours. The salting and drying helps extract moisture from the skin, making good crisp crackling.

Preheat the oven to 170°C (340°F). Remove the pork from the refrigerator and bring to room temperature. Heat the oil in a heavy-based frying pan over a moderate heat. Wipe off any excess salt and moisture from the pork skin and place it in the pan, skin side down. Fry for about 10 minutes until the skin is crisp and golden brown.

Lift the pork out of the frying pan and place on a rack or trivet in a heavy-based roasting pan. Roast for 50 minutes, until just cooked and still tender and pale pink in the centre. The crackling will be extremely crispy, light and puffy. Rest in a warm place for 10 minutes before carving. Use a serrated knife, which will make it easier to cut through the crackling – use the incisions as your guide.

Serve with Spring Onion Creamed Potatoes (page 212), Buttered Sweetcorn (page 224) and Smoked Bacon and Grain Mustard Jus (page 88).

Roasted mulloway (page 204)

Lobster tail roasted on aromatics (page 205)

Roasted mulloway

I don't know why, but some people are a little bit funny about fish skin: in the restaurant I watch time and time again as they peel it away and waste all that lovely crisp, tasty goodness. It's especially sad as the skin and underlying layer of fat are chock-a-block full of health-giving omega fatty acids. From a cooking point of view, it is this layer of fat that helps keep the flesh moist and tender during the cooking process. The fish will continue cooking even after it comes out of the oven, so I usually suggest that people start eating from the thin belly side first, and work their way towards the thicker part of the fish. This cooking technique also works brilliantly with barramundi, snapper, blue eye and kingfish, and, of course, salmon.

serves 4

PREP TIME 5 MINUTES   COOK TIME 8 MINUTES

I like to serve crisp-skinned roasted fish with the pan juices and a Sprout and Chestnut Sauté (page 210).

4 x 180 g (6½ oz) portions of mulloway, skin on

1 tablespoon vegetable oil

salt and pepper

50 g (2 oz) butter

squeeze of lemon

Preheat your oven to 180°C (350°F). Use a very sharp kitchen knife or a Stanley (utility) knife to score the skin. Work from one end to the other, making parallel incisions about 1 cm (½ in) apart. This helps make the skin extra crisp and allows all the tasty pan juices to be absorbed into the flesh.

Heat the oil in a heavy-based oven-proof frying pan over a moderate heat.

Season the fish skin generously with salt and pepper then place in the pan, skin side down. Cook for 3 minutes without moving the fish in the pan, to help the skin caramelise. Transfer to the oven and roast for 4 minutes.

Return the pan to the stove top on a high heat. Add the butter and allow to foam to a light beurre noisette. Use a fish slice or spatula to gently loosen the fish and carefully turn it over. Fry for another minute, basting continuously with the pan juices. The fish should be just cooked through, with delicate pearly-white flesh and crisp golden skin. Finish with a squeeze of lemon and serve hot from the pan with the juices and your choice of accompaniment.

Lobster tail roasted on aromatics

Lobster responds beautifully to being roasted in its shell, and I find this fragrant spice mix really brings out the sweetness of the meat.

serves 4

PREP TIME 10 MINUTES   COOK TIME 12 MINUTES

10 ml (¼ fl oz) cooking oil
2 x 600 g (1 lb 5 oz) lobster tails
Aromatic Spice Mix (page 17)

Preheat your oven to 180°C (350°F). Heat the oil in a heavy-based oven-proof frying pan over a high heat. Add the lobster tails and sauté for a few minutes, turning once or twice, until they turn a deep orangey red.

Scatter on the spice mix and roast in the oven for 12 minutes, until just cooked. Remove from the oven and leave to rest in a warm place for 4 minutes.

Use a lobster cracker or kitchen scissors to cut the tail down the centre of the flat underside. Pull the shell away from the flesh and remove the sweet meat in one whole piece. Slice into large medallions and serve with your choice of accompaniment.

Serve with a squeeze of lemon and a splash of melted butter. If you want to make it into a bigger meal, serve with Béarnaise Sauce (page 92), Sauté of Pea Shoots and White Asparagus (page 221) and Morel and Parmesan Gnocchi (page 216).

Vegetables

In my view, the French tend to make much better use of vegetables than we do in Australia. As anyone who's spent time holidaying in France will tell you, vegetable dishes are not restricted to playing a 'bit part' in a meal.

In France, vegetables are often served as a separate course in their own right, and vegetable dishes feature prominently in the French repertoire of little starters, or hors d'oeuvres.

Visitors to France also speak in wonder of the amazing fresh produce markets. Most French housewives still far prefer to do their fruit and veg shopping at a market where small local producers bring their produce than in a giant, impersonal 'supermarché'. It's fascinating to watch the French in full shopping-mode: prodding, sniffing and firing questions at the store holder. You can tell immediately that these are people who care about the quality of the produce.

When it comes to selecting and buying vegetables, my best advice is to do as the French! Firstly, avoid large supermarkets which bulk-buy and keep their produce cold-stored. I'm a big fan of local and farmers' markets – you know the produce is fresh and you'll get a far greater variety of produce than in a supermarket. Don't be afraid to touch the produce either; pick the vegetables up, inspect them for blemishes, feel their weight, check that they are brightly coloured, crisp and firm. Flabby, tired vegetables are a real no-no. It's also a good idea to buy smaller amounts of vegetables more frequently – that way they are more likely to be of optimum freshness when you cook them.

When you get them home, unpack and store your fresh vegetables away as soon as possible. While most vegetables are best kept in the refrigerator, tomatoes are best stored at room temperature and some root vegetables and onions can also be kept in a cool, dark larder – although not many homes tend to have these any more. Cover or wrap different vegetable types and store them separately. Leafy and delicate vegetables should be wrapped in damp (not wet) kitchen paper or a tea (dish) towel – or even sealed in kitchen storage bags.

When preparing vegetables, in general you should wait to wash, peel or cut them until just before cooking as they begin to deteriorate once exposed to moisture and air. Some vegetables need nothing more than a quick rinse, others need to be peeled.

There are myriad methods for cooking vegetables, and they include many of the techniques touched on in other French Lessons: steaming, braising, pan-frying or deep-frying and so on. Some of my favourite examples are outlined in the recipes below. As a general principle, though, remember that no vegetable improves by being overcooked! Most vegetables should be served with a slight crunch (what the Italians call al dente).

DICING
A broad term to describe cutting vegetables into smallish, even-sized pieces, depending on further use. Generally, the vegetables are first cut into thin slices, then into sticks and then crosswise to achieve small cubes.

MIREPOIX
A rough dice of vegetables which are to be used to enhance the flavour of stocks, soups and sauces. Traditionally a mirepoix consists of carrot, onion, leek and celery, and sometimes fennel and garlic. A white mirepoix is used for white stocks, and contains no carrot.

MACÉDOINE
A medium-size dice (4 mm/¼ in) of mixed vegetables, usually carrots and turnips, that are cooked separately and then tossed together in a little butter, and perhaps fresh herbs. A macédoine is often served as an accompaniment, and may be warm or cold.

BRUNOISE
Perfect tiny dice (2 mm/⅛ in) of vegetables that are used as a garnish for sauces, soups and stuffings.

JULIENNE
A method of cutting vegetables into even-sized thin sticks, a little like skinny matchsticks. They are cut into even slices, around 2 mm (⅛ in) thick, and then cut into strips, around 3 cm (1¼ in) long. A julienne of vegetables may be cooked in a little butter and used as a garnish – especially for soups and consommés. They may also be served raw as an hors d'oeuvre.

JARDINIÈRE
A vegetable, generally root vegetables, cut the same as a julienne except a lot larger, usually about 3 mm (⅛ in) thick and about 3–4 cm (1¼–1½ in) long, resulting in a large baton.

Basic preparation methods

Jardinière

Dicing

Julienne

Root vegetable and game garnishes

Sprout and chestnut sauté

serves 4

/ PREP TIME 5 MINUTES 🍳 COOK TIME 15 MINUTES

500 g (1 lb 2 oz) brussels sprouts, quartered

½ tablespoon cooking oil

12 chestnuts, peeled and cut into eighths

salt and pepper

30 g (1 oz) butter

1 tablespoon chopped parsley

Bring a large saucepan of salted water to the boil. Blanch the sprouts for 2 minutes then refresh in iced water. Tip into a colander to drain, then dry thoroughly on kitchen paper.

Heat the oil in a heavy-based frying pan over a moderate heat. Add the chestnut pieces and lightly sauté until they start to colour. Season well, add the butter and cook it to a light brown foam. Add the blanched sprouts and sauté, basting frequently, until both sprouts and chestnuts are tender and caramelised a deep golden brown, about 10 minutes. Remove the pan from the heat, add the chopped parsley and toss to combine.

Caramelised parsnips

serves 4

/ PREP TIME 5 MINUTES 🍳 COOK TIME 10 MINUTES

4 parsnips

½ tablespoon vegetable oil

salt and pepper

40 g (1 ½ oz) butter

Peel the parsnips and trim off the base end and tip. Slice the parsnip lengthwise around its central core into 4 curved wedges. Cut each wedge in half and slice away any remaining core, which is tough and fibrous.

Heat the oil in a frying pan over a moderate heat. Add the parsnip batons and sauté for a few minutes until they start to colour. Season well, add the butter and cook it to a light brown foam. Continue to sauté the parsnips, basting frequently, until they are caramelised a deep golden brown, about 8–10 minutes.

Confit cabbage and celeriac

serves 4

PREP TIME 15 MINUTES COOK TIME 15 MINUTES

1 celeriac, peeled

¼ cabbage, tough outer leaves removed, cored

60 ml (2 fl oz) duck fat

1 garlic clove, roughly smashed

2 sprigs thyme

salt and pepper

Peel the celeriac and cut to a macédoine (page 208). Dice the cabbage to a similar size. Heat the duck fat in a saucepan over a low heat. Add the celeriac, cabbage, garlic, thyme and seasonings and cook gently for 10 minutes, until the vegetables are tender.

the humble potato

Finding the correct potato to make the perfect purée can be tricky as it depends not only on the variety, but also on the time of year.

In general, I like to use desirée potatoes, which are firm, waxy and buttery, but as their growing season progresses they can sometimes become watery and floury. I might then switch to royal blue, spunta or yukon gold, and as they too start to change in texture I switch back to desirée. It is worth learning how to perfect the basic purée, which can then be flavoured with all kinds of additions, making it a truly versatile accompaniment to any meal. A few of my favourites are included on following pages.

Potato purée

serves 4

PREP TIME 10 MINUTES · COOK TIME 20 MINUTES

2 x 400 g (14 oz) all-purpose potatoes	50 ml (2 fl oz) cream
salt	100 g (3½ oz) cold butter, diced
50 ml (2 fl oz) milk	pepper

Peel the potatoes and cut into even-sized pieces. It doesn't matter what shape they are, but it is important that they are all a similar size so they will cook evenly.

Put the potatoes in a saucepan, cover with cold water and season liberally with salt. Bring to the boil, then lower the heat and simmer gently for 12–15 minutes until the potatoes are tender. Tip into a colander to drain and leave them to air-dry for a few minutes.

Push the potatoes through a potato ricer or drum sieve while still hot. Use a pastry scraper or a large spoon to push them through as swiftly as possible. Take care not to overwork the starch in the potatoes; the resulting purée should be dry.

In a small saucepan, heat the milk, cream and half the butter. When the butter has melted, use a hand blender to whisk and emulsify it, then fold the hot liquid into the potato. Use a rubber spatula to gradually beat in the remaining butter. Taste and season to your liking.

HORSERADISH POTATO PURÉE

Add a few spoonfuls of horseradish cream or grated fresh horseradish to the basic purée.

TRUFFLE POTATO PURÉE

Add a few spoonfuls of finely chopped fresh black truffle and a drizzle of truffle oil to the basic purée.

SPRING ONION CREAMED POTATOES

Finely slice a bunch of spring onions (scallions) and fold them into the purée just before serving. That way you get a lovely contrast in texture and flavour between the hot creamy purée and the delicate crunch and slight sharpness of the onions.

Crushed potatoes (page 218)

Potato purée

Confit kipfler potatoes (page 217)

Sarladaise potatoes (page 214)

Pommes dauphinoise

serves 8

PREP TIME 30 MINUTES COOK TIME 45 MINUTES

200 ml (7 fl oz) cream

3 garlic cloves

3 sprigs thyme

splash vegetable oil

6 all-purpose potatoes, peeled

salt and pepper

50 g (2 oz) grated gruyère and parmesan, mixed

Preheat your oven to 190°C (375°F). Put the cream, garlic and thyme in a small saucepan and heat gently. Simmer for 5 minutes to infuse. Strain through a fine sieve and set the infused cream aside.

Line a small roasting pan, about 15 cm x 20 cm x 4 cm (6 in x 8 in x 1½ in), with baking paper. Brush the sides of the pan with the vegetable oil. Use a mandoline or very sharp knife to slice the potatoes as thinly as possible. Arrange a layer of potato slices on the bottom of the pan. Season with salt and pepper, sprinkle on a little cheese and drizzle with the warm cream. Continue layering to the top of the tin, reserving a little of the cheese. As you go, press the layers down firmly into the base of the pan to eliminate any gaps or air pockets.

Cover with foil and bake for 30 minutes until the potatoes are nearly cooked. Remove the foil and increase the oven temperature to 220°C (430°F). Sprinkle on the remaining cheese and bake until crisp and golden brown. Serve piping hot, or keep in the refrigerator for up to 3 days.

Sarladaise potatoes

serves 8

PREP TIME 20 MINUTES COOK TIME 35 MINUTES

300 ml (10 fl oz) rendered duck fat

8 all-purpose potatoes, peeled

2 tablespoons thyme leaves

salt and pepper

Preheat your oven to 170°C (340°F). Line a small roasting pan, about 15 cm x 20 cm x 4 cm (6 in x 8 in x 1½ in), with baking paper. Brush the sides of the pan with a little of the rendered duck fat.

Use a mandoline or very sharp knife to slice the potatoes as thinly as possible. Arrange a layer of potato slices on the bottom of the pan. Sprinkle on a little thyme, season with salt and pepper and drizzle with duck fat. Continue layering to the top of the tin. As you go, press the layers down firmly into the base of the pan to eliminate any gaps or air pockets.

Cut a rectangle of baking paper to the size of the pan and cover the potatoes. Wrap the whole pan with foil and bake for 35 minutes until the potatoes are tender. Serve piping hot, or keep in the refrigerator for up to 3 days.

POMMES ANNA

Make in the same way as the pommes sarlardaise, but use a round cake tin instead of a rectangular pan. Remove the foil halfway through the cooking time and increase the oven temperature to 220°C (430°F). Dot the surface with a few knobs of butter and bake until crisp and golden brown.

Pommes boulangère

serves 8

PREP TIME 20 MINUTES COOK TIME 35 MINUTES

50 ml (2 fl oz) vegetable oil

3 onions, finely sliced

2 tablespoons thyme leaves

salt and pepper

6 all-purpose potatoes, peeled

200 ml (7 fl oz) White Chicken Stock (page 29)

50 g (2 oz) diced butter

Preheat your oven to 170°C (340°F). Line a small roasting pan, about 15 cm x 20 cm x 4 cm (6 in x 8 in x 1½ in), with baking paper. Brush the sides of the pan with a little of the vegetable oil.

Heat the remaining oil in a heavy-based frying pan. Add the onions, thyme and seasoning and sweat for about 8 minutes, until onion is translucent. Remove from the heat and allow to cool.

Use a mandoline or very sharp knife to slice the potatoes as thinly as possible. Arrange a layer of potato slices on the bottom of the pan, then a layer of onions. Season with salt and pepper and drizzle with chicken stock. Continue layering to the top of the tin. As you go, press the layers down firmly into the base of the pan to eliminate any gaps or air pockets.

Cut a rectangle of baking paper to the size of the pan and cover the potatoes. Wrap the whole pan with foil and bake for 25 minutes until the potatoes are nearly cooked. Remove the foil and baking paper and increase the oven temperature to 220°C (430°F). Dot the surface with a few knobs of butter and bake until crisp and golden brown. Serve piping hot, or keep in the refrigerator for up to 3 days.

Potato and bacon roesti

serves 4

PREP TIME 15 MINUTES COOK TIME 20 MINUTES

2 all-purpose potatoes

50 ml (2 fl oz) rendered duck fat

40 ml (1 ½ fl oz) vegetable oil

1 onion, finely sliced

50 g (2 oz) bacon, finely sliced

1 tablespoon thyme leaves

salt and pepper

Preheat your oven to 190°C (375°F). Place the unpeeled potatoes in a saucepan and cover with cold water. Bring to a gentle simmer and cook for about 8 minutes until the potatoes are barely half-cooked. Remove the potatoes from the water and allow to cool.

Heat the duck fat and oil in a heavy-based frying pan. Add the onion, bacon and thyme leaves and sweat over a medium-heat until soft and translucent, about 5 minutes. Season generously then tip into a mixing bowl and allow to cool.

When the potatoes are cool enough to handle, peel away the skins and grate the potatoes into the onion mix. Mix everything together well, taste and adjust the seasoning to your liking. Divide the mixture into quarters and shape each into a round patty.

Heat a large roasting pan, 4 small roesti pans or an egg poaching pan with four holes in the oven. Add a splash of oil and add the patties. Bake for 8 minutes then turn carefully and bake for another 8 minutes. Serve piping hot.

Morel and parmesan gnocchi

serves 8

PREP TIME 30 MINUTES COOK TIME 20 MINUTES

2 tablespoons salt

1 x 450 g (1 lb) all-purpose potato (this should yield 300 g/10½ oz cooked purée)

90 g (3¼ oz) flour, sieved, plus extra for dusting and rolling

50 g (2 oz) grated parmesan cheese

1 egg yolk

2 tablespoons chopped reconstituted morels

salt and pepper

Preheat your oven to 220°C (430°F). Make a small mound of salt in the base of a small baking tray. Carefully place the unpeeled potato on top and bake for 25 minutes. Turn it over and bake for a further 25 minutes. Test with a skewer – it should be cooked through and soft in the centre.

Cut the potato in half and scoop out the flesh (hold with a tea/dish towel so you don't burn yourself). Leave to air-dry for 3–4 minutes then push the potato through a potato ricer or drum sieve while still hot. Use a pastry scraper or a large spoon to push it through as swiftly as possible. Take care not to overwork the starch in the potato; the resulting purée should be dry.

Add the remaining ingredients and combine gently. Taste and season to your liking. Be very careful not to overwork the potato or it will become gluey and the gnocchi will be dense and heavy.

Divide the mixture into thirds and work with one portion at a time. Dust your hands and work surface with a little flour. Roll the gnocchi mix into a long rope and use a sharp knife to cut into 3 cm (1¼ in) pieces and place them on a sheet of baking paper. Repeat with the remaining mix.

Bring a large saucepan of salted water to the boil. Have a large bowl of iced water ready and add a splash of vegetable oil. Adjust the temperature of the water to a steady simmer and drop in the gnocchi from one sheet of paper, all in one go. As the gnocchi rise to the surface – which will take around 3 minutes – remove them with a slotted spoon and place them in the iced water.

When the gnocchi are cold, drain them well and arrange on a lightly greased tray. Cover with plastic wrap and refrigerate until required. They will keep in the refrigerator for 3 days.

To serve, warm the gnocchi through gently in a saucepan of soup or consommé, or pan-fry in a little oil over a medium heat.

Confit kipfler potatoes

serves 4

PREP TIME 10 MINUTES COOK TIME 12 MINUTES

600 ml (20½ fl oz) olive oil

20 small kipfler (fingerling) potatoes, unpeeled

6 sprigs thyme

4 garlic cloves, roughly crushed

salt and pepper

Warm the oil gently in a large, heavy-based pan, to about 70°C (160°F).

Preheat the oven to 150°C (300°F). Cut the potatoes into slices around 1 cm (½ in) thick. Arrange them in a braising pan and carefully pour on the hot oil. The potatoes should be completely submerged in the oil. Tuck in the sprigs of thyme and the garlic cloves, season well and bake for 10–12 minutes until the potatoes are tender.

Use a slotted spoon to remove the potatoes from the oil and serve straight away. Otherwise, they will keep in the oil, refrigerated, for 3 days. You can reuse the oil several times for cooking other potato dishes.

Truffle-baked nicola potatoes

If you can't find nicola potatoes, substitute another all-purpose potato, preferably with yellowish skin and flesh and a buttery texture.

serves 4

PREP TIME 5 MINUTES COOK TIME 20 MINUTES

4 nicola potatoes

40 ml (1½ fl oz) truffle oil

sea salt and pepper

50 g (2 oz) fresh black truffle

Preheat your oven to 190°C (375°F). Cut out 4 rectangles of foil, around 21 cm x 30 cm (8 in x 12 in). Cut the unpeeled potatoes into large chunks and divide between the foil pieces. Drizzle with truffle oil, season and top with shavings of truffle. Wrap securely to make a parcel and lift onto a baking tray. Bake for 15–20 minutes, until the potatoes are just cooked.

Remove from the oven and carefully lift the parcels onto serving plates. Serve straight away, so that each diner opens their own parcel, releasing the wonderful aroma of fresh truffle.

Crushed potatoes

Nicola potatoes are best for this recipe as they have a soft buttery texture and sweet earthy flavour. Alternatively, use any other all-purpose potato. It is important to cook the potatoes at a very gentle simmer. Above all, don't boil the potatoes, because they will split and become waterlogged.

serves 4

PREP TIME 5 MINUTES — COOK TIME 25 MINUTES

2 nicola potatoes

50 ml (2 fl oz) extra-virgin olive oil

sea salt and pepper

few drops lemon juice

2 tablespoons chopped chives

Place the unpeeled potatoes in a saucepan and cover with cold water. Bring to a very gentle simmer and cook for about 25 minutes until the potatoes are tender. Tip into a colander to drain. When cool enough to handle, peel away the skins.

Place the warm potatoes in a large mixing bowl. Use your hands to gently crush the potatoes, adding seasoning and lemon juice to taste. Add the chives just before serving. The potatoes will keep in the refrigerator for 2 days; to serve, reheat them in a saucepan with a little olive oil.

Pommes fondant

serves 4

PREP TIME 20 MINUTES — COOK TIME 40 MINUTES

4 small all-purpose potatoes

300 g (10½ oz) butter

salt and pepper

Wash the potatoes well, then peel and rinse them again. Lay the potatoes on your chopping board and slice the ends and the two broadest sides flat. Use a small sharp knife to trim the edges so your potatoes are shaped like little barrels.

Slice the butter and put it in the bottom of a heavy-based saucepan or braising dish. Season well and arrange the potatoes on top. Season again.

Place the pan over a high heat and cook until the butter foams up over the potatoes. Cook for a few minutes then remove the pan from the stove and rest for 3 minutes. Return the pan to the heat and foam the butter again, adding more if need be. Cook for a few minutes, then allow to rest.

Repeat several times until the potatoes are tender and have coloured a deep golden brown on the bottom. Serve immediately, golden side upwards.

Vegetable accompaniments

Petit pois à la Française

serves 4

PREP TIME 15 MINUTES COOK TIME 10 MINUTES

100 g (3 ½ oz) shelled small, young peas

½ tablespoon vegetable oil or rendered duck fat

4 shallots, finely diced

40 g (1 ½ oz) sliced bacon, finely diced

1 head baby/little gem lettuce, sliced crosswise

100 ml (3 ½ oz) White Chicken Stock (page 29)

20 g (¾ oz) cold butter, diced

salt and pepper

Blanch the peas in boiling salted water for 2 minutes and then refresh in iced water. Drain and set aside. This can be done ahead of time.

Heat the oil or duck fat in a heavy-based saucepan over a moderate heat. Add the shallots and bacon and sweat for a few minutes until soft. Add the blanched peas, lettuce and chicken stock and bring to the boil. Add the butter and swirl gently to emulsify and thicken the sauce. Season and serve immediately.

Tomato concasse

Add these tomato dice to salads, or as a garnish for sauces and dressings.

serves 4

PREP TIME 2 MINUTES COOK TIME 2 MINUTES

8 tomatoes

Bring a large saucepan of water to the boil. Prepare a large bowl of iced water. Use the sharp point of a small knife to remove the eyes from the tomatoes and score the bottom end with a criss-cross. Plunge the tomatoes into the boiling water for about 30 seconds just to loosen the skins. Using tongs, carefully lift them out of the water and drop them into the iced water to refresh. When cool, remove from the water, drain and pat dry. Quarter the tomatoes and gently slice away the seeds and inner flesh (reserve for stocks, soups and sauces). You will be left with neat little tomato 'petals'. Cut these into small, even dice.

Slow-roasted garlic

Roast garlic makes a great addition to sauces, purées and dressings.

makes 12 cloves

PREP TIME 2 MINUTES COOK TIME 20 MINUTES

12 fat garlic cloves, unpeeled

½ tablespoon vegetable oil

salt and pepper

4 sprigs thyme

Serve roasted garlic cloves with grilled lamb cutlets or Provençale-style dishes. Serve them whole, so that each person can squeeze the lovely soft paste out of the roasted skins.

Preheat your oven to 160°C (320°F). Place all the ingredients in a small roasting pan and toss gently together. Roast for 20 minutes, until the garlic cloves are golden and soft.

219

Choucroute

This famous fermented cabbage dish is a specialty of Alsace and Lorraine and neighbouring areas of Germany, where it is known as sauerkraut. The recipe varies from region to region – this is my version.

makes 1 litre (34 fl oz)

PREP TIME 20 MINUTES · MARINATING TIME 24 HOURS · COOK TIME 3 HOURS

15 juniper berries

10 black peppercorns

3 star anise

1 cinnamon quill

3 garlic cloves

8 sprigs thyme

1 bay leaf

100 g (3½ oz) Wet Citrus Salt (page 19)

1 cabbage, tough outer leaves removed

100 ml (3½ fl oz) rendered duck fat

2 onions, finely sliced

150 g (5½ oz) pancetta

500 ml (17 fl oz) riesling

Put the juniper berries, peppercorns, star anise, cinnamon, garlic, thyme and bay leaf in a mortar and pound until roughly crushed and fragrant. Tip into a large mixing bowl with the salt and rub together well.

Cut the cabbage into quarters and cut out the core. Shred as finely as you can and add to the salt mix. Toss everything together well, cover with plastic wrap and set aside in a warm place to ferment. This can take between 24 and 48 hours – the longer you leave it, the stronger the flavour.

When ready to continue, preheat the oven to 120°C (250°F). Tip the fermented cabbage into a colander and rinse thoroughly under cold running water.

Heat the duck fat in a large casserole or braising pan over a medium heat. Add the onions and sweat gently for 10 minutes until soft and translucent. Add the rinsed cabbage, the pancetta and the wine.

Cut a piece of baking paper to the size of the pan and place on top of the cabbage mixture. Cover the pan with a tight-fitting lid and braise in the oven for 4 hours. Stir every 30 minutes or so, to ensure the contents don't stick and burn. Remove from the oven and leave to cool. Tip out onto a shallow tray and pick out the pieces of crushed spice. Store in a sealed container in the refrigerator for up to 2 weeks.

Sauté of pea shoots and white asparagus

serves 4

PREP TIME 5 MINUTES COOK TIME 5 MINUTES

12 white asparagus spears

1 tablespoon olive oil

100 g (3½ oz) pea shoots

salt and pepper

few drops lemon juice

Peel the asparagus and cut each spear into 4 pieces on an angle. Heat the olive oil in a frying pan over a moderate heat. Add the sliced asparagus and sauté for about 3 minutes until the spears are just cooked but still firm. Add the pea shoots and sauté for a few seconds just to wilt. Season with salt and pepper, sprinkle on the lemon juice and serve immediately.

Lyonnaise onions

makes 200 g (7 oz)

PREP TIME 10 MINUTES COOK TIME 90 MINUTES

60 ml (2 fl oz) rendered duck fat

4 onions, finely sliced

4 sprigs thyme

2 garlic cloves

salt and pepper

Heat the duck fat in a medium-sized saucepan over a moderate heat. Add the remaining ingredients and cook for 60–90 minutes, stirring regularly to ensure the onions don't catch and burn. If the onions become a little dry, add another splash of duck fat. The long slow cooking results in a lovely deep caramelised mess of sweet-savoury onions. The onions will keep refrigerated in a sealed container for up to a month.

Braised borlotti beans and peas

serves 4

PREP TIME 20 MINUTES COOK TIME 2 HOURS

80 g (3 oz) butter

1 onion, finely diced

4 garlic cloves, roughly crushed

4 sprigs thyme

1 bay leaf

300 g (10½ oz) fresh borlotti (cranberry) beans, shelled (to yield around 160 g beans)

1 litre White Chicken Stock (page 29)

salt and pepper

100 g (3½ oz) shelled peas

1 tablespoon chopped parsley

Preheat your oven to 110°C (230°F). Heat the butter in a braising pan over a medium heat until it foams. Add the onion and garlic and sweat gently for about 8 minutes until onion is soft and translucent. Add the thyme, bay leaf, borlotti beans and stock. Season well and bring to a gentle simmer.

Cut a piece of baking paper to the size of the pan and place on top of the bean mixture. Cover the pan with a tight-fitting lid and braise in the oven for 2 hours. Stir every 30 minutes or so, to ensure the contents don't stick and burn.

Bring a large saucepan of salted water to the boil. Blanch the peas for 2 minutes, drain well, then stir into the braised beans. Add the parsley and serve straight away.

221

Mushroom duxelles

makes 500 g (1 lb 2 oz)

PREP TIME 15 MINUTES   COOK TIME 15 MINUTES

1 tablespoon cooking oil

500 g (1 lb 2 oz) button mushrooms, quartered

50 g (2 oz) butter

2 garlic cloves, roughly crushed

4 sprigs thyme

salt and pepper

few drops lemon juice

Heat half the oil in a large frying pan over a medium heat. Add half the mushrooms and sauté until lightly coloured. Add half the butter and allow to foam. Add one of the garlic cloves and 2 sprigs of thyme. Season and sauté for a further few minutes until the mushrooms are golden. Squeeze on a few drops of lemon juice then tip into a colander to drain away any excess oil.

Repeat for remaining ingredients. When all the mushrooms are cooked, tip them out onto a chopping board and pick out the garlic cloves and thyme. Use a sharp knife to chop the mushrooms finely. Taste and adjust the seasoning to your liking.

Parsnip purée

makes 500 ml (17 fl oz)

PREP TIME 10 MINUTES COOK TIME 15 MINUTES

60 g (2 oz) butter

1 onion, finely sliced

2 garlic cloves, finely sliced

3 parsnips, peeled, cored and finely sliced

100 ml (3½ fl oz) cream

50 ml (2 fl oz) milk

salt and pepper

few drops lemon juice

Heat the butter in a heavy-based saucepan over a moderate heat. Add the onion and garlic and sweat for a few minutes until onion is soft and translucent. Add the parsnips and sweat for another few minutes without colouring.

Add the cream and milk to the pan and bring to a gentle simmer. Cook until the parsnips are tender, about 10 minutes. Season well and tip into a blender. Whiz to a velvet smooth purée and finish with a drop of lemon juice. Push through a fine sieve and serve.

Buttered sweetcorn

serves 4

PREP TIME 5 MINUTES COOK TIME 10 MINUTES

4 sweetcorn cobs, outer husks and
  fibres removed

60 g (2 oz) butter

salt and pepper

Bring a large saucepan of salted water to the boil. Use a sharp knife to cut the corn kernels away from the cob. Blanch for 2 minutes then tip into a colander to drain.

Tip the corn into a medium-sized saucepan, add the butter and season to taste. Heat gently for 2 minutes until the butter has melted and the corn is tender.

Roasted baby carrots

serves 4

PREP TIME 5 MINUTES COOK TIME 15 MINUTES

2 bunches baby carrots (or use large carrots cut
  into batons)

1 tablespoon vegetable oil

4 garlic cloves

6 sprigs thyme

salt and pepper

50 g (2 oz) butter

Preheat your oven to 180°C (350°F). Wash and scrub the carrots. Heat the oil in a roasting pan over a moderate heat. Add the carrots and sauté for a few minutes until they begin to colour. Add the remaining ingredients and cook until the butter foams. Place in the oven and roast for 5–8 minutes, until the carrots are golden brown and tender.

Sweet and sour white turnips

serves 4

PREP TIME 10 MINUTES COOK TIME 10 MINUTES

4 large white turnips, stalks trimmed

500 ml (17 fl oz) water

1 teaspoon sugar

40 ml (1 ½ fl oz) chardonnay vinegar

2 garlic cloves

2 sprigs thyme

salt and pepper

Use a vegetable peeler to peel the turnips, keeping as much of the natural round shape as you can. Once peeled, cut the turnips into large chunks.

Put all the remaining ingredients in a large saucepan. Taste and adjust the balance of sweet-sourness to your liking. Add the turnips and bring to a gentle simmer.

Cut a piece of baking paper to the size of the pan and place on top of turnips. Simmer gently for about 15 minutes, until tender.

CARAMELISED SWEET AND SOUR TURNIPS

Prepare the sweet and sour turnips as above then caramelise them in a hot pan in a mixture of oil and butter until they turn a deep golden brown.

Roasted sweet and sour capsicums

serves 4

PREP TIME 5 MINUTES COOK TIME 25 MINUTES

4 red capsicums (peppers)

4 garlic cloves, roughly crushed

6 sprigs thyme

2 tablespoons sherry vinegar

3 tablespoons olive oil

salt and pepper

Preheat your oven to 150°C (300°F). Cut the capsicums in half and scoop out the seeds and membranes. Place in a roasting pan, skin side down. Sprinkle the remaining ingredients into the cavities of the capsicums. Cover with foil and roast for 25 minutes until the skins have loosened from the flesh.

Remove from the oven and place the capsicums in a bowl with all the juices. Cover with plastic wrap and leave the capsicums to steam for 5 minutes; this will loosen the skins further.

When cool enough to handle, peel the skin away from the flesh. Place in a sealed container, strain all the roasting juices over the capsicums and refrigerate.

Pistou of vegetables

serves 4
PREP TIME 15 MINUTES   COOK TIME 5 MINUTES

50 ml (2 fl oz) olive oil

1 Spanish (red) onion, finely diced

2 Asian eggplants (aubergines), finely diced

1 yellow zucchini (courgette), finely diced

1 green zucchini (courgette), finely diced

1 red capsicum (pepper), finely diced

salt and pepper

Heat the oil in a frying pan over a moderate heat. Add the diced vegetables, season well and sauté for 2 minutes until tender. Serve straight away or tip into a sealed container and store in the refrigerator for up to 2 days.

Foie gras and thyme dumplings

serves 4
PREP TIME 20 MINUTES   COOK TIME 8 MINUTES

200 g (7 oz) sifted plain (all-purpose) flour

100 g (3 ½ oz) cooked foie gras, diced

2 tablespoons thyme leaves

salt and pepper

a little cold water

Place the flour, foie gras, thyme and seasoning in a mixing bowl. Rub between your fingers until the foie gras is completely incorporated into the flour. Add a few drops of cold water and work into a soft yet firm dough. Roll into small dumplings. Cook from room temperature: poach gently in broths or consommés for about 8 minutes.

Herb and parmesan purée

This wonderful green purée is incredibly versatile. It makes a delicious sauce for egg dishes or with grilled lamb or roast veal. Or use it to make a vegetarian lasagne or stuffing for cannelloni.

serves 4
PREP TIME 20 MINUTES   COOK TIME 10 MINUTES

200 g (7 oz) butter

1 onion, finely diced

2 garlic cloves, finely diced

2 cups flat-leaf (Italian) parsley leaves

2 cups watercress leaves

3 cups baby spinach leaves

50 g (2 oz) grated parmesan

salt and pepper

few drops lemon juice

Heat 120 g (4½ oz) of the butter in a medium-sized saucepan until it foams to a light golden brown. Allow to cool slightly, then strain through a fine sieve. Set this beurre noisette aside in a warm place.

Heat the remaining butter in a heavy-based frying pan. Add the onion and garlic and sweat for 3 minutes without colouring, until onion is soft and translucent. Add the parsley, watercress and spinach leaves and cook for a few moments until soft and wilted.

Tip everything into a colander and press to extract as much liquid as possible. Tip vegetables into a food processor and process in bursts to a coarse purée. As you process, add the beurre noisette and parmesan. Finally, season to taste, add the lemon juice and serve warm.

Braised shallots

makes 12 shallots

PREP TIME 5 MINUTES 🍲 COOK TIME 25 MINUTES

20 ml (¾ fl oz) vegetable oil

12 large shallots, peeled

salt and pepper

50 g (2 oz) butter

20 ml (¾ fl oz) sherry vinegar

100 ml (3½ fl oz) White Veal Stock (page 30)

2 garlic cloves

3 sprigs thyme

Preheat your oven to 160°C (320°F). Heat the oil in a heavy-based frying pan over a medium heat. Add the shallots and toss in the oil for about 5 minutes until lightly coloured all over. Season with salt and pepper and add the butter to the pan. Heat until it foams to a light golden brown. Continue to sauté the shallots, basting with the foaming butter, until they are caramelised a deep golden brown.

Add the sherry vinegar to the pan and simmer until reduced to a syrup. Swirl the pan gently as you add the veal stock, to emulsify and thicken all the juices. Add the garlic and thyme and cook in the oven for 20 minutes until the shallots are tender. Remove from the oven and serve warm.

Buttered peas

serves 4

PREP TIME 3 MINUTES 🍲 COOK TIME 7 MINUTES

200 g (7 oz) peas

50 g (2 oz) butter

salt and pepper

Blanch the peas in boiling salted water for 2 minutes then tip into a colander and drain. Return the peas to the pan with the butter and seasoning. Toss well and cook on a gentle heat for a further 5 minutes.

If you want to prepare the peas ahead of time, blanch and refresh them in iced water, then set aside until ready to finish.

Buttered spinach

serves 4

PREP TIME 3 MINUTES 🍲 COOK TIME 4 MINUTES

60 g (2 oz) butter

2 garlic cloves, peeled

400 g (14 oz) spinach leaves

salt and pepper

few drops lemon juice

Heat the butter and garlic in a large saucepan over a medium heat. When the butter to begins to foam, add the spinach and toss until wilted and glazed with the butter. Season to taste and finish with a few drops of lemon juice. Remove the garlic just before serving.

Sweet sauces

In the same way that savoury sauces
work to complement and unify the
component parts of a particular dish,
so too do sweet sauces.

Sweet sauces add moisture and flavour to desserts, be it in the form of a basic stock syrup or caramel, a fruit purée or a thin pouring cream. Other thicker sauces, such as custards and whipped creams, go one step further, providing body and structure to a dish.

The techniques you'll learn in basic sauce making are critical, as they form the basis for many other desserts. You can't make sorbets without understanding how to make a syrup or a fruit purée; you can't make ice creams or crème brulées without making a basic crème anglaise (thin custard) or any of the numerous different French pastry desserts without a crème pâtissière (thick custard).

Sugar syrups

Sugar syrups are perhaps the most fundamental and simple element of the French dessert kitchen. Stock syrup – equal weight sugar and water, simmered together briefly – is the basis for numerous French desserts.

I always have a variety of stock syrups on hand, infused with different flavourings, such as citrus, vanilla, spices or even fresh herbs. I use them to poach or macerate fresh fruit or simply to drizzle over just about any dessert.

This basic mixture of sugar and water can be varied and the syrup can be cooked to higher temperatures, which increases the concentration of sugar. It's at this point that we begin to touch upon the very precise art of confectionery making. While it's fairly easy to make light and dark caramel syrups simply by judging the colour by eye, to make candies, boiled sweets or spun sugar decoration you really need a sugar thermometer.

People often complain that their syrups turn cloudy or crystallise and there are a few simple rules to observe if you want to make any sugar syrup successfully. First, you need a good-quality heavy-based pan that distributes the heat evenly and constantly. Pastry kitchens tend to use copper pans, but these do take some effort to clean and maintain. Good-quality stainless steel saucepans in a range of sizes should be perfectly adequate. But before you even start cooking, make sure the pan is spotlessly clean and free from grease.

I guess the next thing you need is patience. The sugar should be heated slowly over a very gentle heat. Never try to make the sugar dissolve faster by stirring it; a little gentle swirling of the pan is the most movement you need. Sometimes grains of sugar spatter up onto the sides of the pan and you should use a wet pastry brush to wipe them down. Always make sure the sugar has completely dissolved before bringing the syrup to the boil and then, once it is boiling, you need to keep a close eye on it. Once the syrup starts to colour around the edges of the pan, it can take only moments for it to reach the desired colour. A few seconds can make the difference between success and burnt, bitter disaster.

Remember, too, that the syrup will continue cooking even after you've taken the pan off the heat, so it's a good idea to have a sink full of iced water ready. Plunge the base of the saucepan into the icy water, which will stop it cooking further.

For more specific types of sugar syrup you'll need a sugar thermometer to accurately gauge the various stages. Some of these are covered in the recipes that follow.

Stock syrup

makes 500 ml (17 fl oz)

/ PREP TIME 1 MINUTE ☞ COOK TIME 2 MINUTES

250 g (9 oz) sugar

250 ml (8½ fl oz) water

Place the sugar and water in a heavy-based saucepan and heat gently until the sugar has completely dissolved. Increase the heat and bring to the boil, then simmer for 1 minute. Remove from the heat and allow to cool. The syrup will keep in a sealed container in the refrigerator for up to 1 month.

LEMONGRASS SYRUP

Pound a stick of lemongrass in a mortar and add it to the syrup once the sugar has dissolved. After simmering, leave the lemongrass in the syrup for a few hours to infuse. Add a squeeze of lemon juice and store in a sealed container in the refrigerator for up to 1 month. Strain before use.

LIME OR LEMON SYRUP

After simmering, add the juice and zest of 2 limes or lemons, as appropriate. Allow to cool, then store in a sealed container in the refrigerator for up to 1 month. Strain before use.

GINGER SYRUP

Add a tablespoon of freshly grated ginger to the syrup once the sugar has dissolved. After simmering, leave the ginger in the syrup for a few hours to infuse. Store in a sealed container in the refrigerator for up to 1 month. Strain before use.

Light caramel syrup

makes 650 ml (22 fl oz)

/ PREP TIME 1 MINUTE ☞ COOK TIME 5 MINUTES

450 g (1 lb) sugar

50 g (1¾ oz) liquid glucose

150 ml (5 fl oz) water

Place all ingredients in a heavy-based saucepan and heat gently until everything has completely dissolved. Increase the heat and bring to the boil, then simmer. You may need to brush down any syrup that splashes up the sides of the pan with a wet pastry brush. Place a sugar thermometer in the pan and cook until the syrup reaches 165ºC (330°F) and turns a light golden brown. Remove from the heat and allow to cool.

The syrup will keep in a sealed container in the refrigerator for up to 1 month.

DARK CARAMEL SYRUP

Use the same method as for the Light Caramel Syrup, but cook the caramel to 180ºC (350°F).

CARAMEL SAUCE

Whisk 100 ml (3½ fl oz) of cream into the finished dark caramel syrup.

BUTTERSCOTCH SAUCE

Whisk 100 g (3½ oz) of diced cold butter into the hot caramel sauce.

Creams

It's hard to imagine dessert without cream. As well as being the classic accompaniment for all kinds of desserts, creams are also used to make many other recipes, such as mousses and bavarois. From thin whipping cream to lightly sweetened crème chantilly or flavoured crème fraîche, cream adds an incomparable richness and smoothness to a dish.

Of course this 'mouth-feel' is all about the fat. Cream is graded according to the amount of butterfat it contains, and it is important to use the appropriate cream as specified in each particular recipe.

In Australia we can generally choose between pure cream (which has a butterfat content of 45% plus) and thickened cream (which contains not less than 35% butterfat), which is generally whipped to thicken and increase its volume. French desserts also make good use of crème fraîche, which has a lactic bacteria added to thicken it and add a slight sour flavour. In this book, I always mean 35% (whipping) cream, unless I specify 45% (double/heavy) cream.

When whipping cream to aerate and lighten it, do make sure that the cream is very cold – straight from the fridge is best. If you're feeling energetic, whisk your cream by hand in a large spotlessly clean stainless-steel or glass bowl with a balloon whisk. In my kitchen apprentice chefs learn to use the traditional figure-eight wrist action that successfully thickens the cream without overheating it and causing it to split.

Although whisking by hand gives you greater control, most people prefer to use an electric mixer. My suggestion is to go slowly. Don't be tempted to crank the speed up too high or you'll turn it to butter!

The cream will progress through several levels of thickness. The first is what we call the ribbon stage. If you lift the whisk out of the cream it should fall in a lightly thickened stream and form a trail or 'ribbon' on the surface below. With further whisking it will reach the soft-peak stage, where it is firm enough to hold soft, floppy peaks; and finally, firm peaks, where the peaks hold their shape without collapsing. Once the cream has reached the required level of stiffness, chill until ready to use.

Vanilla chantilly

The crème fraîche is optional, but I like the slight tang it gives. All kinds of flavourings can be added to this base.

makes 500 ml (17 fl oz)

PREP TIME 3 MINUTES

500 ml (17 fl oz) cream, well chilled

seeds scraped from 1 vanilla pod

45 g (1 ½ oz) icing (confectioners') sugar

1 teaspoon crème fraîche (optional)

Place all the ingredients in a large mixing bowl and whip with a large balloon whisk until soft peaks form (see previous page). Alternatively, whisk using an electric mixer on medium speed.

RASPBERRY CHANTILLY

Whisk in a tablespoon of home-made raspberry jam.

DATE CHANTILLY

Whisk in a tablespoon of Date Purée (page 245).

ORANGE AND RUM CHANTILLY

Whisk in a teaspoon of finely grated orange zest and a splash of dark rum.

LEMON VERBENA CHANTILLY

Whisk in 2 tablespoons finely chopped lemon verbena leaves.

Coffee and mascarpone cream

This is a mixture of heavy cream and mascarpone, which makes for a richer, denser cream.

makes 500 g (1 lb 2 oz)

PREP TIME 5 MINUTES   COOK TIME 5 MINUTES

100 g (3 ½ oz) sugar

50 ml (2 fl oz) water

90 ml (3 fl oz) freshly made espresso coffee

150 ml (5 fl oz) double (heavy) cream

250 g (9 oz) mascarpone

Put the sugar and water in a heavy-based saucepan and heat gently until the sugar has completely dissolved. Increase the heat and bring to the boil, then simmer. Place a sugar thermometer in the pan and cook until the syrup reaches 160°C (320°F) and turns a light golden brown. Remove from the heat and allow to cool for a minute or two.

Add the espresso to the caramel and stir over a medium heat until combined. Increase the heat and simmer until the caramel has reduced by half. Set aside and cool.

Whisk the cool caramel into the cream, then whisk into the mascarpone until very smooth. The cream will keep in a sealed container in the refrigerator for up to 3 days.

Custards and Sabayons

As I touched upon in the lesson on eggs, the yolks and whites of these little nutritional powerhouses are used to very different effect in cooking. In my view it is in dessert cooking that these different uses are most evident.

Yolks, which are high in fat and protein, have the extraordinary ability to thicken and enrich, and they are the key ingredient in making all custards, curds and sabayon sauces.

Custard – or crème anglaise, as it's known in French – is a thin, sweet pouring sauce. Perhaps the all-time favourite dessert sauce, it's made from egg yolks, sugar and milk, and is usually flavoured with vanilla. Crème anglaise is also the most common base for classic ice creams, where extra flavours are added, ranging from liqueurs and chocolate to fruit purées – the possibilities are endless.

Crème anglaise does have a reputation for being 'tricky'. While it's not really difficult to make, there are a few simple rules to follow if you want to avoid lumps or scrambled eggs and, essentially, it comes down to temperature. The basic technique involves pouring nearly boiling milk onto a mixture of yolks and sugar, and whisking it all together well. The sauce is then returned to the pan and cooked very slowly on a very low heat until it thickens to a light cream consistency. If you are impatient, you risk overcooking the yolks, and this is what causes lumps or curdling.

The richness and thickness of crème anglaise depends upon the ratio of egg yolks to milk. The more yolks you use, the thicker the resulting sauce. Many cooks also like to add cream to the cold sauce, which makes it richer, smoother and creamier.

Crème pâtissière – or confectioners' custard – is a thick, glossy custard which is used to fill all those decadent French pastries. It's much easier to make than crème anglaise, as it is stabilised by a little flour or cornflour (cornstarch). The technique is essentially the same as making an anglaise, but it needs to be boiled, so that the flavour of the flour is cooked out. As it boils you need to whisk it vigorously to stop it catching and burning. Unlike an anglaise, any lumps can easily be whisked out.

In baked custards, the same thickening magic occurs, but in the oven. In dishes such as crème brûlée or crème caramel, milk or cream is set with whole eggs and egg yolks. These desserts are usually made in a mould, and they set firm enough to be turned out. Other baked custards are used to fill tarts – think of a classic tarte au citron – but in this case the filling is usually infused before baking with an additional flavouring, and when cooked it is less firm than an unmoulded baked custard. Ideally, it should wobble gently, and just hold its shape when cut.

The sabayon is another type of sweet sauce made from a base of egg yolks and sugar. Unlike custards, which are made with milk or cream, a sabayon is made with wine, champagne or a flavoured liqueur. Sabayons are cooked very gently, ideally over a bain-marie (water bath), whisking all the time until the mix doubles in volume to become a light, foamy mass.

There are various forms of bain-maries. The most common is a double-boiler, where a saucepan of water is placed on a low heat at a very gentle simmer and a bowl is set over the top. This method is essential in the cooking and whisking of sabayons, which require a gentle heat while air is incorporated into your sauce through whisking.

Vanilla crème anglaise

This classic custard is a popular sauce for all sorts of desserts. You can also replace the vanilla bean with myriad other flavours.

makes 500 ml (17 fl oz)

PREP TIME 2 MINUTES COOK TIME 10 MINUTES

200 ml (7 fl oz) cream

200 ml (7 fl oz) milk

1 vanilla pod, split and seeds scraped

4 egg yolks

40 g (1 ½ oz) sugar

Heat the cream and milk in a heavy-based saucepan over a moderate heat. Add the vanilla seeds and scraped pod and bring to the boil. Remove from the heat and leave to infuse for 5–10 minutes.

Put the egg yolks and sugar into a large mixing bowl and whisk together until pale and creamy. Pour the hot liquid onto the egg mixture and whisk gently to combine. Pour back into the saucepan and cook gently over a moderate heat for about 8 minutes. Stir frequently with a wooden spoon until the custard thickens to coat the back of a wooden spoon.

Remove from the heat and strain through a fine sieve. Serve the hot custard straight away or allow to cool and store in a sealed container in the refrigerator for up to 5 days.

Crème brûlée

This must surely be one of the most popular desserts in both French and non-French restaurants. There is something so satisfying about breaking through the glassy caramel sheet on top to the rich creamy custard below.

makes 1 large or 4 small brûlées

PREP TIME 15 MINUTES COOK TIME 35 MINUTES

350 ml (12 fl oz) cream

125 ml (4 fl oz) milk

½ used vanilla pod

7 egg yolks

70 g (2½ oz) sugar

Demerara sugar

Preheat your oven to 110°C (230°F). Place a medium-size gratin dish or 4 x 150 ml (5 fl oz) ramekin dishes in a deep roasting pan. Combine the cream, milk and vanilla pod in a heavy-based saucepan over a medium heat. Bring to the boil, then remove from the heat and set aside to infuse and cool for 5–10 minutes.

In a mixing bowl, whisk together the egg yolks and sugar. Remove the vanilla pod from the cooled cream and pour a little at a time onto the egg mixture. Whisk very gently to combine, without making it frothy.

Strain through a fine sieve into a pitcher. Pour the custard into the gratin dish and pour enough cold water into the roasting pan to come halfway up the side of the dish. Bake for 35–45 minutes, or until the custard is just set. Remove from the roasting pan immediately and allow to rest for at least 2 hours before serving or refrigerate overnight.

Just before serving, sprinkle the surface of the custard with a thin even layer of Demerara sugar. Caramelise the surface with a small kitchen blowtorch until the sugar melts to a shiny caramel glaze. If you don't have a blowtorch, preheat an overhead grill (broiler) to its highest setting. Place the brûlée on a baking tray and slide it under the heat, about 5 cm (2 in) from the heat. Watch carefully to make sure it doesn't burn. Allow to cool for 5 minutes before serving so that the caramel layer will harden to a crisp, crunchy layer.

Baked custards

Use the plain filling or either of the tangy citrus custards that follow to fill a blind-baked tart shell (page 321) made from Sweet Pastry (page 322).

PLAIN CUSTARD FILLING

makes 750 ml (25 fl oz), enough to fill a 22 cm x 2 cm (9 in x 1 in) tart ring

/ PREP TIME 20 MINUTES

500 ml (17 fl oz) cream

75 g (2½ oz) sugar

8 egg yolks

Combine the cream and sugar in a small saucepan over a moderate heat and dissolve. Remove from the heat and allow to cool. Whisk the egg yolks then whisk them into the cooled milk. Use to fill a tart base within 2 days.

LEMON TART FILLING

makes 750 ml (25 fl oz), enough to fill a 22 cm x 2 cm (9 in x 1 in) tart ring

/ PREP TIME 5 MINUTES ✂ INFUSING TIME 24 HOURS

5 whole eggs

1 egg yolk

130 g (4½ oz) sugar

200 ml (7 fl oz) cream

130 ml (4½ fl oz) lemon juice, strained

1 teaspoon grated lemon zest

Combine the eggs, egg yolk and sugar in a large mixing bowl and blitz with an electric hand-blender until well combined. Stir in the cream, lemon juice and zest, cover and leave in the refrigerator overnight to infuse. Use to fill a tart base within 2–3 days.

ORANGE TART FILLING

makes 750 ml (25 fl oz), enough to fill a 22 cm x 2 cm (9 in x 1 in) tart ring

/ PREP TIME 5 MINUTES ✂ INFUSING TIME 24 HOURS

400 ml (13½ fl oz) orange juice, strained

1 teaspoon grated orange zest

4 whole eggs

100 g (3½ oz) sugar

120 ml (4 fl oz) cream

Heat the orange juice in a small saucepan over a high heat. Simmer until reduced to 150 ml (5 fl oz) then remove from the heat and add the orange zest. Set aside.

Combine the eggs and sugar in a large mixing bowl and blitz with an electric hand-blender until well combined. Stir in the cream, orange juice and zest, cover and leave in the refrigerator overnight to infuse. Use to fill a tart base within 2–3 days.

Crème pâtissière

makes 500 ml (17 fl oz)

PREP TIME 5 MINUTES · COOK TIME 10 MINUTES

300 ml (10 fl oz) milk

40 ml (1½ fl oz) cream

1 used vanilla pod

5 egg yolks

100 g (3½ oz) sugar

15 g (½ oz) cornflour (cornstarch)

10 g (¼ oz) plain (all-purpose) flour

Put the milk, cream and vanilla pod in a heavy-based saucepan and bring to the boil. Remove from the heat and leave to infuse for 5–10 minutes.

Put the egg yolks and sugar in an electric mixer and whisk to the ribbon stage (page 233). Fold in the sifted flour and cornflour.

Pour a third of the hot liquid onto the egg mixture and whisk gently to combine. Pour back into the saucepan with the rest of the hot milk and cook gently over a moderate heat for about 5 minutes, whisking all the time. The custard will thicken to a stiff and glossy smooth paste.

Remove from the heat and stand the pan in a sink of iced water. Remove the vanilla pod and whisk vigorously to beat out any lumps. When completely cold, store in a sealed container in the refrigerator for up to 5 days.

Sweet sabayon

This is my foolproof way of making sabayon in an electric mixer. Think of this as a base recipe and vary the flavours to your liking. Either replace the water with white wine (for a traditional sabayon) or other alcohols or flavoured liqueurs, or flavour the base recipe with vanilla, citrus zest … in fact, anything you fancy!

makes 500 ml (17 fl oz)

PREP TIME 2 MINUTES · COOK TIME 10 MINUTES

10 egg yolks

1 whole egg

140 g (5 oz) sugar

100 ml (3½ fl oz) water

Place the yolks, whole egg, sugar and water in a stainless-steel bowl and set it over a pan of simmering water; the base of the bowl should not come into contact with the water. Heat very slowly, without whisking, to about 82–84°C (180–183°F), or until the eggs look as if they're thickening and starting to cook.

Tip the mixture into the bowl of an electric mixer and beat on a medium speed, until pale and creamy. It should be thick enough to form a thick ribbon that leaves a trail across the surface.

WHISKY SABAYON

Replace half the water with the same amount of whisky – or more or less, according to taste! Use the same approach with other spirits or liqueurs. If using wine or champagne, replace all the water with the same amount of wine.

Crème caramel

makes 1 large or 4 small custards

PREP TIME 20 MINUTES   COOK TIME 45 MINUTES

170 g (6 oz) sugar

30 ml (1 fl oz) water

350 ml (12 fl oz) milk

2 eggs

1 egg yolk

Serve with Macerated Strawberries (page 249) or Roasted Golden Peaches (page 254).

Preheat your oven to 160°C (320°F). Lightly oil 1 x 500 ml (17 fl oz) mould or 4 x 120 ml (4 fl oz) dariole moulds or ramekins.

To make the caramel, put 110 g (3¾ oz) of the sugar and the water in a small saucepan over a moderate heat. When the sugar has dissolved, bring to the boil, then simmer to a deep-golden caramel. Be careful not to overcook it.

Remove the pan from the heat and allow the bubbles to subside. Pour the caramel into the base of your mould (or moulds), turning carefully to coat the base evenly. Place in a deep roasting pan and pour in enough cold water to come halfway up the side of the mould.

To make the custard, place the remaining sugar and milk in a small saucepan over a moderate heat and dissolve. Remove from the heat and allow to cool. Whisk together the eggs and egg yolk then whisk them into the cooled milk. Strain the custard into the prepared mould and bake for 45 minutes, until just set. Remove from the roasting pan immediately and allow to rest for at least 2 hours before serving, or refrigerate overnight.

To serve, place a plate over the mould and invert. Shake gently but firmly to release. The custard should be set to a smooth, glossy wobble, and be surrounded by a pool of dark caramel.

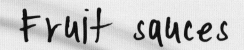

Fruit sauces

Fresh fruit can be used to great effect for intensely flavoured, light and healthy sweet sauces, very much in keeping with contemporary trends.

At their simplest, fruit sauces are simply purées of fresh fruit, although some fruits benefit from being lightly poached in a flavoured stock syrup (page 232) to intensify their flavour.

To achieve that perfect professional smoothness, you need to purée the fruit in small batches in a food processor or blender. When quite smooth, rub the purée through a fine sieve to remove any seeds, stray pieces of skin or fibrous bits.

The smooth purée can then be thinned with a little stock syrup to make a light sauce, also called a coulis, or left thick and used to flavour the base of soufflés, mousses or bavarois.

Fruit sauces freeze very well, so buy up ripe fruits when they are in peak season and freeze them for a delicious hit of summer in the long winter months.

244

Stone fruit coulis

makes 300 ml (10 fl oz)

PREP TIME 5 MINUTES

200 g (7 oz) ripe stone fruit of your choice

50 ml (2 fl oz) Stock Syrup (page 232)

50 ml (2 fl oz) fruit-flavoured liqueur or sweet wine

Peel the fruit and remove the stones. Chop roughly and place in a saucepan with the sugar and liqueur or sweet wine. Bring to the boil and then blend. Pass through a fine sieve and serve straight away. If serving cold, transfer to an airtight container and refrigerate. The stone fruit coulis will keep in a sealed container in the freezer for up to 3 months.

Date purée

This is a wonderfully versatile purée that can be used in both savoury and sweet dishes. I often add a spoonful to finish off soups or sauces for a delicious sweet depth of flavour. Whisk some into Crème Chantilly (page 234), or spread a few spoonfuls over the base of chocolate or caramel tarts to add a lovely rich, toffee top-note.

makes 250 ml (8½ fl oz)

PREP TIME 2 MINUTES   SOAKING TIME 4 HOURS

150 g (5½ oz) dates, stones removed

125 ml (4 fl oz) freshly brewed Earl Grey tea

Place the dates in a bowl and strain the hot tea over them. Cover with plastic wrap and leave for about 4 hours. Tip into a blender and blitz to a fine purée. Push the purée through a fine sieve and store in a sealed container for up to a month.

Berry coulis

makes 300 ml (10 fl oz)

PREP TIME 5 MINUTES

250 g (9 oz) fresh ripe berries of your choice

50 ml (2 fl oz) Stock Syrup (page 232)

Put the raw berries and syrup in a blender in batches and blitz to a smooth purée. Alternatively combine in a saucepan and bring to the boil before blending. Pass through a fine sieve and serve straight away. If serving cold, transfer to an airtight container and refrigerate.

The berry coulis will keep in a sealed container in the freezer for up to 3 months.

Fruit

Fruit is nature's way of sweetening us up!
And we're utterly spoilt for choice when it
comes to the variety of textures, aromas
and flavours of these natural goodies.

Think for a moment about tangy summer berries, or a perfect honeyed peach, dripping with golden juices. Or soft, earthy figs, sun-warmed and sticky, eaten fresh from the tree. Perhaps you prefer the crisp sharpness of an early autumn apple, or that quintessential winter fruit, the quince, poached to a gorgeous ruby-red, until it fills the house with its subtle perfume.

The natural sugars and acids in fruit make them the ideal light finish to any meal. If you are lucky enough to find fruit at the height of the season and in peak condition then it's hard to beat fresh fruit, eaten as is, with no fiddling about. But this perfection and ripeness can be tricky to find and I often find that a little tweaking is needed to bring out the true intensity of flavour. Dust a less-than-ripe peach with a little icing (confectioners') sugar and gently bake it until tender and juicy. Or poach those hard little apricots in a syrup flavoured with cinnamon, vanilla or a touch of lime zest.

Two of the simplest, and most effective, ways to prepare fruit are to toss it gently in a light stock syrup or macerate it in a little alcohol. Both are quick and easy ways of infusing the fruit with complementary flavours and intensifying and releasing the natural juices.

Fruit needs little cooking – a gentle poaching or brief baking is usually all that's needed to soften it to tender juiciness. And once cooked, fruit has many more uses – smooth purées make a natural sweet sauce on their own or folded into creams or custards, and they can be used to flavour jellies (gelatine desserts), mousses, soufflés, sorbets or ice creams. Chunkier compotes can be baked under a cake, pastry or crumble topping. Take the process a step further, and you can roast fruit to a caramelised goodness or dip wafer-thin slices in syrup and dry them in the oven to make an elegant crisp garnish.

Dried fruits – either those you've prepared yourself, or good-quality purchased dried fruits – are similarly versatile and they are a delicious way of varying the range of available fruits during the winter months. Many dried fruits, such as muscatel grapes, tangy apricots or even toffeeish dates, make a wonderful addition to a cheese plate. Most dried fruits also respond particularly well to being macerated in an alcohol-infused syrup, or poached back to softness in a flavoured syrup.

When it comes to selecting and storing fruits, the same principles apply as those discussed in the Vegetable lesson. Buy from farmers' markets or quality greengrocers wherever possible. Only buy fruit that is in season, and choose fruit that is perfumed and blemish-free. Many fruits continue to soften and ripen after they've been picked, so they don't have to be stored in the refrigerator, unless you enjoy eating them chilled.

As far as preparing fruit goes, often it will be need to be washed or peeled, and some fruits have stones, seeds, pips or cores that need to removed. Generally speaking, though, the fruit itself will only need to be neatly sliced or chopped before cooking or serving.

Coupe of macerated strawberries

serves 4

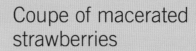 PREP TIME 10 MINUTES

500 g (1 lb 2 oz) strawberries, hulled and
    quartered

50 ml (2 fl oz) Grand Marnier

80 ml (3 fl oz) sauternes or sweet white wine

Combine the strawberries, Grand Marnier and wine in a large mixing bowl and toss gently to combine. Place in the refrigerator for an hour or so to macerate. Serve in chilled martini glasses.

Serve with Vanilla Crème Anglaise (page 237) or Vanilla Milk Sorbet (page 266). Try macerating other berries, such as blueberries or raspberries, when they're in season.

Tropical fruit salad

Fruit salads are light and refreshing, with a pleasing balance of sweetness, perfume and acidity. Always choose fruit in peak condition – and don't just limit yourself to the stock-standards. This salad is lovely with 2–3 tablespoons of pomegranate seeds.

serves 4

/ PREP TIME 20 MINUTES

1 papaya

1 mango

12 lychees

1 young coconut

4 passionfruit

250 ml (8½ fl oz) Lime Syrup (page 232)

Prepare all the fruits, removing peel, seeds and stones as appropriate. Cut the papaya, mango, lychees and coconut into even slices and place in a large mixing bowl. Cut the passionfruit in half, scoop out the seeds and add them to the bowl. Add the lime syrup and toss together gently. Garnish with pomegranate seeds before serving.

This salad of tropical fruit is delicious enough for a dinner party dessert, especially if served with Passionfruit Jelly (page 284) or Verbena Yoghurt Sorbet (page 267).

Poached apricots

Poaching really brings out the intense apricot flavour in what can sometimes be disappointing fruit.

serves 4

⟋ PREP TIME 5 MINUTES ⌾ COOK TIME 10 MINUTES

1 kg (2 lb 3 oz) apricots, halved and stones removed

Stock poaching syrup

300 ml (10 fl oz) water

100 ml (3½ fl oz) white wine

200 g (7 oz) sugar

8 sprigs lemon thyme

a few scraped vanilla seeds or ½ teaspoon vanilla paste

Serve on their own, or with the Lemon Thyme Yoghurt Sorbet (page 267).

Put all the ingredients, except for the apricots, in a large heavy-based saucepan and heat gently until the sugar dissolves. Bring to the boil, then lower the heat and simmer for 5 minutes.

Add the apricots to the pan. Cut a circle of baking paper to the size of the pan to make a cartouche and place on the surface. Cover the fruit and poach gently for 5–8 minutes. Remove the pan from the heat and leave the apricots to cool in the syrup. Serve warm or refrigerate until chilled.

POACHED PEARS OR QUINCES

Use the same syrup to poach pears or quinces, replacing the lemon thyme with a cinnamon stick, 4 cloves, 2 star anise and the zest and juice of a lemon. Peel and core 3 pears or 2 quinces, and poach them whole for 15 minutes or until just tender. For the pears, once cooked, cool them in the refrigerator and then cover with cold poaching syrup. For the quinces, allow them to cool in the hot syrup.

VANILLA POACHED APPLES

Use the same syrup to poach apples, replacing the lemon thyme with the zest and juice of a lemon, and replacing the wine with 200 ml (7 fl oz) medium, alcoholic cider. This makes a lovely light syrup that is not overly sweet. The apples can be used in sweet or savoury dishes.

To prepare, peel and finely slice the apples, and add them to the hot syrup. They don't actually need to be cooked in the syrup; the heat will be enough to soften them without turning them to mush.

Compote of dried and
winter fruits (page 256)

Roasted golden peaches with rosé champagne

serves 4

PREP TIME 10 MINUTES COOK TIME 10 MINUTES

6 golden peaches, halved and stoned

20 ml (¾ fl oz) melted butter

20 g (¾ oz) icing (confectioners') sugar

400 ml (13 fl oz) rosé champagne

Preheat your oven to 180°C (350°F). Arrange the peach halves, skin side up, in a roasting pan. Brush with the melted butter and sprinkle with icing sugar. Roast for 10 minutes until the skins loosen and the peaches are tender.

Remove from the oven and slip off the skins while still warm. Allow to cool, then refrigerate until chilled. When ready to serve, slice the peaches into thin slivers and arrange in dessert bowls. At the table, pour on the champagne and serve straight away.

This exquisitely pretty dessert is delicious served with Palmiers (page 326) and Strawberry Ripple Ice Cream (page 270).

Raviolo of pineapple

serves 4

PREP TIME 20 MINUTES COOK TIME 2 MINUTES

1 pineapple

400 ml (13 fl oz) water

200 g (7 oz) sugar

60 ml (2 fl oz) cream

200 g (7 oz) Crème Pâtissière (page 241)

Serve with fresh raspberries, Lemongrass Jelly (page 285) or Ginger Beer Sorbet (page 266).

Peel the pineapple and slice into wafers as thin as possible. Layer in a deep tray.

Combine the water and sugar in a saucepan and heat gently until the sugar dissolves. Bring to the boil, then lower the heat and simmer for 2 minutes. Pour the syrup over the pineapple and allow to cool. Transfer to the fridge until chilled.

Whip the cream lightly, then fold into the crème pâtissière to lighten it.

Remove the pineapple from the refrigerator and select 8 of the best-looking slices. Finely chop the rest, squeeze out the excess juice and fold into the crème pâtissière.

To serve, lay 4 pineapple slices on your work surface and top each with a neat spoonful of pineapple cream. Carefully place the remaining 4 slices on top. Use a 9 cm (3½ in) pastry cutter to cut neat 'ravioli', and lift onto dessert plates. Serve straight away on their own, or with any of the suggested accompaniments.

Cinnamon-stewed rhubarb, apple and blueberry crumble

Stew the rhubarb and apple on their own or together with the blueberries for a zingy breakfast compote (serve with whipped cream or yoghurt).

serves 4

PREP TIME 10 MINUTES COOK TIME 35 MINUTES

½ bunch rhubarb, trimmed and roughly diced

2 apples, peeled, cored and roughly diced

zest and juice of 1 lemon

150 g (5½ oz) sugar

1 cinnamon stick

1 punnet blueberries

1 quantity uncooked Crumble topping (page 327)

Place the rhubarb and apple in a heavy-based saucepan with lemon zest and juice, sugar and cinnamon. Bring to a simmer then cook for 30 minutes until the rhubarb and apples have broken down to a mush. Add the blueberries and cook for a further 5 minutes.

If making crumble, tip the stewed fruit into the base of an ovenproof dish and sprinkle with the crumble topping. Bake in a 180ºC (350ºF) oven for 10–15 minutes until the crumble is golden brown. Dust with icing (confectioners') sugar and serve straight away with your choice of accompaniments.

Compote of dried and winter fruits

You can use any combination of dried fruits for this lovely winter compote, and you can even dry your own. Simply steep your selection of fruit in a hot stock syrup for 5 minutes. Remove the stones, peel the fruit and cut into large pieces. Dry in a low 60ºC (140ºF) oven for 5 hours. To make it extra-warming, serve with Whisky Sabayon (page 241). For an extra-special presentation, tip the warm compote into a medium-sized gratin dish, pour on the sabayon and gratinée it under a very hot grill (broiler) until golden brown.

serves 4

PREP TIME 20 MINUTES

80 g (3 oz) dried prunes, halved

80 g (3 oz) dried apricots, halved

80 g (3 oz) dried muscatel grapes

2 Poached Quinces (page 251), cut into slices

300 ml (10 fl oz) quince poaching syrup (page 251)

Combine the fruits in a large mixing bowl. Pour on the quince poaching syrup and set aside to macerate for 2 hours.

When ready to serve, tip into a heavy-based saucepan and gently warm through. Serve with whipped cream or your choice of accompaniments.

The compote also makes a delicious crumble. Serve it bubbling hot and golden brown with Vanilla Chantilly (page 234), Vanilla Crème Anglaise (page 237) or Vanilla Ice Cream (page 270).

Fruit purées

I don't use any sugar when making fruit purées, so I achieve maximum intensity and purity of flavour.

They are incredibly versatile – add a few spoonfuls to Crème Chantilly (page 234) or to custards, or use them as a base for mousses (page 290) and hot fruit soufflés (page 304), instead of the more usual custard base.

Fruit purées are easy to make. All you need to do is remove the stones and peel (where appropriate) before simmering quickly in a little water. You want the fruit to be soft and dryish – not stewed to a disintegrated mush. Blitz the fruit in your blender in batches, then push through a fine sieve to make a smooth purée, similar in consistency to a jam rather than a fine coulis.

Soft stone fruits and berries don't need peeling, and because of their higher moisture content they need less water added. Harder fruits, such as apples and pears, do need to be peeled before cooking.

Apricot purée

makes 500 ml (17 fl oz)

PREP TIME 5 MINUTES COOK TIME 15 MINUTES

500 g (1 lb 2 oz) apricots

120 ml (4 fl oz) water

Cut the apricots in half and remove the kernels. Place in a saucepan with the water and simmer over a high heat for 10–15 minutes until the fruit is soft and dryish. Remove from the heat and whiz to a purée in a blender. Push through a fine sieve to remove any skins or fibrous matter.

Sorbets, ices and ice creams

Frozen desserts have got to be one of the all-time favourite sweet treats all around the world, and part of the pleasure is that they come in so many different flavours and forms.

From the purity of a scoop of vanilla ice cream in a cone, to an intensely tangy sorbet or the sophistication of a moulded iced extravaganza, as far as I'm concerned they are all irresistible.

The first frozen desserts were water ices – sorbets (sherbets) – supposedly created in China and then in the Middle East from sweet fruit juices or wines that were frozen with snow. History books tell us that the great traveller Marco Polo brought the technique from China back to Italy in the thirteenth century, starting that country's long-held passion for gelati. The fashion for iced desserts was sparked in the dining rooms of Paris when Catherine de Medici married the soon-to-be king Henri II. By the eighteenth century, the popularity of 'ices' had spread to the streets – most famously in the Parisian Café Procope, where more than 80 different flavours were reputedly served.

The idea of freezing custards emerged towards the end of the eighteenth century. The greater substance and body that eggs, milk or cream gave to the recipe meant that these frozen desserts could be moulded into all sorts of extraordinary shapes. Richest of all were the parfaits, which traditionally have an absurdly high ratio of egg yolks to cream. Coupes, bombes, iced soufflés – all of these were created during the 'belle époque' when a chef's main aim in life was to make a name for himself with some new creation.

These days we can all make our own frozen creations in the comfort of our kitchens. Good-quality ice-cream machines – sorbetières – are readily available from most department stores. In my book these are well worth the outlay for the incomparable result you will achieve.

Granitas

The simplest frozen desserts of all, water-ices or granitas are really refreshing on hot summer days.

They are made from fruit juices or a light syrup that's flavoured with sweet wine or liqueurs and, unlike smooth-textured ice creams and sorbets, they should be crunchy to eat. They are simplicity itself to make: the base liquid is poured into a shallow container and they are lightly beaten with a fork as they freeze, to break up the crystals. They have a light, yet icy texture.

Coffee granita

makes 500 g (1 lb 2 oz)

✏ PREP TIME 5 MINUTES 🍳 COOK TIME 5 MINUTES
❄ FREEZING TIME 8 HOURS

110 ml (3¾ fl oz) water
70 g (2½ oz) sugar
½ tablespoon liquid glucose
350 ml (12 fl oz) strong fresh coffee, cooled

Put the water, sugar and glucose in a heavy-based saucepan and heat gently until the sugar has completely dissolved. Increase the heat and bring to the boil, then simmer for 2 minutes. Remove from the heat and set aside to cool.

Stir in the coffee, pour into a shallow container and freeze. Every few hours take out of the freezer and beat lightly with a fork to mix the frozen crystals into the liquid. By the time it is frozen firm, the texture should be granular with large icy crystals.

Champagne and ginger granita

makes 500 g (1 lb 2 oz)

PREP TIME 5 MINUTES   COOK TIME 5 MINUTES
FREEZING TIME 8 HOURS

110 ml (3¾ fl oz) water

70 g (2½ oz) sugar

1 teaspoon grated fresh ginger (or to taste)

320 ml (10¾ fl oz) champagne

Put the water, sugar and ginger in a heavy-based saucepan and heat gently until the sugar has completely dissolved. Increase the heat and bring to the boil, then simmer for 2 minutes. Remove from the heat and set aside for 10 minutes to infuse.

When completely cold, strain and add the champagne. Pour into a shallow container and place in the freezer. Every few hours take out of the freezer and beat lightly with a fork to mix the frozen crystals into the liquid. By the time it is frozen firm, the texture should be granular with large icy crystals.

Lemon verbena tea granita

makes 500 g (1 lb 2 oz)

PREP TIME 5 MINUTES   COOK TIME 5 MINUTES
FREEZING TIME 8 HOURS

360 ml (12 fl oz) water

140 g (5 oz) sugar

½ cup lemon verbena leaves

1 teaspoon Earl Grey tea leaves

Put the water and sugar in a heavy-based saucepan and heat gently until the sugar has completely dissolved. Increase the heat and bring to a gentle simmer. Remove from the heat, add the lemon verbena and tea leaves and set aside for 15 minutes to infuse.

Strain through a fine sieve and chill. Pour into a shallow container and place in the freezer. Every few hours take out of the freezer and beat lightly with a fork to mix the frozen crystals into the liquid. By the time it is frozen firm, the texture should be granular with large icy crystals.

Sorbets

A level up in sophistication from the water-ice, sorbets (sherbets) really must be churned in an ice-cream machine to ensure they have a fine, silky-smooth texture.

Because they generally have no fat content, sorbets are very much the darling of modern-day health-conscious restaurant menus, and they offer huge scope for the creative cook. It can be a little tricky to achieve that perfect smoothness, which depends on using the correct proportion of sugar to other ingredients. Sorbets are at their best when freshly made as the flavours start to lessen after a few days. They should be allowed to soften at room temperature for about 10 minutes before eating, to really bring out the intensity of the flavours.

The simplest sorbets are made from pure fruit juice, mixed with a little stock syrup and glucose, which prevents the sorbet becoming icy and helps achieve the desired velvety smoothness.

Use the mandarin sorbet recipe opposite as a base and experiment with other fresh juices as the fancy takes you. My other favourites are ruby grapefruit sorbet, blood orange, lemon, lime and tequila or even passionfruit-orange. The quantity of stock syrup needed may vary slightly, depending on the sweetness and acidity of the fruit juice. Add the syrup to the juice gradually, tasting as you go until you achieve your preferred level of sweetness.

Mandarin sorbet

makes 600 g (1 lb 5 oz)

PREP TIME 5 MINUTES

200 ml (7 fl oz) Stock Syrup (page 232)

400 ml (13 fl oz) fresh mandarin juice

50 g (2 oz) glucose

Stir the syrup into the mandarin juice then whisk in the glucose. Tip into an ice-cream machine and churn according to the manufacturer's instructions. Transfer to a plastic container and freeze for up to 3 days.

Chocolate sorbet

makes 500 g (1 lb 2 oz)

PREP TIME 5 MINUTES   COOK TIME 5 MINUTES

300 ml (10 fl oz) water

120 g (4½ oz) sugar

20 g (¾ oz) liquid glucose

150 g (5½ oz) good-quality dark chocolate

Put the water, sugar and glucose in a heavy-based saucepan and heat gently until the sugar has completely dissolved. Increase the heat and bring to the boil, then simmer for 2 minutes. Remove from the heat and set aside to cool slightly.

Break the chocolate into small pieces and place in a heatproof bowl with a few tablespoons of the hot syrup. Stir until the chocolate is smooth and melted. Trickle in the remaining syrup, whisking with a hand blender to emulsify – a bit like making mayonnaise. Set aside to cool.

Tip into an ice-cream machine and churn according to the manufacturer's instructions. Transfer to a plastic container and freeze for up to 3 days.

Granny Smith apple sorbet

makes 500 g (1 lb 2 oz)

PREP TIME 5 MINUTES   COOK TIME 5 MINUTES

200 ml (7 fl oz) water

100 g (3½ oz) sugar

60 g (2 oz) liquid glucose

140 g (5 oz) Granny Smith apples

lemon juice to taste

Place the water, sugar and glucose in a heavy-based saucepan and heat gently until the sugar has completely dissolved. Increase the heat and bring to the boil, then simmer for 2 minutes. Remove from the heat and set aside to cool.

Cut the apples in half and remove the cores, but do not peel them. Dice them roughly and blitz them in batches in a blender or food processor, gradually adding the cold syrup to make a fine smooth purée. Add the lemon juice to taste then push the purée through a fine sieve. Use a rubber spatula or the back of a ladle to push and extract as much juice as possible.

Tip into an ice-cream machine and churn according to the manufacturer's instructions. Transfer to a plastic container and freeze for up to 3 days.

Peach sorbet

makes 500 g (1 lb 2 oz)

PREP TIME 10 MINUTES COOK TIME 2 MINUTES

400 g (14 oz) finely chopped peach flesh

80 ml (3 fl oz) water

100 g (3½ oz) sugar

30 g (1 oz) liquid glucose

½ tablespoon lemon juice

Put the chopped peaches in a heavy-based saucepan with the water, sugar and glucose. Heat gently until the sugar has completely dissolved. Increase the heat and bring to the boil, then simmer for 2 minutes. Remove from the heat and set aside to cool slightly.

Blitz in batches in a blender or food processor to make a fine smooth purée. Add the lemon juice to taste then push the purée through a fine sieve. Use a rubber spatula or the back of a ladle to push and extract as much juice as possible. Set aside to cool completely.

Tip into an ice-cream machine and churn according to the manufacturer's instructions. Transfer to a plastic container and freeze for up to 3 days.

Ginger beer sorbet

makes 500 g (1 lb 2 oz)

PREP TIME 5 MINUTES COOK TIME 5 MINUTES
INFUSING TIME 3 HOURS

200 ml (7 fl oz) Stock Syrup (page 232)

120 g (4½ oz) liquid glucose

30 g (1 oz) grated fresh ginger

150 ml (5 fl oz) ginger beer

lime juice to taste

Place the syrup, glucose and grated ginger in a heavy-based saucepan and heat to a gentle simmer. Remove from the heat and set aside to infuse for 3 hours.

Strain the infused syrup and stir in the ginger beer and lime juice to taste. Tip into an ice-cream machine and churn according to the manufacturer's instructions. Transfer to a plastic container and freeze for up to 3 days.

Vanilla milk sorbet

makes 500 g (1 lb 2 oz)

PREP TIME 5 MINUTES

350 ml (12 fl oz) milk

50 g (2 oz) liquid glucose

seeds scraped from 2 vanilla pods

100 ml (3½ fl oz) stock syrup (page 232)

lemon juice to taste

Put the milk, glucose and vanilla in a heavy-based saucepan and bring to a gentle simmer. Remove from the heat and set aside to infuse for 10 minutes. When the milk is cold, stir in the stock syrup and lemon juice to taste. Tip into an ice-cream machine and churn according to the manufacturer's instructions. Transfer to a plastic container and freeze for up to 5 days.

Vanilla, marmalade and mascarpone sorbet

makes 500 g (1 lb 2 oz)

🔪 PREP TIME 5 MINUTES 🍲 COOK TIME 15 MINUTES

220 ml (7½ fl oz) water

70 g (2½ oz) sugar

35 g (1¼ oz) liquid glucose

seeds scraped from 2 vanilla pods

170 g (6 oz) mascarpone

lemon juice to taste

50 g (2 oz) Seville Orange Marmalade (page 132)

Place the water, sugar and glucose in a heavy-based saucepan and heat gently until the sugar has completely dissolved. Increase the heat and bring to the boil, then remove from the heat, add the vanilla and set aside to infuse for 10 minutes.

When the syrup is cold, add the mascarpone and use a hand blender to blitz it to a smooth purée. Add the lemon juice to taste. Tip into an ice-cream machine and churn according to the manufacturer's instructions.

Towards the end of the churning time, swirl in the marmalade. Serve straight away or transfer to a plastic container and freeze for up to 5 days.

Verbena yoghurt sorbet

There are many derivatives of this delicate, tangy sorbet. Simply replace the lemon verbena with the herb of your choice. Lemon thyme or lemon basil both work beautifully, for instance.

makes 500 g (1 lb 2 oz)

🔪 PREP TIME 5 MINUTES 🍲 COOK TIME 15 MINUTES

200 ml (7 fl oz) water

60 g (2 oz) sugar

30 g (1 oz) liquid glucose

1 cup lemon verbena leaves

150 g (5½ oz) natural yoghurt

lemon juice to taste

Put the water, sugar and glucose in a heavy-based saucepan and heat gently until the sugar has completely dissolved. Increase the heat and bring to a gentle simmer. Remove from the heat, add the lemon verbena leaves and set aside for 10 minutes to infuse.

Strain through a fine sieve and chill. Add the yoghurt and use a hand blender to blitz it to a smooth purée. Add the lemon juice to taste. Tip into an ice-cream machine and churn according to the manufacturer's instructions. Serve straight away or transfer to a plastic container and freeze for up to 5 days.

Ice creams

By definition, commercially manufactured ice creams must have a minimum dairy fat content (usually 10%) to give them that desirable cold, rich creaminess.

But slightly belying their name, they are not simply frozen cream, which would be too heavy and dense. Most ice creams are made using a base of crème anglaise (see page 237), a custard made from eggs, sugar and hot milk. This crème anglaise is the base for myriad flavours, which can be achieved through infusions (of herbs or spices), by adding fruit purées, melted chocolate or liqueurs. And then you can have fun by adding texture, in the form of crumbled biscuit (cookie) or meringue, crunchy praline or flaked chocolate.

The secret to achieving a velvety-smooth texture is, once again, an ice-cream machine. As the mixture churns, air is incorporated into it – on a commercial scale, the amount of air is much larger than in domestic machines, and basically, the cheaper the ice cream, the more air there is in it. Home-made ice creams are much denser and richer than commercially manufactured ice cream.

Ice cream base

makes 500 g (1 lb 2 oz)

PREP TIME 2 MINUTES COOK TIME 10 MINUTES

| 150 ml (5 fl oz) cream |
| 225 ml (7½ fl oz) milk |
| 5 egg yolks |
| 60 g (2 oz) sugar |

Put the cream and milk in a heavy-based saucepan and bring to a gentle simmer. Remove from the heat.

Whisk together the egg yolks and sugar until thick and creamy.

Gradually pour in the hot milk, whisking continuously. Return the mixture to the saucepan. Cook over a low heat for around 8 minutes, stirring frequently until it thickens to coat the back of the spoon.

Remove from the heat and strain through a fine sieve. You can infuse all manner of different flavours while the base is still warm. Alternatively, chill in a sink of iced water then refrigerate for up to 5 days until ready to churn.

VANILLA ICE CREAM

Infuse the seeds from 2 vanilla pods in the warm base recipe for around 20 minutes.

THYME ICE CREAM

Infuse ½ bunch thyme in the warm base recipe for 1–2 hours as it cools.

STRAWBERRY RIPPLE ICE CREAM

Make the base ice cream recipe. Towards the end of the churning time, add a few spoonfuls of home-made Strawberry Jam (page 133), or indeed any good home-made berry jam, to the ice cream and churn briefly to make it 'ripple'.

SEVILLE ORANGE MARMALADE ICE CREAM

Make the base ice cream recipe. Towards the end of the churning time, add a few spoonfuls of home-made Seville Orange Marmalade (page 132) to the ice cream and churn briefly to make it 'ripple'.

CHOCOLATE BROWNIE ICE CREAM

Make the base ice cream recipe. Towards the end of the churning time, crumble in 100 g (3½ oz) of Chocolate Brownie (page 350).

Armagnac and caramel ice cream

makes 500 g (1 lb 2 oz)

PREP TIME 2 MINUTES · COOK TIME 10 MINUTES

125 g (4½ oz) sugar

150 ml (5 fl oz) cream

225 ml (7½ fl oz) milk

Armagnac to taste

Put the sugar in a heavy-based saucepan and heat gently to dissolve. Increase the heat and cook gently until it forms a dark brown caramel. Whisk in the cream and milk – carefully, as it will spit and bubble. Bring the mixture back to the boil and whisk gently until it is smooth. Remove from the heat and set aside to cool.

Strain the cooled caramel milk through a fine sieve. Use a hand blender to blitz the mixture before adding Armagnac to taste. Tip into an ice-cream machine and churn according to the manufacturer's instructions. Transfer to a plastic container and freeze for up to 3 days.

Banana ice cream

makes 500 g (1 lb 2 oz)

PREP TIME 5 MINUTES · COOK TIME 20 MINUTES

140 g (5 oz) chopped bananas

120 ml (4 fl oz) milk

120 ml (4 fl oz) cream

3 egg yolks

50 g (2 oz) sugar

20 ml (¾ fl oz) dark rum

Place the chopped bananas in a heavy-based saucepan with the milk and cream. Heat to just below a simmer and cook for 10 minutes. Remove from the heat, stir bananas and liquid together well and push through a fine sieve to achieve a very smooth purée.

Whisk together the egg yolks and sugar until thick and creamy. Gradually pour on the hot banana milk, whisking continuously. Return the mixture to the saucepan. Cook over a low heat for around 8 minutes, stirring frequently until it thickens to coat the back of the spoon.

Remove from the heat, strain once more into a bowl and chill in a sink of iced water. Stir in the rum and store in the refrigerator for up to 3 days. When ready to churn, tip into an ice-cream machine and churn according to the manufacturer's instructions. Transfer to a plastic container and freeze for up to 3 days.

Frozen parfaits

If you don't have an ice cream machine, don't despair. There are still a number of frozen desserts that can be made very successfully without one, and the parfait is a prime example.

Parfaits – or semi-freddos, to give them their Italian name – are not churned, but frozen in individual moulds or a large mould. These days, moulds come in all manner of fancy shapes and sizes, from cones to spheres to triangles, but most popularly, parfaits tend to be frozen in large, terrine-style moulds. They are turned out and cut into slices just before serving.

The base for a parfait is usually a sabayon or pâte bombe, which provide a stable foamy base. Both are made in a similar way, with egg yolks and sugar whisked together over a pan of simmering water to cook the foam. Whipped cream and flavourings are folded into the foam base to make it delicate, yet rich and creamy.

Date and Earl Grey parfait

While I love the combination of toffeeish dates with Earl Grey tea, I encourage you to think of this as a base recipe and experiment with your own variations. For instance, replace the Earl Grey with a herbal infusion, and the dates with chopped dried apricots or raspberry jam.

serves 8

♻ INFUSING TIME OVERNIGHT ⁄ PREP TIME 30 MINUTES ✸ FREEZING TIME 8 HOURS

10 g (¼ oz) Earl Grey tea leaves

100 ml (3½ fl oz) cream

4 egg yolks

65 g (2¼ oz) sugar

splash Grand Marnier

200 ml (7 fl oz) double (heavy) cream

80 g (3 oz) fresh pitted dates

Infuse the tea leaves in the cold cream overnight. Line a 1 litre (34 fl oz) terrine mould or loaf tin with plastic wrap.

Put the egg yolks and sugar in a stainless-steel bowl and set it over a pan of simmering water; the base of the bowl should not come into contact with the water. Whisk gently and heat very slowly to about 85°C (185°F), or until the eggs look as if they're thickening and starting to cook.

Tip the mixture into the bowl of an electric mixer and beat on a medium speed, until it cools to room temperature and is pale and creamy. It should be thick enough to form a thick ribbon that leaves a trail across the surface. Stir in the Grand Marnier.

Strain the tea-infused cream through a fine sieve. Combine with the double cream and whip to soft peaks.

Fold the sabayon into the cream, then fold in the chopped dates. Tip into the prepared mould and freeze. The parfait will keep in the freezer for up to 3 weeks.

To serve, dip the mould into warm water for a few seconds, cover with a board or large plate and invert. Remove the mould and peel away the plastic wrap. Use a sharp knife to cut into slices and serve straight away.

Frozen soufflé (page 276)

Cherry and pistachio nougat
glacé (page 277)

Frozen fruit soufflés

These are iced desserts that superficially resemble hot baked soufflés. They are made in a large mould or individual ramekin dishes, whose height is increased by a band of paper. After freezing the band is removed to create the look of a traditional 'risen' soufflé. An iced soufflé is made from a flavoured ice cream or parfait mix, and they are often tizzed up with piped Crème Chantilly (page 234), crystallised fruits or finely chopped nuts.

Frozen soufflé

The flavour options for frozen soufflés are infinite. Use 1 kg (2 lb 3 oz) of any ice cream, parfait or mousse base. Some of my favourites are the Date and Earl Grey Parfait (page 273), any fruit mousse (page 291) or Nougat Glacé (opposite).

makes 4 soufflés

PREP TIME 30 MINUTES ✪ FREEZING TIME 8 HOURS

Lightly oil 4 x 200 ml (7 fl oz) soufflé moulds. Tie a strip of baking paper around the dish to form a collar that rises 5 cm (2 in) above the rim of each mould.

Fill each mould up to the top of the paper collar and freeze for 8 hours. Once frozen, decorate the top and peel away the paper band to reveal the frozen soufflé in all its splendour. Serve immediately.

Nougat glacé

One of my favourite frozen desserts. Nougat glacé is similar to a parfait, but uses Swiss meringue base (page 297) instead of a pâte bombe or sabayon. This gives quite a different texture, which is a bit gooey and almost chewy – like a bar of nougat. Traditional nougat glacé is lightened with whipped cream, flavoured with honey and given textural interest with the addition of dried fruits and nuts. Use the recipe as a base and experiment with any combination of dried or candied fruits and nuts that you like. Avoid fresh fruit as the higher water content causes the parfait to become icy. Nougat glacé is usually frozen in a terrine mould and served in slices, like a parfait.

Cherry and pistachio nougat glacé

serves 8

✂ PREP TIME 30 MINUTES ❀ FREEZING TIME 6 HOURS

3 egg whites
125 g (4½ oz) sugar
25 ml (¾ fl oz) whisky
190 ml (6½ fl oz) cream
100 g (3½ oz) glacé cherries or griotte cherries, roughly chopped
50 g (2 oz) unsalted pistachios, blanched and peeled

Line a 1 litre (34 fl oz) terrine mould or 8 x 120 ml (4 fl oz) ramekin dishes with plastic wrap and place in the freezer to chill.

To make the Swiss meringue, put the egg whites and sugar in a stainless-steel bowl and, whisking lightly, warm slowly to 65°C (150°F) in a bain-marie or over a pan of gently simmering water. Tip into the bowl of your electric mixer and whisk at the highest speed until the mixture stops steaming. Reduce the speed to medium and continue whisking until the mixture is just warm. Reduce the speed again to the lowest setting, and continue whisking until the mixture reaches room temperature. Briefly stir in the whisky.

In another bowl, whisk the cream to soft peaks (page 233), then fold it into the meringue. Fold in the cherries and pistachio until just evenly distributed and pour into the prepared moulds. Freeze until firm. The parfait will keep in the freezer for up to 3 weeks.

To serve, dip the mould into warm water for a few seconds, cover with a board or large plate and invert. Remove the mould and peel away the plastic wrap. Use a sharp knife to cut into slices and serve straight away.

Gelatine

Not the most trendy of ingredients, gelatine-based food tends to remind us of childhood parties (think of those little individual strawberry jellies set in paper cups) or of old-fashioned moulded savoury dishes coated in aspic.

But to be honest, I think of gelatine as a bit of a wonder ingredient – especially when it comes to desserts. I adore those shimmering, jewel-like, pure jellies that quiver so sexily on the plate; not to mention the delectable creamy wobble of a bavarois or a light-as-air mousse – all of which make for a deliciously light end to a rich meal. Best of all, they can be made well ahead of time, making them the ideal dinner party dessert.

Clear jellies and fruit terrines use fresh fruit juice or a light syrup that is set with gelatine. The possibilities are endless and they can be visually spectacular, with pieces of fresh fruit suspended within the crystal-clear jelly. If you're making your own fruit jellies from fresh fruit juice you should avoid certain fruits: pineapple, paw paw and kiwi fruit all contain an enzyme that breaks down the animal protein in gelatine, making it impossible to set.

Bavarois (also known as Bavarian cream) and pannacottas are both set with gelatine and are quite similar in look and texture. They both have a silky sheen and both should be set only to a soft shivering consistency. The difference is that a bavarois is based on custard, while a pannacotta is simply set cream (modern versions also use buttermilk or yoghurt).

Mousses – both savoury and sweet – are another sort of soft, wobbly dessert, but they tend to be lighter than a bavarois as they have air incorporated into the mix. Some mousses are not set with gelatine at all, but rely on whipped egg whites and cream to set them to a dense, creamy texture. They are lighter, airier and creamier than either a bavarois or a pannacotta, and again, the range of flavourings is almost limitless.

Gelatine is a natural product that is derived from the bones and skin of animals as they cook. Long slow cooking – as is needed for making stocks and braises – causes this natural savoury jelly to be released. When reduced and concentrated down it forms aspic, which is used in many savoury mousses and terrines.

Sweet jellied desserts are made from commercially manufactured gelatine which comes in powdered or sheet form. I always use sheet gelatine as it's easier to work with and has a much better flavour. You can buy sheet gelatine from many supermarkets and good delis – but be warned, there are different varieties from different countries, all of which are classified in different ways … and not surprisingly, this can lead to some confusion! I always weigh my gelatine sheets and work in grams. If you follow the measurements exactly the recipes will work.

All gelatine sheets need to be pre-soaked in cold water for a few minutes before use. This softens them and helps to remove any gelatine taste. The softened gelatine is then squeezed to extract any excess water and added to the hot liquid it is intended to set. It should be well stirred to make sure it melts completely, and then strained through a fine sieve, just in case a few tiny lumps and bumps remain.

Mandarin jelly

Heating fresh fruit juices alters their flavour, so only heat the few tablespoons necessary to dissolve the gelatine. This is a lovely, clean dessert for a warm summer evening. Serve with segments of mandarin and grapefruit or with Mandarin Sorbet (page 265). Decorate with fresh sorrel leaves for an unusual presentation.

serves 4

PREP TIME 10 MINUTES   COOK TIME 3 MINUTES
SETTING TIME 4 HOURS

18 g (²/₃ oz) gelatine sheets

400 ml (13 fl oz) mandarin juice

80 ml (3 fl oz) Stock Syrup (page 232)

1 tablespoon lemon juice

Lightly oil 4 x 120 ml (4 fl oz) jelly moulds. Soak the gelatine in a large bowl of cold water for 5–10 minutes to soften. Drain and squeeze out as much excess water as you can.

Place a few tablespoons of the mandarin juice in a saucepan with the gelatine and heat gently over a moderate heat, stirring until the gelatine dissolves. Remove the pan from the heat and stir in the remaining mandarin juice, the stock syrup and the lemon juice. Strain through a fine sieve then pour into your prepared moulds. Allow to cool to room temperature then refrigerate until set.

Campari and blood orange jelly

serves 4

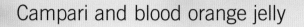 PREP TIME 10 MINUTES ☞ COOK TIME 3 MINUTES
⊛ SETTING TIME 4 HOURS

18 g (⅔ oz) gelatine sheets

350 ml (12 fl oz) blood orange juice

110 ml (3¾ fl oz) Stock Syrup (page 232)

40 ml (1⅓ fl oz) Campari

Follow the same method as the Mandarin Jelly
(opposite). A fun way to serve this vibrant red-orange
jelly is in martini or wine glasses. Top with a generous
scoop of Granny Smith Apple Sorbet (page 265) and
a few Vanilla Poached Apple slices (page 251).

Passionfruit jelly

serves 4

PREP TIME 10 MINUTES   COOK TIME 3 MINUTES
SETTING TIME 4 HOURS

25 g (1 oz) gelatine sheets

150 ml (5 fl oz) orange juice

250 ml (8½ fl oz) passionfruit juice

100 ml (3½ fl oz) Stock Syrup (page 232)

Follow the same method as the Mandarin Jelly
(page 282). Serve with a drizzle of fresh passionfruit,
a scoop of Champagne and Ginger Granita (page
263) and a Spiced Tuile (page 353).

Chocolate jelly

Everyone loves chocolate, especially in such an unexpected form! To increase the fun factor, cut the jelly into interesting shapes.

serves 4

✎ PREP TIME 10 MINUTES ⌣ COOK TIME 3 MINUTES
✿ SETTING TIME 4 HOURS

18 g (²⁄₃ oz) gelatine sheets

300 ml (10 fl oz) water

100 ml (3½ fl oz) Stock Syrup (page 232)

30 g (1 oz) unsweetened cocoa powder

30 ml (1 fl oz) Muscat wine

Lightly oil a small shallow tray. Soak the gelatine in a large bowl of cold water for 5–10 minutes to soften. Drain and squeeze out as much excess water as you can.

Put the water, syrup and cocoa powder in a saucepan and bring to the boil over a moderate heat. Remove the pan from the heat, add the gelatine and stir until it dissolves. Allow to cool a little, then add the Muscat. Strain through a fine sieve then pour into your prepared tray.

Allow to cool to room temperature then refrigerate until set. Cut into shapes and serve with your choice of accompaniment.

Serve with runny cream or with Chocolate Sorbet (page 265).

Lemongrass jelly

serves 4

✎ PREP TIME 10 MINUTES ⌣ COOK TIME 3 MINUTES
✿ SETTING TIME 4 HOURS

280 ml (9½ fl oz) water

140 g (5 oz) sugar

60 g (2 oz) lemongrass stalks, roughly crushed

18 g (²⁄₃ oz) gelatine sheets

Put the water, sugar and lemongrass stalks in a saucepan and bring to the boil over a moderate heat. Remove the pan from the heat and leave to infuse for 15 minutes.

Lightly oil a small shallow tray. Soak the gelatine in a large bowl of cold water for 5–10 minutes to soften. Drain and squeeze out as much excess water as you can.

Add the gelatine to the infused syrup and stir until it dissolves. Allow to cool a little then strain through a fine sieve and pour into your prepared tray.

Allow to cool to room temperature then refrigerate until set. Cut into shapes and serve with your choice of accompaniment.

This has a delicate lemon flavour and is delicious served as a garnish for fruit salads or with Raviolo of Pineapple (page 254).

Bavarois

Use the Vanilla Bavarois recipe as a base to create all sorts of different flavoured bavarois. Add fruit purées, liqueurs and so on to an anglaise base, up to the 300 ml (10 fl oz) quantity specified.

Vanilla bavarois

serves 4

🖊 PREP TIME 15 MINUTES ⊛ SETTING TIME 4 HOURS

5 g (¼ oz) gelatine sheets

300 ml (10 fl oz) Vanilla Crème Anglaise
  (page 237)

200 g (7 oz) double (heavy) cream

Lightly oil 4 x 120 ml (4 fl oz) dariole (cylindrical)
moulds. Soak the gelatine in a large bowl of cold
water for 5–10 minutes to soften. Drain and squeeze
out as much excess water as you can.

Put the vanilla anglaise in a saucepan and heat
gently over a moderate heat. Add the softened
gelatine and stir until it dissolves. Remove the pan
from the heat and cool to room temperature.

Whip the cream to form soft peaks (page 233)
and fold into the anglaise. Pour into your prepared
moulds, allow to cool to room temperature then
refrigerate until set.

Serve with slices of
fresh plum, a drizzle
of fresh passionfruit
or with Peach Sorbet
(page 266).

Sauternes pannacotta

Instead of sauternes, you can substitute any flavoured liqueur of your choice.

serves 4

✐ PREP TIME 10 MINUTES ☐ COOK TIME 3 MINUTES
✿ SETTING TIME 4 HOURS

10 g (⅓ oz) gelatine sheets

80 ml (3 fl oz) milk

100 g (3½ oz) sugar

25 g (1 oz) liquid glucose

100 ml (3½ fl oz) sauternes or sweet white wine

160 ml (5½ fl oz) cream

Lightly oil 4 x 120 ml (4 fl oz) dariole (cylindrical) moulds. Soak the gelatine in a large bowl of cold water for 5–10 minutes to soften. Drain and squeeze out as much excess water as you can.

Put the milk, sugar and glucose in a saucepan and heat gently over a moderate heat until dissolved. Add the softened gelatine and stir until it dissolves. Remove the pan from the heat and cool to room temperature. Stir in the wine and the cream.

Strain through a fine sieve and pour into your prepared moulds. Allow to cool to room temperature then refrigerate until set. Serve with your choice of accompaniment.

Serve with Dark Caramel Syrup (page 232) and orange slices macerated in hot caramel.

Mascarpone and vanilla pannacotta

For a lighter and less rich pannacotta replace the mascarpone with yoghurt or crème fraîche. Serve with finely sliced fresh figs and a drizzle of Raspberry Coulis (page 245).

serves 4

✐ PREP TIME 10 MINUTES ☐ COOK TIME 3 MINUTES
✿ SETTING TIME 4 HOURS

200 ml (7 fl oz) milk

100 ml (3½ fl oz) cream

50 g (2 oz) sugar

2 vanilla pods, seeds scraped

10 g (⅓ oz) gelatine sheets

140 g (5 oz) mascarpone

Put the milk, cream, sugar and vanilla pods in a saucepan and heat gently over a moderate heat until dissolved. Remove the pan from the heat and leave to infuse for 15 minutes.

Lightly oil 4 x 120 ml (4 fl oz) dariole (cylindrical) moulds. Soak the gelatine in a large bowl of cold water for 5–10 minutes to soften. Drain and squeeze out as much excess water as you can.

Remove the vanilla pods from the infused milk, add the softened gelatine and stir until it dissolves.

Strain through a fine sieve then cool to room temperature. Add the mascarpone and use a hand blender to blend it in thoroughly. Pour into your prepared moulds and refrigerate until set. Serve with your choice of accompaniment.

mousses

Dark chocolate mousse

serves 4

PREP TIME 10 MINUTES ⬤ COOK TIME 3 MINUTES ⬤ SETTING TIME 4 HOURS

5 g (¼ oz) gelatine sheets

150 g (5½ oz) dark chocolate

200 ml (7 fl oz) cream

150 ml (5 fl oz) Sweet Sabayon (page 241)

Lightly oil 4 x 120 ml (4 fl oz) dariole (cylindrical) moulds. Soak the gelatine in a large bowl of cold water for 5–10 minutes to soften. Drain and squeeze out as much excess water as you can.

Melt the chocolate in your microwave or in a bowl set over simmering water. When just melted, stir and remove from the heat.

Warm half the cream in a small saucepan, then add the softened gelatine. Stir until dissolved and add to the melted chocolate.

Whip the remaining cream to soft peaks (page 233). Fold the sabayon into the chocolate mixture, then gently fold in the whipped cream. Spoon the mousse into your prepared moulds and refrigerate until set.

Fruit-based mousse

serves 4

🥄 PREP TIME 10 MINUTES 🍳 COOK TIME 3 MINUTES
❄ SETTING TIME 4 HOURS

150 ml (5 fl oz) cream

250 g (9 oz) Fruit Purée (page 257)

100 g (3½ oz) Italian Meringue (page 296)

Lightly oil 4 x 120 ml (4 fl oz) dariole (cylindrical) moulds. Whip the cream to soft peaks (page 233). Mix the fruit purée through the Italian meringue and then fold in the cream. Spoon into your prepared moulds and refrigerate until set.

White chocolate mousse

serves 4

🥄 PREP TIME 10 MINUTES 🍳 COOK TIME 3 MINUTES
❄ SETTING TIME 4 HOURS

5 g (¼ oz) gelatine sheets

100 ml (3½ fl oz) milk

200 g (7 oz) white chocolate

220 ml (7½ fl oz) cream

Lightly oil 4 x 120 ml (4 fl oz) dariole (cylindrical) moulds. Soak the gelatine in a large bowl of cold water for 5–10 minutes to soften. Drain and squeeze out as much excess water as you can.

Warm the milk in a small saucepan, then add the softened gelatine. Stir until dissolved then strain through a fine sieve.

Put the chocolate in a bowl and stir in the hot milk, little by little, until melted and velvety smooth. Allow to cool to room temperature.

Whip the cream to soft peaks (page 233) and fold into the chocolate mixture. Spoon into your prepared moulds and refrigerate until set.

meringues and soufflés

Meringues and soufflés are what I think of
as the 'sweet-nothings' of the dessert world.
Both look stunning, all puffed up like airy clouds,
and both dissolve into a delicate sweet lightness
on the tongue.

This magic occurs when air is whisked into egg whites. As they cook, the heat causes the tiny air bubbles to expand and it sets the egg white protein firm around them. In the lesson on gelatine we touched on this whisking and aerating technique in making mousses. The difference is that mousses are not cooked, and the whisked egg whites are 'set' with gelatine or with whipped cream.

Meringues are one of the simplest desserts of all to make, as they need only two ingredients: sugar and egg whites. And although this sounds as if it might be a little restricting, meringues are extraordinarily versatile. Pastry cooks love meringue and it is used to make all manner of imaginative concoctions. It's not just an essential building block of the soufflé, but think too of oeufs à la neige (floating islands), baked Alaska, vacherin, Genoese sponge, Mont Blanc and the great Aussie and Kiwi dessert classic, pavlova.

The versatility is achieved because different methods of combining the two basic ingredients result in three quite different types of meringue – French, Italian and Swiss.

French meringue – or meringue ordinaire – is the simplest, and is made by beating sugar into whisked egg whites to form snow-white, shiny peaks. Whisked egg whites can expand up to eight times their original volume and the sugar helps to stabilise them, making them less likely to collapse. The only thing to remember when making French meringue is to add the sugar gradually (usually after the whites have been whipped to about four times their original volume) and to make sure each batch is thoroughly dissolved into the whites, or the meringues will 'weep' as they bake. French meringue can be used as is for a soufflé or for making oeufs à la neige, or it can be piped or shaped into shells, discs or fingers and baked.

Italian meringue is the meringue of choice of professional pastry chefs. It is virtually indestructible (unlike French meringue, which will break down if not used straight away), so it can be pre-prepared and kept for several hours in the fridge. The stability is achieved by pouring boiling sugar syrup into the whisked egg whites and continuing to whisk them until they cool. The heat from the syrup causes the whites to puff up and 'cook'. Italian meringue has an even smoother, finer texture than French meringue. It is mainly used as the base for other sweet recipes, but it's also used to make a range of petits fours, as a topping for tarts, in sweet icings (frostings), and as a base for some sorbets (sherbets), ice creams and iced soufflés.

Swiss meringue – or meringue cuite – is somewhat trickier to make, and tends to be left to professional pastry chefs. It's made in a similar way to Italian meringue, but is cooked over a pan of simmering water. It requires a fair amount of muscle power, but the resulting meringue is stiff and very stable. I use Swiss meringue to make nougat glacé (page 277).

Sweet or savoury, hot soufflés have earned a bit of a reputation for being tricky and unpredictable. A fallen soufflé is probably every cook's nightmare. But they really are not difficult as long as you observe the basic principles.

Hot soufflés as distinct from iced soufflés (page 276) are all are made using the same component parts: a flavoured base and whisked egg whites to aerate. Savoury soufflés are usually based on a béchamel sauce (page 80). Sweet soufflés are based on pure fruit purées or a flavoured crème pâtissière (page 241), folded together with French meringue. In all cases, it is important that both base mixture and whisked egg whites should be of the correct consistency, and they should be folded together gently to maintain maximum volume and lightness.

The prepared soufflé mixture is then spooned into lightly buttered ramekins or a large soufflé dish and baked in a hottish oven to quivering splendour.

A slightly simpler and more foolproof version of the soufflé is the omelette soufflé. These follow the same basic principle of folding whisked egg white into an egg yolk base, but they are baked in an oven-proof omelette pan instead of the traditional soufflé mould.

294

Tips for whisking egg whites

✳ In general, eggs are easier to separate when they are super-fresh, but the whites whip better when they are older and lightly warmed. I recommend separating them as soon as you take them out of the refrigerator, then leave the egg whites in a covered bowl and allow them to come to room temperature before whisking. Even better, leave them at room temperature for a couple of days; they will begin to liquefy a little, which makes them easier to whisk to even greater volume and they will also be less likely to collapse.

✳ Both your whisk and bowl should be scrupulously clean. Any traces of dirt – and especially any oil or grease – will prevent the whites from whisking successfully.

✳ When whisking egg whites, always start at a low speed. Whisk until they are foamy, with large loose bubbles, then increase your speed to medium-high then high. If the egg whites are beaten too quickly from the beginning the structure of the foam will not be as strong and you will not achieve the maximum volume.

✳ There are several distinct stages that whisked egg whites go through: foamy – when there are large, loose cloudy bubbles but the whites are still quite liquid; soft peaks – when the bubbles have tightened into a white foam, form a ribbon and can be pulled into a peak, but will not hold the shape; firm peaks – glossy, firm and smooth, and will form a peak that curls over at the top; stiff peaks – glossy and very stiff, peaks will hold firm and are stiff enough to slice.

meringues

Swiss meringue

makes 450 g (1 lb)

✏ PREP TIME 2 MINUTES 🥘 COOK TIME 5 MINUTES

250 g (9 oz) sugar
5 egg whites

Put the egg whites and sugar in a stainless-steel bowl and warm gently to 65°C (150°F) in a bain-marie or over a pan of gently simmering water. Tip into the bowl of your electric mixer and whisk at the highest speed until the mixture stops steaming. Reduce the speed to medium and continue whisking until the mixture is just warm. Reduce the speed again to the lowest setting, and continue whisking until the mixture reaches room temperature.

Italian meringue

makes 500 g (1 lb 2 oz)

✏ PREP TIME 10 MINUTES 🥘 COOK TIME 5 MINUTES

110 g (3¾ oz) water
220 g (7¾ oz) sugar
4 egg whites

Put the sugar and water in a heavy-based saucepan and heat gently until the sugar has completely dissolved. Increase the heat and place a sugar thermometer in the pan. Boil the syrup for around 7 minutes until it reaches 128°C (262°F), or until a little of the syrup dropped into a glass of cold water forms a hard clear ball – the 'hard ball' stage.

Put the egg whites in a scrupulously clean electric mixer. Start whisking at low speed, until the mixture begins to foam. With the beaters on slow, gradually trickle in the boiling syrup and continue whisking for 5–10 minutes until the meringue cools to room temperature. It should be smooth, shiny and white. Use straight away.

Oeufs à la neige – Floating islands

French meringue

makes 600 g (1 lb 5 oz)

PREP TIME 10 MINUTES

5 egg whites
200 g (7 oz) sugar
200 g (7 oz) icing (confectioners') sugar

Put the egg whites and a few tablespoons of sugar into a scrupulously clean electric mixer. Start whisking at low speed, until the mixture begins to foam. Then increase the speed to high and whisk until the foam thickens to form smooth, soft glossy peaks. Sift on the remaining sugar, a little at a time, and continue whisking until the meringue stands in firm peaks. Finally, sift on the icing sugar and whisk in briefly until it is incorporated. Use straight away.

OEUFS À LA NEIGE – FLOATING ISLANDS

COOK TIME 5 MINUTES

Bring a large saucepan of milk to a gentle simmer. Use 2 hot dessert spoons to shape the French meringue into quenelles and drop into the hot milk. Poach around 4 at a time, for 3–5 minutes, turning them in the milk so they poach evenly. Use a slotted spoon to remove the meringues from the milk and leave to dry on a clean tea (dish) towel.

To serve, fill a shallow dessert bowl or individual serving bowls with a pool of frothy Vanilla Crème Anglaise (page 237) and float the soft meringues on top.

This dessert can be made ahead of time and kept in a cool place until ready to serve. As a final flourish, swirl some Berry Coulis (page 245) into the custard or accompany with fresh berries or stone fruit.

VACHERINS

COOK TIME 90 MINUTES

Preheat the oven to 120°C (250°F). Line 2 baking sheets with a silicone baking mat or baking paper and draw on 10 cm (4 in) circles to act as a template.

Spoon the French meringue into a piping bag and pipe in concentric circles to fill the drawn circle. Pipe another ring on the outer edge of each disc to create a basket.

Bake for 1½ hours until the vacherins are ivory and crisp. Leave to cool for 10 minutes before carefully lifting them onto a wire rack to cool completely. When ready to serve, fill with flavoured Crème Chantilly (page 234) and Macerated Berries (page 249).

Champagne chiboust

serves 4

5 g (¼ oz) gelatine sheets

210 ml (7⅓ fl oz) milk

2 egg yolks

20 g (¾ oz) cornflour (cornstarch)

120 g (4½ oz) sugar

3 egg whites

50 ml (2 fl oz) champagne

Serve with fresh raspberries and Raspberry Coulis (page 245).

Soak the gelatine in a large bowl of cold water for 5–10 minutes to soften. Drain and squeeze out as much excess water as you can.

Combine the milk, egg yolks and cornflour in a heavy-based saucepan and add a tablespoon of the sugar. Bring to a simmer, whisking continuously.

Place the egg whites in a scrupulously clean electric mixer with the rest of the sugar and whisk to soft peaks (page 295).

Dissolve the gelatine in the hot milk then quickly whisk in a third of the meringue and all the champagne. When completely amalgamated, gently fold in the remaining meringue and spoon into a piping bag.

Arrange 4 x 8 cm (3 in) pastry rings on a tray. Pipe the chiboust into the rings then transfer to the refrigerator to set for about 4 hours.

When ready to serve, remove the chibousts from the refrigerator and toast the surface of each with a small kitchen blowtorch, so that they resemble toasted marshmallows. Carefully unmould and place on the centre of dessert plates. Serve straight away with your choice of accompaniment.

Soufflés

Sweet soufflés are based on pure fruit purées or a flavoured crème pâtissière folded together with French meringue. In all cases, it is important that both base mixture and whisked egg whites should be at the correct temperature (room temperature) and consistency, and they should be folded together gently to maintain maximum volume and lightness.

Hot soufflés are baked in a large soufflé dish or small individual ramekins. They need to be properly prepared so that the soufflé mixture rises up the sides of the dish evenly. Brush the base and the inside of the moulds with melted butter in an upwards direction – it may sound silly, but it does make a difference! Then dust evenly with sugar, shaking off any excess. Refrigerate to set the butter while you prepare the mix.

Fill the moulds generously, then level off the top with a spatula to form a smooth, even surface. Use the tip of a knife to run a small indentation around the rim; this helps the soufflé to rise evenly, without catching on the sides.

Crème pâtissière base

This base is made in the same way as a traditional Crème Pâtissière (page 241), but with less sugar. Remember that it is combined with French Meringue (page 297) as well as other sweet flavourings, and you don't want to give your guests toothache!

makes 500 g (1 lb 2 oz)

/ PREP TIME 5 MINUTES ☐ COOK TIME 5 MINUTES

360 ml (12 fl oz) milk

4 egg yolks

30 g (1 oz) sugar

20 g (¾ oz) plain (all-purpose) flour

20 g (¾ oz) cornflour (cornstarch)

Put the milk in a heavy-based saucepan and bring to the boil. Remove from the heat and set aside.

Put the egg yolks and sugar in an electric mixer and whisk to the ribbon stage (page 295). Fold in the sifted flour and cornflour.

Pour a third of the hot milk onto the egg mixture and whisk gently to combine. Pour back into the saucepan with the rest of the hot milk and cook gently over a moderate heat for about 5 minutes, whisking all the time. The custard will thicken to a stiff, glossy smooth paste.

Remove from the heat and stand the pan in a sink of iced water. Whisk vigorously to beat out any lumps. When completely cold, store in a sealed container in the refrigerator for up to 5 days.

Prune and Armagnac soufflé

The classic combination of dark sticky prunes and Armagnac works brilliantly in a soufflé and is one of my favourites. Serve with Vanilla Crème Anglaise (page 237) flavoured with Armagnac and a scoop of Armagnac and Caramel Ice Cream (page 271). When you serve the soufflés dollop a scoop of ice cream on top of each one. It will gradually sink into the hot soufflé, making a wonderful contrast in temperatures as you eat.

serves 4

PREP TIME 10 MINUTES   COOK TIME 8 MINUTES

250 g (9 oz) Crème Pâtissière Base (page 301)

20 ml (¾ fl oz) Armagnac

80 g (3 oz) prunes, pitted and chopped

7 egg whites

140 g (5 oz) sugar

Preheat your oven to 190°C (375°F). Prepare 4 individual soufflé dishes. Beat the crème pâtissière base to soften it, then stir in the Armagnac and chopped prunes.

Put the egg whites and sugar in a scrupulously clean electric mixer and whisk to soft peaks (page 295). Fold into the crème pâtissière and spoon into the prepared dishes. Level the surface with a palette knife and run it around the rim to create a small groove.

Place the soufflés on a baking tray and bake for 8 minutes until risen and golden. Serve straight away with your choice of accompaniment.

Fruit soufflé base

makes 500 g (1 lb 2 oz)

✐ PREP TIME 10 MINUTES ☕ COOK TIME 8 MINUTES

360 g (12 ½ oz) Fruit Purée (page 257)
3 egg yolks
30 g (1 oz) sugar
20 g (¾ oz) plain (all-purpose) flour
20 g (¾ oz) cornflour (cornstarch)

Make in the same way as the Crème Pâtissière Base (page 301), substituting the fruit purée for the milk.

Apricot soufflé

Make your fruit soufflé base with apricots – or indeed any other fruit, such as peach, raspberry or rhubarb.

serves 4

✐ PREP TIME 10 MINUTES ☕ COOK TIME 8 MINUTES

250 g (9 oz) Fruit Soufflé Base (above)
40 g (1 ½ oz) apricot liqueur
7 egg whites
140 g (5 oz) sugar

Make in the same way as the Prune and Armagnac Soufflé (page 303), substituting the fruit soufflé base for the crème pâtissière base.

OMELETTE SOUFFLÉS

Use either a crème pâtissière or fruit base for these fun soufflés. The difference is really in the presentation. As the omelette pans are shallower it removes some of the anxiety about whether or not the soufflé will rise.

Preheat your oven to 190ºC (375°F) and grease small individual ovenproof omelette pans. Spoon in the soufflé mix and place the pan on a high heat for 30 seconds, just to colour the base. Bake in the oven for 5 minutes.

Chocolate

There's no doubt that for many people their sweet treat of choice begins and ends with chocolate. Chocolate desserts are always the most popular items on a restaurant menu and, indeed, there are entire books, web sites and even movies devoted to its virtues.

Part of the appeal of chocolate is the variety of flavours – from being so bitter it makes you shiver, to cloyingly sweet; and colours – from darkest brown to palest ivory. Its uses are equally diverse, from hot drinks, and elegant hand-made confectionery to tarts, cakes, cookies, pastries, creams and ice creams – the list goes on and on.

Chocolate is made from the ground nib of the cacao bean, which is then combined with sugar and cocoa butter in varying ratios. It can come in a powder form (as unsweetened cocoa) or as a solid or liquid. Liquid chocolate is mainly used by the confectionary industry for coatings or moulds. Solid chocolate is the most commonly used product, and ranges in quality from fine couverture to common-or-garden candy bars. Milk chocolate is lighter in colour and sweeter than dark because it contains milk.

The quality of chocolate is determined by the type of cocoa bean used in its manufacture and in the ratio of cocoa solids to cocoa butter. The higher the percentage of cocoa solids the stronger and more intense will be the chocolate flavour. At the high end (which can reach as high as 75–80%) chocolate can be a little too bitter for many palates. At the mass confectionery end of the spectrum, the percentage of cocoa solids can be as low as 30%. For most desserts I use a chocolate with a minimum of 60% cocoa solids. And remember that white chocolate is not really chocolate at all as it contains no cocoa solids. It is an amalgam of cocoa butter and vanilla, which gives it a unique sweet flavour and silky smooth texture.

In the end, whether it's chocolate for eating or chocolate for use in cooking, it will come down to personal preference. One of the most highly regarded (and most expensive) chocolate available is the French brand Valrhona, but there are others, such as Callebaut and Lindt, which I think are almost as good, and you won't have to mortgage your house to buy them.

Chocolate should be stored in a cool, dry cupboard, away from the light. It needs to be well wrapped and kept in an airtight container, as it has a tendency to absorb odours from other nearby foods. Sometimes you might notice a white 'bloom' appearing on the surface of the chocolate. Sugar bloom is caused by a humid environment: water particles come into contact with the chocolate and dissolve some of the sugar; as the water evaporates the sugar crystals are left behind. Fat bloom occurs with sudden fluctuations in temperature that alter the structure of the chocolate: particles of cocoa butter are released and make their way to the surface where they create a fatty film. Neither type of bloom will affect the taste or usability of the chocolate.

Melting chocolate

Break the chocolate up into small even-sized pieces and place them in a large heatproof bowl. Sit the bowl over a pan of very gently simmering water. The heat from the steam should be sufficient to melt the chocolate. The base of the bowl should not come into contact with the water as too high a temperature can burn it and taint its flavour. Most importantly of all, don't allow any water or steam to come into contact with the chocolate or it will seize up into a tight grainy mass. Stir from time to time until it has melted to a smooth shiny consistency, then remove the bowl from the pan and leave the chocolate to cool.

You can also melt chocolate very successfully in a microwave oven. Again, break it into small even-sized pieces and heat on high or medium in bursts of around 30 seconds. Stir in between until it all melts to a smooth, shiny consistency.

Whichever method you use, if you need to add liquid – such as alcohol or cream – then add it at the beginning and stir gently to combine as you heat it. If you add it at the end, the chocolate will seize up.

Tempering

A word filled with mystery and science. Tempered chocolate is used in professional restaurant kitchens and in the process of hand-making high-quality chocolates when that extra-glossy sheen is required. The process involves heating, lowering and reheating the chocolate to very precise temperatures and then maintaining it at an even 31°C (88°F) for use. To temper chocolate successfully you really need a special machine and I wouldn't recommend it for the home cook.

Warm rich chocolate pudding

This pudding is delicious served with softly whipped cream, but enters another heavenly realm when served with the Cherry and Pistachio Nougat Glacé (page 277).

serves 6

PREP TIME 10 MINUTES   COOK TIME 30 MINUTES

melted butter

4 eggs

60 g (2 oz) liquid glucose

100 g (3½ oz) sugar

60 g (2 oz) ground almonds

90 g (3 oz) plain (all-purpose) flour

30 g (1 oz) unsweetened cocoa powder

1 teaspoon baking powder

100 ml (3½ fl oz) cream

60 g (2 oz) clarified butter

40 ml (1½ fl oz) dark rum

60 g (2 oz) best-quality dark chocolate

Preheat your oven to 160°C (320°F). Brush the inside of a large pudding basin (steamed pudding mould) or brioche mould with a little melted butter. In a large mixing bowl, beat together the eggs, glucose and sugar. Add the almonds, then sift on the flour, cocoa and baking powder and mix to combine. Stir in the cream and butter.

Break the chocolate into small pieces and place in a heatproof bowl with the rum. Microwave on medium in 30-second bursts, or stand the bowl over a pan of simmering water until the chocolate has melted. Stir until smooth then mix into the pudding batter. Spoon the batter into your prepared mould and bake for 25–30 minutes.

Remove from the oven and allow to cool for a few moments. To unmould the pudding, run a knife around the sides to loosen it, then invert onto a serving plate. Cut into wedges and serve warm with the accompaniment of your choice.

Chocolate tuiles

Another dessert stalwart, these delicate little lacy tuiles are the perfect accompaniment to all sorts of ice creams, mousses or baked custards.

makes around 30

PREP TIME 10 MINUTES ⊨ RESTING TIME 12 HOURS ⌸ COOK TIME 10 MINUTES

250 g (9 oz) sugar

50 g (2 oz) unsweetened cocoa powder

50 g (2 oz) ground almonds

50 g (2 oz) plain (all-purpose) flour

125 g (4½ oz) softened butter

125 ml (4¼ fl oz) fresh orange juice

In a large mixing bowl, stir together the sugar, cocoa, almonds and flour then sieve into the bowl of an electric mixer. Add the softened butter and mix until well combined. Mix in the orange juice then transfer the bowl to the fridge and chill for 12 hours.

When ready to bake, preheat the oven to 160°C (320°F). Line a baking sheet with a silicone baking mat or baking paper. Using a teaspoon, place small balls of the mixture on the prepared sheet, allowing about 5 cm (2 in) between them. They will melt and spread out in the heat of the oven – like a brandy snap.

Bake for 6–10 minutes until the tuiles start to darken around the edges. Leave for a few seconds before lifting the tuiles off with a spatula. They will crisp up as they cool.

Caramelised chocolate pots

serves 4

PREP TIME 10 MINUTES COOK TIME 40 MINUTES

500 ml (17 fl oz) milk
20 g (¾ oz) unsweetened cocoa powder
100 g (3½ oz) liquid glucose
100 g (3½ oz) best-quality dark chocolate, grated
4 egg yolks
Demerara sugar

Preheat your oven to 180°C (350°F). Stand 4 x 120 ml (4 fl oz) dariole (cylindrical) moulds, ramekin dishes or coffee cups in a deep roasting pan. Put the milk, cocoa and glucose in a heavy-based saucepan and bring to the boil. Remove the pan from the heat and stir in the chocolate until melted and smooth. Allow to cool. Stir in the egg yolks, then strain the mixture through a fine sieve.

Pour the mixture into the prepared moulds. Pour enough cold water into the roasting pan to come halfway up the side of the moulds. Cover loosely with foil and bake for 15 minutes. Lower the heat to 160°C (320°F), remove the foil and cook for a further 20 minutes.

Remove from the oven and allow to cool for about 20 minutes; the creams will still be quite wobbly. When ready to serve, sprinkle the surface of each chocolate pot with a thin, even layer of Demerara sugar. Caramelise the surface with a small kitchen blowtorch until the sugar melts to a shiny caramel glaze. If you don't have a blowtorch, preheat an overhead grill (broiler) to its highest setting. Place the brûlée on a baking sheet and slide it under the heat, about 5 cm (2 in) from the heat. Watch carefully to make sure it doesn't burn. Allow to cool for 5 minutes before serving so that the caramel layer will harden to a crisp, crunchy layer.

Chocolate fondants

These fondants have a soft liquid chocolate centre and are superb with Banana Ice Cream (page 271).

serves 4

PREP TIME 10 MINUTES COOK TIME 8 MINUTES

200 g (7 oz) bittersweet chocolate (70% cocoa solids)

50 g (2 oz) butter

5 egg whites

65 g (2 ¼ oz) sugar

3 egg yolks, lightly beaten

Break up the chocolate and place in a heatproof bowl with the butter. Microwave on medium in 30-second bursts, or stand the bowl over a pan of simmering water until the chocolate has melted. Stir until smooth.

Put the egg whites and sugar in the bowl of an electric mixer and whisk to soft peaks (page 295). Spoon a little into the melted chocolate to slacken it, then add the beaten egg yolks to the chocolate and whisk until smooth. Fold in the remaining egg whites, taking care to maintain the airiness.

Butter 4 x 8 cm (3 in) pastry rings and line with a strip of baking paper, extending 2 cm (¾ in) above the top of the ring. Arrange them on a baking sheet lined with baking paper. Spoon the chocolate fondant into a piping bag and pipe in enough to just fill the rings. Cover with plastic wrap and refrigerate until ready to bake. You can make the fondants to this stage 2–3 days ahead of time.

When ready to bake, preheat the oven to 180°C (350°F). Bake the fondants for 8 minutes. The outside should be firm, but they should still be liquid in the centre. Carefully remove the ring moulds and the paper and serve the fondants straight away.

Chocolate ganache

This is an indispensable item in any pastry or dessert kitchen. Use it to ice (frost) or fill cakes and pastries or fold into whipped cream to make a simple mousse. I also use it to make little petits fours: set the ganache in an ice tray and scoop out little balls with a melon baller; roll in cocoa or dip in melted chocolate and serve with coffee.

makes 500 g (1 lb 2 oz)

PREP TIME 5 MINUTES   COOK TIME 5 MINUTES

200 ml (7 fl oz) cream

40 g (1½ oz) liquid glucose

240 g (8½ oz) bittersweet chocolate (70% cocoa solids), grated

½ tablespoon Armagnac, cognac, brandy or rum

Combine the cream and glucose in a small saucepan and bring to the boil. Remove the pan from the heat and stir in the chocolate until melted and smooth. Stir in the alcohol and leave to cool. Cover and refrigerate until ready to use. It will keep up to 2 weeks.

Chocolate sauce

makes 500 ml (17 fl oz)

PREP TIME 5 MINUTES   COOK TIME 2 MINUTES

250 ml (8½ fl oz) cream

200 g (7 oz) chocolate

50 g (2 oz) butter

Put the cream in a heavy-based saucepan and bring to the boil. Break the chocolate into pieces and add to the hot cream. Stir until all melted then add the butter. Leave to cool at room temperature, then refrigerate until required. The sauce will keep in a sealed container in the refrigerator for up to 5 days.

Chocolate mille-feuille

An extravaganza of chocolate puff pastry, coffee cream and chocolate ganache. For the ultimate dinner party dessert, serve with a scoop of Chocolate Sorbet (page 265) on the side. Make all the component parts ahead of time and assemble at the last minute.

serves 4

✎ PREP TIME 15 MINUTES 🍲 COOK TIME 10 MINUTES

200 g (7 oz) Chocolate Puff Pastry (page 325)

200 g (7 oz) Coffee and Mascarpone Cream
  (page 234)

200 g (7 oz) Chocolate Ganache (page 316)

100 g (3½ oz) Butterscotch Sauce (page 232)

Preheat your oven to 180°C (350°F). Roll out the pastry to a thickness of 5 mm (¼ in). Cut into 4 neat rectangles about 5 cm x 12 cm (2 in x 5 in) and bake for 10 minutes until the pastry has puffed up to a rich dark brown. Remove from the oven and transfer to wire racks to cool.

Split each pastry rectangle into 3 layers at the natural seams. Lay the 4 bottoms out on your work surface. Pipe a layer of coffee cream and a layer of chocolate ganache onto each and carefully place the middle pastry layer on top. Pipe another layer of coffee cream and chocolate ganache onto the middle pastry layer and finish with the top layer of pastry.

Carefully lift each mille-feuille onto a dessert plate. Spoon the butterscotch sauce around the plate and serve straight away.

Pastry

Although it's often considered an art,
in my view pastry making is actually more
of a science, and a simple science at that.

Pastries

The very thought of making pastry is enough to make some people break out in a sweat.

There's so much hoo-hah about the right and wrong ways: whether your hands are the correct temperature, using the appropriate flour, whether you can make pastry in a food processor or do you absolutely have to get your hands dirty. And then there are all the different types of pastry: short, sweet, puff (to name but a few). It's no wonder people get nervous. However, it's really just about observing a few simple principles and, most critically, weighing your ingredients precisely.

Most of the pastries in this lesson can indeed be made in a food processor, although I personally find there is something very satisfying and relaxing about getting into the mix with your hands, rubbing in the butter, perhaps working in an egg yolk and gently bringing it all together to form a smooth ball in the palm of your hands.

All of the dough recipes below can be made in large quantities, divided into batches and frozen. And to be honest, some can also be purchased if you really don't feel up to the challenge of making it yourself. This is especially true of puff pastry, which can be tricky to get right at home. My tip is to source a good baker or pastry shop which sells fresh, good-quality puff pastry.

General tips

* The quicker the better is the overriding rule when making pastry. Unlike bread doughs, pastry needs minimal gluten development, so there's no kneading, stretching or working required. This is one reason why pastries are successfully made in a food processor – it speeds up the amalgamation process.

* Rest and chill the pastry each time it's handled and it won't shrink in the tart tin. I recommend an hour in the refrigerator once the dough's made, and then another 30 minutes once it's been rolled out and lines the tin.

* When rolling out the pastry, use a heavy, lightly floured rolling pin and make sure your work surface is clean. Roll out only as much dough as you need using downward pressure and rolling it away from you. Lift and rotate the dough a quarter turn every so often until you achieve the desired shape at a thickness of between 3–5 mm (⅛–¼ in). Don't worry if it's uneven; you can patch it together in the tin using extra scraps if need be.

* Butter the tart tin with melted butter and place it on a large heavy-based baking tray. Use your rolling pin to lift the pastry up and over the tin. Use your fingers to gently push the pastry into the bottom and up the sides of the tin. Trim the excess pastry, leaving an overhang of about 1–2 cm (½–¾ in). Prick the base all over with a fork.

* To avoid soggy pastry, most tarts are baked 'blind' before the filling is added. This means that they are partly or completely cooked, depending on whether the filling itself also needs to be cooked. To blind bake, you need to line the tart with a circle of baking paper and fill it with dried beans (you can buy special ceramic or metal beans for just this purpose, but any old dried pulses will do just as well). The tart is then baked in a preheated oven. After about 20 minutes, the tart will be partially baked. If it is to be filled with a wet filling, such as a custard, the paper and beans are removed and the filling poured in. Once the filling is poured into the tart shell, it should be cooked immediately.

Shortcrust (pie) pastry

This is the workhorse of the French pastry kitchen, the basic dough used for making savoury quiches and tarts, and also some sweet dessert tarts. The ideal shortcrust pastry should be thin, yet strong enough to safely contain its filling, delectably crumbly and melting in the mouth.

makes 500 g (1 lb 2 oz)

PREP TIME 15 MINUTES

300 g (10½ oz) plain (all-purpose) flour, sifted

1 teaspoon salt

150 g (5½ oz) cold butter, diced

1 egg yolk

60 ml (2 fl oz) water

Combine the flour, salt and butter in a food processor and pulse to a fine sandy consistency. Add the egg yolk and pulse quickly. Then add enough cold water to just bring the pastry together in a ball. Tip the dough out onto a lightly floured work surface and use your hands to shape it into a smooth, flattened ball. Wrap in plastic wrap and refrigerate for at least 30 minutes before rolling out. This pastry can also be frozen for up to 2 months.

Sweet pastry

Pâte sucrée is a sweet variation of the basic shortcrust. It's one of the most popular types of pastry in the French kitchen and I use it for all my favourite sweet tarts. Pâte sablé (page 351) is another type of sweet pastry that uses even more sugar, which makes it very fragile and crumbly. It tends to be reserved for fine patisserie items and biscuits (cookies). Both these sweet shortcrust (pie) pastries are often enriched with egg yolks for an even more delectable result.

makes 500 g (1 lb 2 oz)

PREP TIME 20 MINUTES

140 g (4½ oz) cold butter, diced

100 g (3½ oz) icing (confectioners') sugar

pinch of salt

1 egg, lightly whisked

230 g (8 oz) plain (all-purpose) flour

20 g (¾ oz) cornflour (cornstarch)

Put the butter and icing sugar in the bowl of your electric mixer and beat until lightly creamed. Add the salt and drizzle in the egg, a little at a time, beating until it comes together as a smooth mass. Sift on the flour and cornflour and mix briefly until it just comes together.

Tip the dough out onto a lightly floured work surface and use your hands to shape it into a smooth, flattened ball. Wrap in plastic wrap and refrigerate for at least 45 minutes before rolling out. This pastry can also be frozen for up to 2 months.

Choux pastry

Choux pastry is quite different from other pastries and far and away the easiest to make. It's one of the essential items of French patisserie, used to make crisp hollow pastry shells that neatly contain rich creamy fillings. Unlike other pastries, choux is cooked twice. First butter is melted with water and brought to the boil. Flour is then tipped in and vigorously beaten to form a panade – a dryish ball that comes away from the sides of the pan. Eggs are added one by one – and this part does require a bit of elbow-grease – and the smooth, shiny dough is then piped into little mounds or long fingers to bake. One of the most important things to remember about cooking choux is not to take it out of the oven too soon. It invariably looks done before it is sufficiently dry and crisp – there is nothing worse than soggy choux!

makes 500 g (1 lb 2 oz)

/ PREP TIME 10 MINUTES ☞ COOK TIME 20 MINUTES

160 ml (5⅓ fl oz) water	65 g (2¼ oz) butter
pinch salt	100 g (3½ oz) plain (all-purpose) flour, sifted
pinch sugar	4 eggs, lightly beaten

Combine the water, salt, sugar and butter in a large heavy-based saucepan and heat gently over a moderate heat until the butter melts. Bring to the boil. Add the flour all at once and beat vigorously with a wooden spoon until the dough is smooth.

Lower the heat and continue to beat the dough for another couple of minutes. It will begin to thicken and dry until eventually it will come away from the side of the pan in a ball. Tip the dough into the bowl of your electric mixer and allow to cool for 5 minutes.

With the mixer on low speed, gradually add the eggs, a quarter at a time. Beat well after each addition so that it is thoroughly incorporated before you add the next. Continue beating until you have a smooth paste, the texture of a stiff cake mix. Use straight away.

BABY PROFITEROLES

makes 40–50

☞ COOK TIME 15 MINUTES

Preheat the oven to 220°C (430°F). Line a baking sheet with a silicone baking mat or baking paper. Spoon the choux pastry into a piping bag and pipe into small, 2.5 cm (1 in) rounds. Leave about 5 cm (2 in) between them to allow for expansion as they cook. Bake for 5 minutes. Prop the oven door ajar with a wooden spoon and continue baking for a further 10 minutes. The choux buns will be puffed and golden. Remove from the oven and transfer them to a wire rack to cool. Make a small slit in the sides of each bun to release the hot air – this stops them going soggy. When cool, use a sharp knife to split the choux buns and fill them with Crème Chantilly (page 234). Serve immediately.

Puff pastry

The word feuillettée means 'many-leaved', which perfectly describes a good puff pastry. It should be golden brown, light as a feather, delicate and flaky – a multi-layered triumph. In traditional puff pastry a flour and water dough – the détrempe – is used to encase a block of butter. The whole thing is rolled, turned and folded, rolled, turned and folded with meticulous precision to achieve the many layers. True puff pastry is a challenge even for accomplished pastry chefs, so for home-baking I use a simplified version, known as a 'rough puff'.

makes 1.2 kg (2 lb 10 oz)

⫻ PREP TIME 20 MINUTES

500 g (1 lb 2 oz) firm butter

500 g (1 lb 2 oz) plain (all-purpose) flour (plus a little extra for dusting)

pinch salt

250 ml (8½ fl oz) iced water

Remove the butter from the fridge 1 hour before using so it is firm but not rock-hard. Cut into small cubes. Sift the flour into a bowl and make a well in the centre. Place the butter and salt in the well and use your fingertips to rub it into the consistency of coarse sand.

Add the water, a little at a time, and work it into the dough gently until it comes together as a firm dough, flecked with small bits of butter.

Place the pastry on a lightly dusted work surface and roll it out away from you to form a long rectangle, about 20 cm x 40 cm x 5 mm (8 in x 16 in x ¼ in) thick. Fold the 2 short ends in upon each other to make 3 layers.

Rotate the pastry a quarter-turn (90º) and roll it away from you again to form a long rectangle, the same size as before. Fold into thirds again. This is the first 'double turn'.

Wrap the pastry in plastic wrap and refrigerate for 30 minutes. Repeat the 'double turn' as described, then chill again for 30 minutes before using. Alternatively, the pastry can be wrapped in plastic wrap and kept in the refrigerator for 2 days, or up to a week in the freezer.

CHOCOLATE PUFF PASTRY

500 g (1 lb 2 oz) unsalted butter

70 g (2 ½ oz) unsweetened cocoa powder

Soften the butter and beat in the cocoa powder thoroughly.
Refrigerate until firm, but not rock hard, then proceed as
described in the basic puff pastry recipe above but
substituting this chocolate butter for the butter.

Palmiers

makes 20

🔪 PREP TIME 5 MINUTES ⛉ COOK TIME 10 MINUTES

100 g (3 ½ oz) Puff Pastry (page 324)

sugar

icing (confectioners') sugar

Preheat the oven to 180°C (350°F). Line a baking
sheet with a silicone baking mat or baking paper.

Roll out the puff pastry to a rectangle about 30 cm
x 20 cm x 5 mm (12 in x 8 in x ¼ in) thick. Sprinkle
liberally with sugar and roll each of the long sides into
the centre. Turn this long double log a quarter turn
away from you, so it is standing on one side, and
gently flatten it. Use a sharp knife to cut into slices
about 1 cm (½ in) thick.

Roll the slices very lightly and lay them out on the
prepared baking sheet, so the flat, swirly surface is
facing upwards. Dust with icing sugar and bake for
8–10 minutes until the pastry is crisp, and
caramelised a delectable golden brown.

Who can resist a cinnamon-spiked apple or orange-scented rhubarb crumble, served piping hot from the oven with a good slosh of cream? Crumbles are deservedly one of the most popular home-made desserts.

The dough is made from the same ingredients as sweet shortcrust pastry – flour, butter and sugar – which is rubbed together to form large crumbs. Unlike other pastries, crumbles don't need to rest and can be used straight away, scattered over the top of par-cooked fruits or fruit compotes and baked in the oven to form a crisp, golden topping. I also like to scatter crumble mix out onto a baking tray and cook it on its own to serve with ice cream or stewed fruit.

Crumble

makes 500 g (1 lb 2 oz)

🔪 PREP TIME 10 MINUTES   🍲 COOK TIME 15 MINUTES

| 250 g (9 oz) plain (all-purpose) flour |
| 1/2 teaspoon salt |
| 125 g (4 1/2 oz) chilled butter, diced small |
| 125 g (4 1/2 oz) soft brown sugar |

Preheat your oven to 200°C (400°F). Line a baking tray with baking paper.

Sift the flour and salt into a large mixing bowl. Add the diced butter and use your fingers to rub it into the consistency of coarse sand. Add the brown sugar and quickly rub it in with your fingers until it is roughly incorporated – don't overwork or the butter will melt.

Scatter the crumble mixture over your prepared baking tray and bake for 15 minutes, turning every now and then so it cooks evenly to crunchy golden crumble.

tarts

Caramel tart

makes 1 x 22 cm (9 in) tart, to serve 8

✎ PREP TIME 15 MINUTES 🍲 COOK TIME 40 MINUTES

2 eggs

4 egg yolks

100 g (3 ½ oz) Caramel Powder (opposite)

550 ml (19 fl oz) cream

200 g (7 oz) Sweet Pastry (page 322)

egg wash – 1 egg whisked with a few tablespoons milk

icing (confectioners') sugar (optional)

Serve this tart with ice cream and fresh fruit, and a drizzle of Dark Caramel Syrup (page 232).

Put the eggs, yolks and caramel powder in a bowl and use a hand blender to blitz until smooth. Add the cream and blitz again. Cover with plastic wrap and refrigerate for 1–2 hours.

Meanwhile, roll the pastry out on a lightly floured work surface to about 2 mm (⅛ in) thick. Butter a 22 cm x 2 cm (9 in x 1 in) tart tin with a little melted butter and place on a baking tray. Roll the pastry up over the rolling pin and carefully lift it onto the tart ring. Press the pastry into the bottom and up the sides of the tin. Trim the excess pastry, leaving an overhang of about 1–2 cm (½–¾ in). Patch any holes with the pastry trimmings. Prick the base all over with a fork and refrigerate for 1–2 hours.

When ready to cook the tart, preheat the oven to 180ºC (350°F). Line the tart with baking paper and baking beans and blind bake for 7 minutes. Remove the paper and beans and brush the inside of the tart with a little egg wash and bake for a further 3 minutes or until golden and crisp. Remove from the oven and sit on a wire rack for a few minutes to cool. Use a sharp knife to slice away the pastry overhang, leaving a nice even edge. (These trimmings make a delicious treat for the kids with jam and vanilla ice cream – and don't forget a few sneaky bites for yourself!)

Reduce the oven temperature to 125ºC (260°F). Pour the chilled caramel filling into the tart shell and bake for 30 minutes until just set and still quite wobbly. Rest on a wire rack for at least 30 minutes before serving.

Serve as it is, or dust the surface with an even layer of icing sugar and caramelise the surface with a small kitchen blowtorch until the sugar melts to a shiny caramel glaze. Allow to cool for 5 minutes before serving so that the caramel layer will harden to a crisp, crunchy layer.

Caramel powder

makes 100 g (3 ½ oz)

PREP TIME 5 MINUTES   COOK TIME 10 MINUTES

75 g (2 ½ oz) sugar
25 g (1 oz) butter

Put the sugar in a heavy-based saucepan and heat gently until the sugar has completely dissolved. Increase the heat and bring to the boil, then simmer to a medium caramel.

Remove the pan from the heat and whisk in the butter. Pour into a greased baking tray and leave to cool. When it has set hard, break into pieces and blitz in a food processor to a fine powder. Store in an airtight container in a cool, dry place for up to 3 weeks.

I like to use this mix for Caramel Tart and Tarte Tatin (page 334).

Almond and blueberry frangipane tart

The filling for this tart can be made and the tart baked ahead of time, making it a great dinner party dessert.

makes 1 x 22 cm (9 in) tart, to serve 8

PREP TIME 20 MINUTES COOK TIME 12 MINUTES

blind-baked Sweet Pastry tart shell (page 322)

115 g (4 oz) icing (confectioners') sugar

115 g (4 oz) ground almonds

25 g (1 oz) plain (all-purpose) flour

115 g (4 oz) butter, softened

2 eggs, lightly whisked

25 ml (1 fl oz) dark rum

2 cups blueberries

Serve cold or warm with Vanilla Crème Anglaise (page 237) and Blueberry Ripple Ice Cream (page 270).

Preheat your oven to 180°C (350°F). Prepare a tart shell using Sweet Pastry (page 322), and blind bake, following the same method as for the Caramel Tart (page 328).

Sieve the sugar, almonds and flour into the bowl of an electric mixer. Turn the beaters on low and add the softened butter. Mix until just incorporated, but do not overwork the butter. Gradually mix in the eggs, a little at a time, followed by the rum. Cover and refrigerate for 30 minutes.

Pour the filling into the blind-baked tart shell and smooth the surface. Scatter on the blueberries, and press them lightly into the filling. Bake for 12 minutes then remove from the oven and rest on a wire rack for at least 30 minutes before serving.

Caramelised citrus curd tart

makes 1 x 22 cm (9 in) tart, to serve 8

PREP TIME 20 MINUTES COOK TIME 35 MINUTES

blind-baked Sweet Pastry tart shell (page 322)

750 ml (25 fl oz) Lemon Tart Filling (page 240)

icing (confectioners') sugar

Preheat your oven to 180°C (350°F). Prepare a tart shell using Sweet Pastry (page 322), and blind bake, following the same method as for the Caramel Tart (page 328).

Pour the lemon filling into the blind-baked tart shell and smooth the surface. Bake for 35 minutes. Remove from the oven and rest on a wire rack for at least 30 minutes before serving.

When ready to serve, dust the surface with an even layer of icing sugar. Caramelise the surface with a small kitchen blowtorch until the sugar melts to a shiny caramel glaze. Allow to cool for 5 minutes before serving so that the caramel will harden to a crisp, crunchy layer.

Serve this tart with Vanilla, Marmalade and Mascarpone Sorbet (page 267) and Confit Citrus Rind (page 133).

Flourless chocolate tart

makes 1 x 22 cm (9 in) tart, to serve 8

PREP TIME 20 MINUTES COOK TIME 15 MINUTES

blind-baked Sweet Pastry tart shell (page 322)

250 g (9 oz) best-quality dark chocolate

200 g (7 oz) butter

4 eggs

3 egg yolks

60 g (2 oz) sugar

Preheat your oven to 180°C (350°F). Prepare a tart shell using Sweet Pastry (page 322), and blind bake, following the same method as for the Caramel Tart (page 328).

Break the chocolate into small pieces and place in a heatproof bowl with the butter. Microwave on medium in 30–second bursts, or stand the bowl over a pan of simmering water until the chocolate has melted. Stir until smooth.

Make a thick Sweet Sabayon (page 241) with the eggs, yolks and sugar.

Fold one-third of the sabayon into the melted chocolate and mix well. Gently fold the chocolate mix into the remaining sabayon.

Pour into the blind-baked tart shell and smooth the surface. Bake for 12 minutes, just until the sabayon is set – remember it is already cooked. Remove from the oven and rest on a wire rack for at least 30 minutes before serving.

Serve the chocolate tart with Banana Ice Cream (page 271), Chocolate Sauce (page 316) and Chocolate (page 311).

Tarte fine of figs

This simplest of puff pastry tarts can be made with just about any fresh fruit, from finely sliced bananas to peaches, nectarines or apples.

serves 4

PREP TIME 10 MINUTES COOK TIME 20 MINUTES

200 g (7 oz) Puff Pastry (page 324)

8 fresh figs

icing (confectioners') sugar

Roll out the pastry to a large rectangle about 3 mm (⅛ in) thick. Cut out 4 x 12 cm (5 in) circles, and lift them onto a baking sheet lined with a silicone baking mat or baking paper. Rest in the refrigerator for 1 hour.

Preheat your oven to 180°C (350°F). Finely slice the figs and arrange them in overlapping circles on top of the pastry. Dust with plenty of icing sugar. Bake for 15–20 minutes until the pastry is puffed up and golden brown.

Serve with Thyme Ice Cream (page 270) and Lemon Syrup (page 232).

Mini tartes Tatin

This is the easiest dessert in the world to throw together – especially if you have a jar of caramel powder on hand in the pantry, as I always do! There's no messing around with sputtering sugar and butter – simply scatter the powder into the base of an ovenproof pan, throw in some sliced fruit, tuck a sheet of puff pastry over the top and bang it into the oven. For a dinner party, I like to make mini tartes Tatin in little roesti pans.

serves 4

PREP TIME 10 MINUTES COOK TIME 20 MINUTES

200 g (7 oz) Puff Pastry (page 324)

100 g (3½ oz) Caramel Powder (page 329)

4 large pears or apples

Roll out the pastry to a large rectangle, about 3 mm (⅛ in) thick. Lift onto a tray and rest in the refrigerator for 1 hour.

Preheat your oven to 190°C (375°F). Lightly butter 4 roesti pans or individual round baking tins and divide the caramel powder between them, so that the bottom is completely covered.

Peel the pears and cut them into thick wedges, slicing away the cores.

Arrange the pear wedges in the prepared pans, leaving a 5 mm (¼ in) gap around the edge. Remove the pastry from the refrigerator and cut out 4 circles, a little bigger than the roesti pans. Drape the pastry over the pears, tucking the edges down the sides of the pan. Bake for 15–20 minutes until the pastry is crisp and golden.

To serve, place a dessert plate on top of each pan and quickly invert it. The pears should be a gorgeous golden brown, and sticky with a caramel glaze.

334

Serve with a generous scoop of Vanilla Ice Cream (page 270).

Breads and yeast doughs

The famous French breadsticks –
baguettes – are a constant presence at
just about every French dining table.

My memories of France are filled with baguettes spread with cold unsalted French butter and a dollop of apricot jam, smeared with a wedge of creamy triple cream cheese or a slathering of pork rillettes, or dunked into a rich, flavoursome sauce at dinner.

In my view, the art of baking reaches a peak in France, where the boulanger hones his craft from a tender age. Even the humblest neighbourhood bakery boasts an irresistible range of croissants, escargots, pains au chocolat and other fancy breads as well as the ubiquitous baguette (and its variants, the ficelle, flute and épi). For the most part, baking is not really something that people ever contemplate doing at home. And after all why would you, when such quality baked goods are so readily available?

It's probably more the fancy breads, such as brioche or savarin, or the famous Kugelhopf from Alsace, that are made at home for special occasions. Or simpler Italian-inspired breads, such as the pissaladière or fougasse, both of which are popular in the south of France.

Irrespective, the lessons involved in baking are pretty much the same. All of these risen breads rely on yeast – a living-wonder ingredient that causes a simple flour-and-water dough to puff and expand in the oven. And because yeast is a living

ingredient, it needs to be treated with respect. In fact, this is probably the most important tip I can give you about baking: it requires care. First, choose good-quality ingredients: good strong bread flour, fine-flavoured sea salt and carefully stored fresh yeast; second, don't rush the process. If you understand what is actually happening as you mix, knead, prove, shape and bake, you will almost certainly achieve good results, and the enormous satisfaction of knowing that you did it yourself.

Yeast

Yeast is a microscopic fungus that multiplies rapidly in suitable conditions and produces tiny bubbles of carbon dioxide. These bubbles are what causes bread to rise and expand in the oven.

Yeast is readily available as dried granules or fresh. In general I prefer to use fresh yeast as I think it is more reactive and has a more delicate aroma and flavour than the dried version. You can buy fresh yeast from health food shops, delis and good food stores, but I always buy mine from my local baker. I know it's fresh and good quality. Both fresh and dried yeast should be stored in an airtight container in the refrigerator.

Flour

When making yeast doughs, it is important to use the appropriate flour. Bread flour should have a high gluten content, which gives elasticity to the dough and helps give the baked bread a fine, even texture.

For straightforward breads choose a good-quality strong or 'bread' flour that's made from hard wheat. Don't assume that all flours taste the same; if you can source an artisanal flour from a local mill you'll certainly notice the difference in flavour.

Enriched doughs, such as brioche, are not so dependent on a high gluten content and plain flour will do perfectly well.

Mixing

Before you start, make sure all the ingredients are at room temperature. In a small bowl, whisk together the fresh yeast and water until completely dissolved. In another large bowl, mix together the flour and salt. Pour in the yeast liquid and use your hands to stir and mix it all together as quickly as you can, to make a sticky dough. Make sure all the flour is mixed in, then cover the bowl with a cloth and leave it for 10 minutes before you start to knead.

Kneading

This is the crucial step that works the yeast evenly into the dough and develops the gluten – both of which are critical for a fine, even texture and an even rise. I usually work on a lightly oiled work surface, and make sure that my hands are also lightly coated in oil. Shape the dough into a round then begin to work it. Use the heel of your hand to press the dough firmly down and away from you to stretch it. Lift and rotate it a quarter turn and repeat. Continue with the turning and kneading until the dough begins to change in consistency. You'll feel it becoming softer and lighter and it will feel silky and elastic.

While I enjoy the process of kneading by hand (and it's a great stress reliever), you can use the dough hook on an electric mixer if you prefer. Whichever method you use, you definitely need to familiarise yourself with the feel of the bread at some stage.

Rising

Most doughs are left to rise twice; this is a key stage in the fermentation process. After the dough has been kneaded, place it in a lightly oiled bowl, cover it and leave it in a warm spot for an hour. It is important not to rush this process. The dough should not be allowed to get too hot – 25–30°C (77–86°F) is about right – or the yeast will go crazy and the dough will spill out over the top of your bowl! A long, slow rise to about one and a half times its original volume is ideal for the development of good flavour and texture.

After the initial rise the dough is lightly kneaded again – this is when it's 'knocked back' – to slightly deflate the air bubbles. Now the dough can be divided, shaped to your liking and transferred to a lightly oiled tin. Before baking it is left for the second rise. At this stage the surface of the dough should be covered lightly with a cloth or sheet of plastic wrap. This prevents a skin forming and helps maintain moisture in the dough. During the second rise the dough should, again, increase in bulk by at least one and a half times.

Baking

Not many of us have a traditional wood-fired baker's oven to give that authentic, earthy flavour. But you can still bake delicious bread in a domestic oven. It's essential to preheat the oven to a high heat – 220°C (430°F) – which immediately kills the yeast and stops the dough rising further. Before you put the bread in the oven, use a sharp knife to slash the surface, which will help it rise evenly. Most commercial ovens inject steam into the oven to create a moist environment. A few sprays with a mister over the surface of the bread go some way to replicating this humidity and will help form the desired crisp, hard crust.

Is it done?

Perfectly cooked bread is a deep golden brown with an appetising – irresistible – aroma. But beware of undercooking – gluggy, soggy bread will only give you stomach ache. The tried and true way to test if a loaf of bread is cooked is to tip it out of its tin into a tea towel held in your hand. It should feel light and sound hollow when you knock the base of the loaf with your knuckles.

Basic yeast dough

This is a great quick and easy dough, perfect for making the classic Provençal snack, pissaladière – the French equivalent of pizza. Vary the toppings depending on what you've got lurking in the refrigerator – sun-dried tomatoes and olives, rosemary and red (Spanish) onions, artichokes and anchovies – all these Provençal-style toppings are great.

makes 500 g (1 lb 2 oz)

/ PREP TIME 20 MINUTES ☐ COOK TIME 15 MINUTES

1 teaspoon fresh yeast
185 ml (6 ¼ fl oz) water
310 g (11 oz) strong bread flour
1 teaspoon salt

Before you start, make sure all the ingredients are at room temperature. In a small bowl, whisk together the fresh yeast and water until completely dissolved.

Put all the ingredients into your electric mixer. With the dough hook attached, knead on the lowest speed for 4 minutes. Make sure the flour is mixing in completely and increase the speed to medium. Continue kneading for a further 4 minutes, or until the dough is soft and silky. Cover the bowl with a cloth and leave in a warm place for 30 minutes to prove.

When ready to bake, preheat the oven to 180ºC (350°F). Scoop the dough out on a lightly floured work surface and roll out to a circle or rectangle about 1 cm (½ in) thick; carefully transfer to a baking tray. Refrigerate for 10 minutes to rest, then top with the ingredients of your choice (see next recipe for one suggestion) and bake.

PISSALADIÈRE

100 g (3 ½ oz) Lyonnaise Onions (page 221)
50 g (2 oz) anchovies
½ cup black olives
olive oil

Spread the onions onto the prepared dough (above) in a thick layer. Arrange the anchovy strips across the surface to form a diamond pattern and stud each diamond with an olive. Drizzle with olive oil and bake for 20 minutes at 180ºC (350°F) until the base is crisp and golden brown.

Crunchy ficelles

This is another simple bread dough that we use to make long, crunchy breadsticks to serve as an accompaniment with soups, salads and cheese plates – so much more interesting than boring old croutons. The dough is left to prove in the refrigerator for 24 hours. This subdues the activity of the yeast and prevents the dough from rising too quickly and too much. To make traditional ficelles, rather than this crunchy version, simply allow the dough to prove for a second time (15 minutes or so) after rolling into long, thin breadsticks.

makes 500 g (1 lb 2 oz)

PREP TIME 20 MINUTES   COOK TIME 12 MINUTES

110 ml (3¾ fl oz) water
10 g (⅓ oz) salt
½ teaspoon fresh yeast
½ teaspoon sugar
300 g (10½ oz) strong bread flour
50 ml (2 fl oz) clarified butter
90 g (3¼ oz) softened butter
sea salt

TRUFFLE FICELLES

Mix 2 tablespoons chopped fresh truffle and a few drops of truffle oil into the basic dough while kneading.

MUSHROOM FICELLES

Mix 2 tablespoons cep (porcini) powder into the basic dough while kneading.

OLIVE FICELLES

Mix 3 tablespoons finely chopped green or black olives into the basic dough while kneading.

Before you start, make sure all the ingredients are at room temperature. In a small bowl, whisk together the fresh yeast and water until completely dissolved.

Put all the ingredients except clarified butter and sea salt into your electric mixer. With the dough hook attached, knead on the lowest speed for 5 minutes. Make sure the flour is mixed in completely. Cover the bowl with a cloth and refrigerate for 24 hours.

When ready to cook, preheat the oven to 180ºC (350°F). Scoop the dough out on a lightly floured work surface and roll out to a rectangle, around 1 cm (½ in) thick. Use a sharp knife to cut long thin strips, about 2 cm (¾ in) wide. Roll each strip on the work surface to make long, thin breadsticks.

Transfer to a baking tray. Brush each breadstick with a little clarified butter and sprinkle with sea salt. Bake for 12 minutes until golden brown. Remove from the oven and lift the ficelles onto wire racks to cool. They can be kept in an airtight container for up to a week.

Rum baba

These should be made a day ahead of time, giving them a chance to dry out a little. This will make them absorb the hot syrup better.

Serves 4

⟋ PREP TIME 1 HOUR ☐ COOK TIME 20 MINUTES

65 ml (2 ¼ fl oz) milk	210 g (7 ½ oz) flour
35 ml (1 ¼ fl oz) cream	2 eggs, lightly whisked
½ teaspoon salt	65 g (2 ¼ oz) butter
15 g (½ oz) sugar	500 ml (17 fl oz) Stock Syrup (page 232)
15 g (½ oz) fresh yeast	100 ml (3 ½ fl oz) dark rum

Grease 4 x 120 ml (4 fl oz) dariole (cylindrical) moulds. Combine the milk and cream in a small saucepan and warm gently to about 30°C (85°F). Add the salt, sugar and yeast and whisk gently to dissolve.

Sift the flour into the bowl of your electric mixer. Stir in the warm milk and half of the eggs. Mix in the sifted flour and then half of the remaining egg mixture. With the dough hook attachment, knead on slow speed for a couple of minutes.

Add the rest of the egg and knead for another minute until absorbed. Heat the butter until just barely melted and pour into the dough, but don't mix it in. Cover the bowl and leave in a warm place for 15–20 minutes until the butter has pooled underneath the dough at the bottom of the bowl.

Use a spatula to mix the dough by hand until smooth. Spoon into the prepared moulds so that they are two-thirds full. Cover loosely and leave in a warm place to prove for about 15–20 minutes, until the dough has risen above the top of the moulds.

Meanwhile, preheat your oven to 200°C (400°F). Bake the babas for 3 minutes, then lower the temperature to 170ºC (340°F) and bake for further 10 minutes, until babas are firm and golden brown. Leave in the tin for a few minutes then tip out onto a wire rack to cool.

Cover loosely with a tea (dish) towel and leave them overnight.

Just before serving, warm the stock syrup and stir in the rum. Drop the babas in the syrup and leave for about 5 minutes to absorb the syrup. Turn them every minute or two. Lift them out of the syrup and serve in a dessert bowl with lashings of Vanilla Chantilly (page 234). The rest of the syrup can be strained and reused another day. It will keep in the refrigerator for up to a month.

Brioche

To my way of thinking, brioche is the perfect combination of sweet and savoury. You can eat it toasted – to serve with pâtés and terrines – or use it in puddings. All the butter means that it takes a long time to rise – but it's well worth the wait.

Makes 1 loaf

PREP TIME 1 HOUR   COOK TIME 45 MINUTES

1 ½ teaspoons fresh yeast

50 ml (2 fl oz) warm milk

350 g (12 oz) plain (all-purpose) flour, sifted

40 g (1 ½ oz) sugar

1 teaspoon salt

3 eggs

250 g (9 oz) butter, very soft

1 egg, whisked (for egg glaze)

Before you start, make sure all the ingredients are at room temperature. In a small bowl, whisk together the fresh yeast and milk until completely dissolved.

Put the flour, sugar and salt into your electric mixer. With the dough hook attached, mix briefly to combine. Add the warm milk and the eggs and knead at a medium speed. With the motor running, slowly dollop in the butter and knead for 5 minutes, making sure the flour is mixed in completely. The dough should be shiny and come away cleanly from the bowl. Cover the bowl with a cloth and leave in a warm place to prove. It should double in bulk.

Knock back the dough with your fists, then return to the bowl, cover and leave to prove again for 40–45 minutes, this time in the refrigerator. This slow prove allows the butter to set firm and stabilise, and the dough will be less likely to split.

Grease a 24 cm x 11 cm (9½ in x 4½ in) loaf tin. Remove the dough from the refrigerator and knock it back for a second time. Divide the dough into thirds and roll each piece to a round ball. Place the dough balls in the prepared tin and leave in a warm place until they rise up to the top of the tin, about 20 minutes.

While the dough is proving for the third time, preheat the oven to 180°C (350°F). When ready to bake, brush the surface with the egg glaze and bake for 40–45 minutes until risen and golden brown. Carefully turn the loaf out of the tin and leave to cool on a wire rack. Wait until completely cold before slicing (although if you're like me, you'll just rip off big chunks and eat it warm from the oven). Wrap the brioche in plastic wrap and keep in the refrigerator for 3 days, or up to a month in the freezer.

Brioche pudding with candied fruits

✎ PREP TIME 10 MINUTES ☗ COOK TIME 20 MINUTES

Make in the same way as the Brioche (page 343).
Before you knock the dough back for the first time,
stir in 2 cups of mixed dried fruit and candied peel.
Then proceed as described above.

When ready to bake, preheat oven to 180ºC (350°F).
Divide the dough into 8 portions, roll each into a
small ball and place in lightly buttered dariole
(cylindrical) moulds to bake. Bake in an oven for
about 20 minutes. Serve the puddings warm,
drizzled with Light Caramel Syrup (page 232), and
with a generous scoop of Armagnac and Caramel
Ice Cream (page 271).

Rum baba (page 342)

cakes, biscuits and petits fours

I find that even the most reluctant cook will get excited at the thought of a bit of home baking.

A light sponge cake, sandwiched with jam and cream or dripping with chocolate icing, is one of the easiest ways to celebrate a birthday or special occasion, while a melt-in-the-mouth shortbread biscuit or a delicate madeleine cake is the perfect accompaniment to an afternoon cuppa – or a tisane, if you're feeling particularly Proustian!

In France, these sweet bakery items are known generically as gâteaux, a term that encompasses all manner of patisserie items, from pastry-based concoctions such as mille-feuilles, to whisked Genoese sponges, fragile meringues, dainty wafers or exquisite little petits fours.

While the trend in modern-day cooking is for lighter, less-rich eating, sweet bakery goods are one area of the kitchen where the use of eggs, butter, flour, sugar and cream is simply not to be compromised. However, it is probably true to say that pièces montées – the multi-layered, buttercream-rich, elaborate constructions that reached the height of popularity in the eighteenth and nineteenth centuries – have been replaced in our affections by simpler cakes and biscuits (cookies).

I've covered some patisserie items in the lesson on pastry and tarts, where we looked at different kinds of pastry, so in this lesson I'll focus on the techniques involved in making various sorts of sponge cakes and biscuits (what the French call gâteaux secs). Some items straddle both categories, and are simply miniature versions of the original recipe. These dainty petits fours are often served with coffee after a meal, as part of a buffet table or with morning or afternoon tea.

All sponge cakes are made with the same four basic ingredients: butter, sugar, flour and eggs. The basic batter is prepared in such a way as to incorporate air in varying degrees, making the finished product soft and light, or dense and rich. Sometimes a rising agent, such as yeast or baking powder, is used; other cakes, like the famous Genoese sponge, are leavened with whisked egg whites. A variety of other ingredients, such as nuts, fruit, chocolate or spices, are added, making the range of flavours and textures immense.

While biscuits are usually made from the same basic ingredients, the end result is quite different: they are typically flat, crisp and crunchy, without being dry in the mouth.

cakes

Genoese sponge

A light and airy whisked fatless sponge cake, a Genoese is soft and moist, but fairly plain in flavour, so it provides the perfect base for all kinds of creamy fillings and fancy layered cakes. I usually make it in thin largish rectangles and cut them to size, according to each recipe. But you can just as easily make a more traditional round sponge, split it and spread with the filling of your choice.

makes 2 x thin sponges

PREP TIME 10–15 MINUTES   COOK TIME 5 MINUTES

6 eggs, lightly whisked
160 g (5⅔ oz)
100 g (3½ oz) plain flour, sifted
50 g (2 oz) cornflour, sifted

Preheat your oven to 200°C (400°F). Line 2 shallow non-stick baking trays with baking paper. Alternatively, if you want a deeper, more traditional sponge, grease and line a 24 cm x 6 cm (9½ in x 2½ in) cake tin.

Put the eggs and sugar in a stainless-steel bowl and set it over a bain-marie or a pan of simmering water; the base of the bowl should not come into contact with the water. Heat very slowly to about 50°C (120°F).

Tip the mixture into the bowl of an electric mixer and beat on a high speed for 2 minutes until pale and creamy. It should be thick enough to form a thick ribbon that leaves a trail across the surface. Reduce the speed and continue whisking until the batter cools to room temperature. Use a large spatula to gently fold in the sifted flours.

Pour the batter into your prepared tins, to a thickness of about 1 cm (½ in). Bake in the pre-heated oven for 5–6 minutes. If making the thicker cake, bake for 8–10 minutes. When the cake is golden brown and firm to the touch, remove from the oven and cool for a moment before turning it out onto a wire rack. Carefully peel away the greaseproof paper – brushing with a little water helps to loosen it from the surface. Allow to cool completely before cutting into the desired shapes. Alternatively, wrap in plastic wrap and refrigerate for up to 3 days, or freeze for up to a month.

Chocolate brownie

Some of my fondest childhood memories involve brownies! My mum was a great home-baker and I was always hanging around the kitchen to lick the bowl. One of my other great tricks was to steal the odd piece, hot from the oven. If I'm honest, it's something I still do to this day.

makes 10–12 brownies

PREP TIME 20 MINUTES   COOK TIME 25 MINUTES

180 g (6½ oz) dark chocolate

125 g (4½ oz) butter

50 g (2 oz) plain (all-purpose) flour

60 g (2 oz) unsweetened cocoa powder

3 eggs

100 g (3½ oz) sugar

75 g (2½ oz) hazelnuts, roasted, peeled and roughly chopped

icing sugar (optional)

Preheat your oven to 150°C (300°F). Line a brownie tin or a 22 x 14 x 4 cm (9 x 5½ x 1½ in) baking tin with greaseproof paper.

Break up the chocolate and place in a heatproof bowl with the butter. Microwave on medium in 30–second bursts, or stand bowl over a pan of simmering water until the chocolate has melted. Stir until smooth. Sift together the flour and cocoa powder.

Whisk together the eggs and sugar to the ribbon stage (page 295), then mix into the chocolate. Gently fold in the sifted flour, then stir in the hazelnuts.

Pour the batter into the prepared tin and bake for 25 minutes until firm. The brownie will still be soft and a bit gooey in the middle, but don't worry; as it cools it will firm up to a wonderful squidgy consistency. Remove from the oven and leave to cool in the tin before cutting into squares. To serve, cut the brownie into squares using a knife dipped in hot water. Dust with a little icing sugar if you feel like it.

Biscuits

Brittany shortbread

Although I like to serve these baby shortcakes as petits fours, you could make them larger and serve them for dessert.

makes 24

⁄ PREP TIME 20 MINUTES ☞ COOK TIME 8 MINUTES

2 egg yolks
130 g (4½ oz) sugar
180 g (6½ oz) plain (all-purpose) flour
1 teaspoon baking powder
pinch salt
130 g (4½ oz) butter, softened

Serve with crème fraîche and a dollop of Strawberry Jam (page 133).

Whisk together the egg yolks and sugar until pale and creamy. Sift together the flour, baking powder and salt.

Beat the softened butter into the beaten eggs then stir in the sifted ingredients. Shape the dough into a ball, wrap in plastic wrap and refrigerate for 30 minutes to rest.

When ready to cook, preheat your oven to 160°C (320°F) and line a baking tray with a silicone baking mat or baking paper. Roll the dough out on a lightly floured work surface to a thickness of 1 cm (½ in). Use a 4 cm (1½ in) cookie cutter to cut out little round cakes (or fingers if you prefer) and bake for 8 minutes until golden brown.

Sablé biscuits

Pâte sablé is a very fragile and crumbly pastry. It gets its name – sablé, meaning 'sandy' – because of the high amount of sugar used. These little biscuits (cookies) are one of my all-time favourite treats, served warm from the oven with a sprinkling of vanilla sugar and a strong cup of tea.

makes 24

⁄ PREP TIME 15 MINUTES ☞ COOK TIME 15 MINUTES

225 g (8 oz) plain (all-purpose) flour
25 g (1 oz) cornflour (cornstarch)
100 g (3½ oz) icing (confectioners') sugar
pinch salt
200 g (7 oz) cold butter, diced
1 small egg yolk
1 teaspoon double (heavy) cream
Vanilla Sugar (page 24)

Combine the flour, cornflour, icing sugar and salt in a food processor and pulse a few times to mix. Add the diced butter and pulse until barely combined, followed by the egg yolk and cream. Tip the dough out onto a lightly floured work surface and use your hands to shape it into a smooth ball.

Divide the pastry into two, wrap in plastic wrap and refrigerate for 45 minutes before using. This pastry can also be frozen for up to 2 months. When ready to bake, preheat the oven to 180°C (350°F). Line a baking sheet with a silicone baking mat or baking paper.

Roll each piece of dough into a log, and use a sharp knife to cut into slices, about 1 cm (½ in) thick. Arrange the slices on the prepared baking sheet and bake until golden brown, around 15 minutes. Halfway through the baking, dust with vanilla sugar. Transfer to a wire rack to cool.

Tuiles

makes around 20

PREP TIME 10 MINUTES COOK TIME 10 MINUTES

100 g (3½ oz) plain (all-purpose) flour

100 g (3½ oz) icing (confectioners') sugar

3 egg whites

100 g (3½ oz) butter, melted

Sift the flour and sugar together into a large mixing bowl. Lightly whisk the egg whites then stir into the flour and sugar. Stir in the melted butter until smooth. Cover and refrigerate for 2 hours.

When ready to bake, preheat your oven to 170°C (340°F). Line a baking sheet with a silicone baking mat or baking paper. Using a teaspoon, place small balls of the mixture on the prepared sheet and smear the mixture out as thin as you can. For a perfect look, you can create a simple template using the lid of a plastic ice cream container. Use a Stanley (utility) knife to cut a circle – or any shape you like.

Bake for 6–10 minutes, until golden brown. Leave for a few seconds before lifting the tuiles off with a spatula. They will crisp up as they cool.

To shape the tuiles, while warm from the oven, drape them over a rolling pin to form curls or over the bottom of a glass to form baskets.

Spiced tuiles

makes around 20

PREP TIME 10 MINUTES COOK TIME 10 MINUTES

125 g (4½ oz) butter, softened

250 g (9 oz) sugar

1 tablespoon grated fresh ginger

125 g (4½ oz) golden syrup (light treacle)

125 g (4½ oz) plain (all-purpose) flour

1 teaspoon five-spice powder

1 teaspoon cinnamon powder

Put the butter and sugar in a food processor and blend for 3–4 minutes until well combined. Add the ginger and golden syrup and pulse to combine. Add the flour and spices and pulse again until everything is mixed together thoroughly.

Scrape the dough into a bowl, cover with plastic wrap and refrigerate for 2 hours to rest. You can make in advance to this stage and store the dough in the refrigerator for up to 2 weeks.

When ready to bake, preheat your oven to 160°C (320°F). Line a baking tray with a silicone baking mat or baking paper. Using a teaspoon, place small balls of the mixture on the prepared sheet, allowing about 5 cm (2 in) between them. They will melt and spread out in the heat of the oven – like a brandy snap.

Bake for 6–10 minutes, until the biscuits start to darken around the edges. Leave for a few seconds before lifting them off with a spatula. They will become crisp as they cool.

Petits fours

We make macaroons by the bucketful to serve as petits fours with coffee. Known as macaron in French, they are delicate biscuits made from ground almonds, sugar and egg whites, sandwiched together with flavoured cream. The macaroons themselves can be flavoured and tinted with specially purchased baker's pastes and they are as pretty as a picture. But it's easy enough to make vanilla, lemon or chocolate macaroons without all that fuss.

Macaroons

makes 50 mini or 25 medium-sized macaroons

⁄ PREP TIME 20 MINUTES ⌐ COOK TIME 15 MINUTES

125 g (4½ oz) ground almonds

225 g (8 oz) icing (confectioners') sugar

3 egg whites

60 g (2 oz) sugar

zest of 1 lemon (optional)

Line 2 baking sheets with a silicone baking mat or baking paper. Sift the ground almonds and sugar together into a large mixing bowl. In another bowl, whisk the egg whites and sugar to stiff peaks and stir in the lemon zest if using.

Use a large spatula to gently fold the sifted ingredients into the egg whites. Spoon the mixture into a piping bag fitted with a medium-sized nozzle. Pipe neat little mounds on the baking sheets – about 1.5 cm (¾ in) for mini macaroons or 2.5 cm (1 in) for medium-sized macaroons. Leave to stand for 15–20 minutes, until a skin forms on the surface.

Preheat your oven to 140°C (275°F). Bake the macaroons for 12–15 minutes until they have a firm outer shell. The perfect macaroon is crisp on the outside and slightly chewy in the centre. Leave to cool on the baking tray for a few minutes then carefully transfer them to a wire rack to cool completely. At this stage the macaroons can be stored in an airtight container for up to 2 days.

When ready to serve, sandwich pairs of macaroons together with Crème Pâtissière (page 241). For lemon macaroons you might like to flavour the filling with a little grated lemon zest – or any citrus zest for that matter.

CHOCOLATE MACAROONS

Sift 20 g (¾ oz) of unsweetened cocoa powder in with the ground almonds and icing sugar (and don't include the lemon zest). Sandwich them with Chocolate Ganache (page 316).

Financiers

Sometimes called friands, these little cakes are made with ground almonds and beurre noisette, which gives them a lovely toasted nut flavour. They are traditionally baked in little oval or rectangular shapes.

makes 50 small financiers

PREP TIME 20 MINUTES COOK TIME 5 MINUTES

125 g (4½ oz) Beurre Noisette (page 93)

75 g (2½ oz) ground almonds

60 g (2 oz) plain (all-purpose) flour

150 g (5½ oz) sugar

4 egg whites, at room temperature

Gently heat the beurre noisette to around 50°C (120°F).

Mix together the dried ingredients then stir in the egg whites. Gradually stir in the melted butter until smooth. Cover and refrigerate for 2 hours.

When ready to bake the financiers, preheat your oven to 210°C (410°F). Grease 2 financier tins or mini muffin pans and dust lightly with flour.

Spoon the batter into the moulds, so that they are three-quarters full. Bake for 5 minutes until firm and golden brown. Remove from the oven and leave to cool in the tins for a few minutes. Turn out onto a wire rack and eat while still warm. Financiers are best eaten on the day they are made, but will keep in an airtight container for up to 3 days.

Madeleines

These little cakes are easily recognised by their unique shell-like form. Yes, you do need a special tin to bake them in, but they are so pretty and delicate that it's worth it.

makes 50 small cakes

PREP TIME 20 MINUTES COOK TIME 5 MINUTES

75 g (2½ oz) butter

40 g (1½ oz) ground almonds

80 g (3 oz) plain (all-purpose) flour

80 g (3 oz) sugar

3 egg whites, lightly whisked

Gently heat the butter until it is melted, then set aside to cool a little.

Mix together the dried ingredients then stir in the egg whites. Gradually stir in the melted butter until batter is smooth. Cover and refrigerate for 2 hours.

When ready to bake the madeleines, preheat your oven to 210°C (410°F). Grease 2 madeleine tins and dust lightly with flour.

Spoon the batter into the moulds and bake for 5 minutes until firm and golden brown. Remove from the oven and leave to cool in the tins for a few minutes. Turn out onto a wire rack and eat while still warm. Madeleines are best served freshly baked with a cup of tea, but will keep in an airtight container for up to 3 days.

the cheese course

The cheese course is a very important
part of the French dining structure.

The cheese course can be served as a selection of various cheeses and appropriate garnishes, or as an individual slice of one cheese and a garnish. Traditionally, it is served before dessert but this decision is of course entirely up to you. Cheese can take the place of dessert, or be served after it. It can also appear at the beginning of a meal as part of an hors d'oeuvre selection.

When considering your cheese selection, aim to include a good balance of styles. We have access to some fantastic artisan cheeses, both locally crafted and from around the globe. Your choice can include cow's milk, goat's milk, ewe's milk and mixed milk cheeses. You also have the choice of soft cheeses, including rich triple and double creams; cooked cheeses such as beaufort and gruyère; washed rinds such as livarot, munster and époisses; stilton, gorgonzola, roquefort and other blue cheeses; and semi-hard cheeses such as cantel, reblochon and cheddar.

When purchasing cheese, be guided by quality farmhouse cheeses, crafted according to traditional methods. Avoid mass-produced, factory-made cheeses – they're great for cheese on toast but should never be included in a quality cheese course. Also consider seasonal variations affecting quality and availability, and purchase your cheese from a reputable store that specialises in sourcing quality local and international cheeses. These specialists will have the passion and knowledge to help you make your selection, offering you blue cheese that's moist, triple creams oozing with lusciousness, and washed rinds redolent with that distinct ripe aroma. Most specialist stores will wrap your cheeses in waxed paper, which will allow them to breathe.

When you bring your cheeses home, leave them wrapped in the waxed paper and store them in your refrigerator's dairy compartment. This will prevent the strong odours of your ripe cheeses mingling with the contents of your fridge. Keep any strong cheeses in an airtight container, so the flavour of more delicate cheeses is not affected.

Blue cheese

ROQUEFORT

Alternatives: valdeón (Spanish), stilton (English) or gorgonzola (Italian)

One of the most famous of all French cheeses, roquefort is a pungent ewe's milk blue cheese from the south of France. The crumbly, slightly moist white cheese has distinctive veins of blue mould running through it, which provide a sharp tang. Roquefort has a characteristic odour and flavour, with a notable taste of butyric acid. The overall flavour sensation begins slightly mild, before waxing sweet, then smoky, and fading to a salty finish. The cheese has no rind; the exterior is edible and slightly salty. Roquefort is high in fat, protein and minerals, with each kilogram (2 lb 3 oz) of finished cheese requiring around 4.5 litres (152 fl oz) of milk. A typical wheel of roquefort weighs between 2.5 and 3 kg (5½ and 6½ lb), and is about 10 cm (4 in) thick.

In 1925 roquefort was the first cheese to obtain an Appellation d'Origine Contrôlée (AOC) label, guaranteeing that the traditional production methods and geographical origins of the cheese are controlled. The ewe's milk used to produce the cheese is also under strict AOC control. The benchmarks for production have been set by producers such as the Carles family, who have been making the cheese for generations, according to rigorous methods and entirely by hand. The cheese is ripened in cellars beneath the village of Roquefort sur Soulzon, and has a minimum affinage (maturation period) of four months.

Washed-rind cheese

ÉPOISSES

Alternatives: munster (French), taleggio (Italian) or livarot (French)

A perennial favourite of fans of strong-smelling cheese – reputedly including Napoleon – époisses is a pungently flavoured washed-rind cheese from Burgundy. The remarkable cheese was first made by monks in the Abbaye de Citeaux, in the heart of the region. Its spoonable, silky paste has salty and creamy notes, achieved through rather complicated traditional production methods.

Époisses is one of the last remaining French cheeses to involve milk coagulation in its production. The cheese is first washed in salty water, then stored in a humid cellar. After a month, it is washed several times with a mix of rainwater and marc de Bourgogne brandy.

Semi-hard/hard cheese

COMTÉ GRUYÈRE

Alternatives: beaufort (French), Quickes cheddar (English) or cantal (French)

This cow's milk cheese is one of the richest and most popular cheeses in France. It is traditionally produced in the mountains of the Jura, where local farmers bring their milk down to the local cooperatives (fruitières) which are managed by a group of villages. Production is strictly controlled by the AOC, being restricted to the Franche-Comte, eastern Bourgogne, and parts of Lorraine, Champagne and the Rhône-Alps.

The cheese has a firm pate with a sweet, nutty tang, and is regularly rubbed and wiped with brine during its production. Comté is rich in milk, requiring as many as 530 litres (140 gallons) of milk to produce just one cheese.

Soft cow's milk cheese

DELICE DE BOURGOGNE

Alternatives: bouche d'affinois (French), brie de Nangis (French) or rouzaire coulommiers (French)

This triple cream cow's milk cheese from Bourgogne is covered in a fine, fluffy white mould. When ripe, the outside of the cheese will be soft, leaving the middle firm. The pate is soft, sweet and buttery, though you may also notice a slight sourness.

Cream is added to the milk stock during curd production, resulting in a minimum fat content of 75%. Double cream cheeses have a fat content of 60 to 70%.

Ewe's milk cheese

OSSAU-IRATY

Alternatives: fleur du maquis (French), manchego (Spanish) or romero (Spanish)

This traditional hard-crusted cheese is made from new season's milk collected by the bergers of the Ossau Valley and Iraty region in the Basque country. Ossau-Iraty is made according to methods that date back 4000 years, and it's claimed to be the world's oldest surviving traditional means of cheese-making. The cheese was granted an AOC label in 1980.

The lightly pressed cheese has a washed and hand-salted rind, and is matured in a humid cellar for at least 90 days. It has an oily textured pate and a nutty, fruity, olive-like flavour.

Goat's milk cheese

DELICE DE BOURGOGNE

Alternatives: st maure caprifeuille (French), florette (French) or st maure de touraine (French)

Fresh chèvre is made almost entirely by using lactic coagulation, which takes 24 hours. The chèvre is then carefully ladled by hand, in order to avoid destroying the delicate curd matrix. The white curd has a moist, mousse-like, fluffy consistency, with retained sweetness, a delicate balance of acidity and a mild, clean, creamy finish. The curd has an average fat content of 45%.

Some recipes for your cheese course

The following ideas feature interesting cheeses that are generally readily available from good cheese stores. The recommended serving size when preparing a cheese course with an accompaniment is 60 g (2 oz) per person – 240 g (8½ oz) will serve four.

AN IDEA FOR BLUE CHEESE is to bring 240 g (8½ oz) roquefort to room temperature, then serve with 200 g (7 oz) Spiced Cherries (page 17). I prefer the cherries to be served chilled, and moistened with a little of their pickling juices.

A WASHED-RIND CHEESE such as époisses can be served with Crunchy Ficelles (page 341). Bring 240 g (8½ oz) of the cheese to room temperature before serving, so that it is oozing its sweet, luscious pate. Crunchy Ficelles are also fantastic with a little toasted crushed cumin seeds added to the basic ficelle dough.

ON A LAZY SUMMER'S DAY there's nothing better than a large chunk of bitey aged cheddar, a jar of Piccalilli (page 131) and chunks of warm, fresh, rustic country-style bread.

FOR A TASTE SENSATION IN THE EVENING, place 160 g (5½ oz) seedless dried muscatel grapes in a bowl and cover with 80 ml (3 fl oz) Pedro Ximenez sherry and 120 ml (4 fl oz) warm, strong Earl Grey tea. Leave the muscatels to marinate for a couple of hours, until juicy and plump, then serve with 240 g (8½ oz) room temperature goat's milk delice de bourgogne.

AT ANY TIME OF DAY, Ossau-iraty is marvellous on warm slices of freshly toasted fruit and nut bread.

FINALLY, AS AN ALTERNATIVE TO DESSERT, serve big spoonfuls of fresh chèvre with 100 g (3½ oz) fresh, sweet almonds and 100 g (3½ oz) honeycomb. Delicious!

Planning a menu

One of the things that excites me the most about having a restaurant is the fun I have putting together dishes and entire dégustation menus.

To my mind, balancing the flavours, textures and colours of a dish is as important a lesson as any other cooking technique.

In classic French cooking, there are certain expectations about the ways in which ingredients are put together to produce a dish or a meal. Thankfully, the modern emphasis has shifted away from rigidly following these 'rules' towards a more flexible reinterpretation of tradition, reflecting our faster-paced lifestyles. However, a number of non-negotiable aspects of the French meal remain: food is always accompanied by bread, and most meals include a salad or a vegetable dish.

As I discussed in the very first French Lesson, flavour is where it all starts. It may seem like common sense, but putting different flavours together on a plate or within a meal requires a bit of experience. While some of our flavour preferences are innate, it's also about developing what I call your 'cook's brain' – that is, the part of your brain that tells you which things taste good

together, and which things do not.

It all comes with practice, of course, which is why I emphasise over and over again the importance of tasting your food. The analogy I use with the apprentice cooks I work with is that you need to build a tasting palette in your brain – a bit like a painter's palette. Over time, you will create an enormous memory bank of flavours. You will also develop the ability to mix these flavours together and imagine what they will taste like.

Similarly, the more you taste different dishes and ingredients, the more you'll learn about their intrinsic textures. You'll learn how to 'feel' these textures in your brain – and you'll begin to understand the ways in which these textures and flavours are affected by various cooking techniques.

Whether you are planning a simple family supper or a fancy six-course dinner party, the same principles apply when you're putting together a menu. In the same way that you plan a journey by learning to read a map, in order to create a meal you need to engage in a bit of 'mind-mapping'. You need to be able to imagine the cooking journey and the final destination – the way each dish will look, the way it will 'feel' and the way it will taste.

As I've said, it does take a bit of practice – but hey, it's not exactly a chore! As you'll have noticed, most of the recipes in *French Lessons* include suggestions about accompaniments. In the section that follows, I've put together some ideas for creating menus for different occasions. Once you develop a bit of confidence in this 'mind-mapping', you can start to mix and match the various techniques and garnishes in your own way, to create wonderful menus for your family and friends.

Sunday Brunch

Slow-Cooked Eggs with Mushroom Duxelles and Toasted Brioche

Salad of Golden Frisée and Smoked Trout

Tarte Fine of Figs

∽

Friends for a Barbecue

Pissaladière

Grilled Scampi Tails with Lemon and Parsley Butter

Grilled Lamb Cutlets with Gremolata

Grilled Wagyu Entrecôte Steak with Béarnaise Sauce

Flourless Chocolate Tart with Banana Ice Cream

Rum Baba with Vanilla Chantilly

∽

Family Weekend Picnic

Lamb's Lettuce with Lardons and Chicken Confit

Pâté de Campagne with Piccalilli and Crusty Bread

Whole Roasted Baby Chicken

Chocolate Brownie

∽

Breezy Late Outdoor Lunch

Spring Pea Nage

Ragoût of Mussels, Leeks and Saffron with Croutons and Aioli

Duck Legs Braised with Port, Orange and Thyme

Caramelised Citrus Curd Tart

∽

Working Lunch

Smoked Ham Broth

Grilled Entrecôte Steak with Pommes Anna and
Café de Paris Butter

Salade Simple

Tarte Tatin with Vanilla Ice Cream

∽

Big Celebration Lunch

Warm Citrus-Marinated Ocean Trout
Confit with Parsley and Fennel Coulis

Grilled Scampi Tails with Lemon
and Parsley Butter

Confit Belly of Pork

Roast Rib of Dry-Aged Beef with
Bordelaise Sauce

Sarladaise Potatoes

Roasted Golden Peaches with
Rosé Champagne
and Strawberry Ripple Ice Cream

∽

Afternoon Tea

Madeleines

Palmiers

Chocolate Macaroons

Profiteroles Filled with Crème Pâtissière
and Chocolate Sauce

Brittany Shortbread with Crème Frâiche
and Strawberry Jam

∽

Cocktail Evening and Light Snacks

Deep-Fried King Prawn Beignets
with Lemon
and Chervil Mayonnaise

Roast Venison Sausages with Tomato
Chutney

Butterflied Quail Grilled with Garlic and
Rosemary Butter

Lobster Tail Roasted on Aromatics

Campari and Blood Orange Jelly

Vacherins with Vanilla Chantilly and
Strawberry Coulis

∽

Light Healthy Dinner

Potage Quat' Saisons

Salade Simple with Lemon Vinaigrette

Steamed Coral Trout with Lemon
Verbena and Crushed Potatoes

Tropical Fruit Salad

∽

A Quick Dinner for 2

Fricassée of Chicken with Morels
and Leeks

or

Pan-Fried John Dory with Caponata
Dressing

Crushed Potatoes

Sauternes Pannacotta with Caramel
Oranges

∽

A Cold Romantic Winter Evening

Salade Provençale

Red Mullet 'En Papillote'

Daube of Beef with Caramelised
Parsnips

or

Slow-Roasted Pork Rump with
Crackling

Potato Purée

Chocolate Fondants with Cherry
and Pistachio Nougat Glacé

∽

An Extravagant Evening Feast

Lobster Consommé

Asparagus Salad with Hazelnuts
and Tatsoi with Pickled Beetroot

Steamed Zucchini Flowers
and Scallop Mousse

Pan-Fried Swordfish with
Grilled Scampi Tails and
Verbena Tea Vinaigrette

Confit Chicken Wings with
Seared Scallops, Peas
and Albufera Sauce

Roast Loin of Venison with
Périgueux Sauce

Truffle-Baked Nicola Potatoes

Prune and Armagnac Soufflé with
Caramel Ice Cream

∽

Acknowledgements

James Metcalfe – head chef at Bécasse – with another book under our ever-expanding belts (or should I say aprons!), once again thank you for your assistance with this project. And for 6 wonderful and fun years – your loyalty, professionalism and constant search for excellence are inspiring to us all.

Richard Guerin – chef pâtissière at Bécasse, now living back in France – thank you for 2 great years, and for your assistance with this book. I know just how hard you worked to meet the deadlines, so thank you for helping to make this possible.

Tristan Robertson – thank you for your passion, enthusiasm and loyalty for the last 2 years, and for taking the time to perfect these recipes.

Toru Kiuchi – 5 fantastic years, thank you for your support and hard work. Your humour is what often keeps us sane – well, almost sane!

And a special thank you to all the kitchen brigade and front-of-house staff at Bécasse, a very special team. It is great to share such a wonderful vision with immensely dedicated, talented and focused people as yourselves. So many different personalities but with the common thread of a love of great produce and intelligent cooking, fantastic service and wonderful wines. Thank you all … if nothing else, it's good fun!

And to the amazing chefs I've been lucky enough to work for, learn from, steal recipes from and copy things from. Above all, thank you for the inspiration you all gave me, for giving me insight into such an amazing craft. It was from the shoulders of Raymond Blanc and Liam Tomlin that I gained such a spectacular view when I was an impressionable young man, and I will never be able to thank you both enough. You turned my craft into an obsessive art.

This book would just not have been possible without the very special people who gave so much. To my wonderful editor Lucy Malouf: you made the complex, simple and the frustrating, fun. You're an absolute gem to work with – thank you. Under the direction of Mary Small, thank you once again, to Hardie Grant Books for supporting another title and making this great book possible. I hope it is not the last.

And a very special thanks to photographer Steve Brown, and to designer Gayna Murphy for making every page so bloody damn gorgeous!

The ingredient is everything, so thank you to the many suppliers we deal with on a daily basis, for sourcing such great produce. Thank you to Vic's Premium Quality Meat, Anthony and Vic, Jamie and Barry at Fratelli, Simon Johnson and Victoria Lush, Lyn and Robin at Oz on a Plate, Frank and Jason at De Costi, Peter and Derek at Nicholson and Saville, and George from GJ Foods.

And to all the small, honest, passionate growers and producers – I just hope you know how much you are loved and admired by our industry, and relied upon by so many great chefs.

Index